THE ETHICS OF SCIENCE

"If anyone still believes that scientific research is a value-free zone, *The Ethics of Science* will disabuse them. David B. Resnik uses a wealth of actual and hypothetical examples in a clear philosophical discussion that illuminates the range of ethical concerns that scientists need to face. This is one area where philosophical argument can serve a practical need: the more scientists who think carefully about the issues Resnik raises, the better."

Peter Lipton
Professor of History and Philosophy of Science
University of Cambridge

"Science faculty and students – and an interested public – will find *The Ethics of Science* admirably clear, balanced, and richly comprehensive. Resnik's clarity shows itself not only in his unpretentious, straight-forwardness, but by being philosophically sophisticated yet avoiding jargon. An extremely useful aspect of the book is that virtually every kind of ethical question that arises in and about science is addressed."

Hans Oberdiek
Swarthmore College

David B. Resnik is an Associate Professor of Philosophy and the Director of the Center for the Advancement of Ethics at the University of Wyoming. This is his first book.

Philosophical Issues in Science
Edited by
W.H. Newton-Smith
Balliol College, Oxford

THE ETHICS OF SCIENCE

An Introduction

David B. Resnik

London and New York

First published 1998
by Routledge
11 New Fetter Lane, London EC4P 4EE

Simultaneously published in the USA and Canada
by Routledge
29 West 35th Street, New York, NY 10001

Typeset in Aldus by RefineCatch Limited, Bungay, Suffolk
Printed and bound in Great Britain by
Creative Print and Design (Wales), Ebbw Vale

British Library Cataloguing in Publication Data
A catalogue record for this book is available from the British Library

Library of Congress Cataloging in Publication Data
Resnik, David B., 1962–
The ethics of science: an introduction/David B. Resnik.
p.   cm.
Includes bibliographical references and index.
1. Science – Moral and ethical aspects.   2. Research – Philosophy.
I. Title.
Q175.35.R46   1998
174'.95—dc21   97–40514

ISBN 0–415–16697–7 (hbk)
ISBN 0–415–16698–5 (pbk)

⌊14133⌋

In memory of my grandmother,
Muriel Resnik,
who encouraged me to write.

Contents

Acknowledgments

I would like to thank the following people for comments on drafts of this book: David Hull, Scott O'Brien, W.H. Newton-Smith, Marshall Thomsen, and several anonymous reviewers. I would also like to thank the following people for comments and criticism: Stephanie Bird, Ron Canterna, Michael Davis, Clark Glymour, Alvin Goldman, Susanna Goodin, Fred Grinnell, Michael Harkin, A.C. Higgins, Dale Jamieson, Audrey Kleinsasser, Helen Longino, Claudia Mills, Kenneth Pimple, Michael Resnik, Geoffrey Sayre McCord, Ed Sherline, Linda Sweeting, Robert Switzer, and my class on ethical issues in scientific research which I taught at the University of Wyoming in the Spring of 1996. I also would like to mention that the National Science Foundation helped to provide partial support for this work through grants SBR-960297, SBR-9511817, SBR-9223819, and AST-9100602.

CHAPTER 1
Science and Ethics

During the past decade, scientists, laypeople, and politicians have become increasingly aware of the importance of ethics in scientific research. Several trends have contributed to these growing concerns. First, the press has covered stories on ethical issues raised by science, such as the United States (US) government's secret experiments on human beings during the Cold War, genetic engineering, the Human Genome Project, studies on the genetic basis of intelligence, the cloning of human embryos and animals, and global warming. Second, scientists and government officials have investigated, documented, and adjudicated cases of ethical misconduct and ethically questionable conduct in many aspects of research, and a perceived lack of ethics in science has threatened the stability and integrity of research (PSRCR 1992, Hilts 1996, Hedges 1997). These cases include allegations of plagiarism, fraud, violations of the law, mismanagement of funds, exploitation of subordinates, violations of recombinant DNA regulations, discrimination, conflicts of interests, and problems with the FBI's crime lab. Despite a growing body of evidence on unethical research, the data still indicate that the frequency of misconduct in science is quite low when compared to the frequency of misconduct in other professions, such as business, medicine, or law (PSRCR 1992).[1]

A third reason why ethics has become a pressing concern is that science's increasing interdependence with business and industry has generated ethical conflicts between scientific values and business values (PSRCR 1992, Reiser 1993). These conflicts have raised concerns about the funding of science, peer review, scientific openness, the ownership of knowledge, and the sharing of resources. Universities have expressed concerns about scientists who use their facilities to conduct secret research for private industry or personal economic gain (Bowie 1994). In some cases, universities have fought lengthy court battles with businesses and individuals over patents and intellectual property rights. University administrators also complain that scientists who work for business are spending less time on their other duties, such as education. Scientists in various fields worry that the relationship between science and business will redirect research toward the solution of applied problems and that basic research will suffer. Government watchdogs have objected to allowing companies to profit from publicly funded research (Lomasky 1987).

In response to concerns about ethical improprieties and issues in science, various scientific institutions and societies, such as the National Science Foundation (NSF), the National Institutes of Health (NIH), the American Association for the Advancement of Science (AAAS), the National Academy of Sciences (NAS), and Sigma Xi have commissioned committees to study ethical issues and improprieties in science and make policy recommendations (Sigma Xi 1986, 1993, AAAS 1991, PSRCR 1992, Committee on the Conduct of Science 1994). Additionally, universities, businesses, and scientific societies have sponsored workshops and conferences that address ethical issues in science, scientists have initiated efforts to integrate ethics into the science curriculum at the graduate and undergraduate level of instruction, scholars from various sciences and the humanities have written books and articles about the ethics in research, and new journals have been started that address ethical issues in science (Reiser 1993, Bird and Spier 1995, Garte 1995). Finally, scientific societies and organizations have adopted codes of ethics and have recommended that scientists integrate ethics into the science curriculum (Sigma Xi 1986, US Congress 1990, PSCRC 1992).

Despite this new awareness about the importance of ethics in science, some scientists do not take ethical improprieties very seriously because they regard misconduct as very rare and insignificant and view confirmed reports of misconduct as isolated incidents or anomalies. Some scientists invoke the "psychological pathology" theory to explain misconduct: scientists who behave unethically must be mentally deranged because only a crazy person would think that they could get away with fraud, plagiarism, and other forms of misconduct (Broad and Wade 1993). Crime does not pay in science, because the scientific method, the peer review system, and the public nature of scientific research serve as mechanisms for catching people who break science's ethical rules. Thus, misconduct is not a problem in science because it does not occur often, and when it does, it does not reflect any significant flaws in the research environment.

Many scientists believe that no significant ethical issues arise in science because they view science as "objective." Science studies facts, employs objective methods, and produces knowledge and consensus. Ethics, on the other hand, involves the study of values, employs subjective methods, and produces only opinion and disagreement. Hence, scientists need not concern themselves with ethical issues in conducting research or in teaching science. As members of society, scientists will of course need to confront ethical issues. But as members of the scientific community, scientists do not need to address these issues. Scientists need to follow ethical standards, of course, but these rules are clear cut. Scientists do not need to engage in a philosophical/ethical discussion in order to know that they should not fabricate or falsify data. Thus, science provides an objective sanctuary from the ethical issues and ambiguities that beleaguer other spheres of human existence.

Even those scientists who take ethical improprieties and issues seriously may believe that scientists do not need to have any formal instruction in ethics. Some people hold that scientists need no formal instruction in ethics because they believe that people learn ethics when they are very young. There is little, if anything that a person can learn about ethics and morality by the time she enters college. If a person is already ethical when she enters the scientific profession, she will continue to be ethical; if she is not ethical when she enters science, then no amount of instruction can make her become ethical. Even those scientists who think that some kind of ethical learning can take place in science may still believe that there is no need to teach ethics because students learn ethics by example, practice, and osmosis. Since ethical knowledge in science is informal and tacit, scientists do not need to spend valuable class time going over ethical standards and concepts. Scientists can teach ethics by showing students how to do good science and by modeling ethical conduct in science.

All of these views I have just discussed erect barriers to the serious study of the ethics of science, and they are all deeply misguided. As more research surfaces concerning the nature of science and scientific misconduct, it is becoming increasingly clear that the science's research environment plays a role in contributing to misconduct and in generating ethical issues (PSRCR 1992, LaFollette 1992, Grinnell 1992, Shrader-Frechette 1994, Macrina 1995, Woodward and Goodstein 1996). If science's research environment contributes to misconduct, then reports of misconduct reflect some structural problems in the research environment and cannot be treated as isolated incidents of pathological behavior.

Several aspects of the research environment may contribute to ethical improprieties and issues. First, science is, for most scientists, a career. A successful career in science is achieved through publications, grants, research appointments, tenure, and awards. Most scientists who have academic appointments face the pressure to "publish or perish" before they earn tenure or get promoted. Nearly all tenure and promotion committees assess a scientist's research efforts based largely on the quantity of his or her publications – the more the better. Even scientists who have earned tenure need to continue publishing at a high rate in order to gain a promotion or add to their prestige. Thus, some scientists may be tempted to violate ethical principles in order to advance their careers.

Second, government funding for research is tighter than ever, due to smaller budgets and more scientists seeking funding. In order to receive funding and to continue receiving it, scientists must produce results. If an experiment is not going well or the results have been ambiguous, scientists may gloss over these problems in applying for grants or in reporting results. Third, research in many sciences carries economic rewards. A person who patents a new process, technique, or invention can earn thousands or even millions of dollars. Thus, economic incentives may also contribute to unethical practices in science. Fourth, science's highly touted self-correcting mechanisms – peer review, publication, and replication – often do not succeed in detecting fraud or error. Referees who review proposals or papers do not have time to thoroughly examine them for errors or fraud, many papers that are published are never read, and most experiments are not repeated (Broad and Wade 1993, Kiang 1995, Armstrong 1997).

Finally, it may also be the case that science education contributes to unethical behavior. As I noted earlier, many scientists believe that they do not need to make a serious attempt to teach research ethics. If students do not learn how to be ethical scientists, then it should come as no surprise that many of them behave unethically when they pursue careers in science. Moreover, educational practices and academic pressures can conspire to encourage misconduct (Petersdorf 1986, Sergestrale 1990, Browning 1995). Many laboratory exercises reward students for getting the right results, regardless of how they get them. Since students often know the results they are supposed to get, they may be tempted to fudge, fabricate, or trim data in order to get those results. Most students are under pressure to get good grades and they may cheat in order to get them. This is especially true among premedical students, who must get very high grades in order to be admitted to medical school.

Thus, ethical improprieties in science cannot be viewed as an anomaly since they probably result from factors operating within the research and learning environment. Although it is difficult to estimate the incidence of scientific misconduct, any misconduct should be taken seriously (PSRCR 1992). Even if misconduct is still very rare in science, the fact that it occurs at all is cause for concern since any misconduct damages science's public image and erodes public support for science.

Ethical issues and controversies can arise in science because science is a cooperative activity that takes place within a larger social and political context (Longino 1990). Scientists cannot escape from the ethical quandaries and issues that arise in other walks of life. Purely objective science is a myth perpetuated by those who would flee from fuzzy, controversial, and vexing questions. Ethical dilemmas and issues can also arise in science because scientists often do not agree on the standards of conduct that should govern science or how standards should be interpreted or applied (Whitbeck 1995a). For instance, publication practices are an area of ethical dispute in science because they often involve disputes about how to allocate credit and responsibility (Rose and Fisher 1995). Ethical issues also arise as a result of science's interaction with the public because scientific research often has important social, moral, and political consequences (Committee on the Conduct of Science 1994).

There are several reasons why science students need some kind of formal instruction in ethics. First, although a great deal of ethical learning takes place in childhood, evidence from developmental psychology indicates that people continue to learn about ethics and moral reasoning throughout life (Rest 1986). College age students and older adults can learn to recognize ethical issues, make moral choices in novel situations, and reason about ethics and morality. They can also learn ethical concepts, theories, and principles, they can appreciate different points of view, and they can even develop moral virtues. Moreover, some ethical concepts and principles can only be learned by understanding and practicing an occupation or profession. For example, the doctrine of "informed consent" in medical research requires some special ethics education beyond what one would learn in kindergarten or grade school. In order to learn about informed consent in research, one must begin to understand and practice medical research. Thus, some ethical learning can take place in undergraduate, graduate, and professional education (Rest and Narvaez 1994).

Second, although informal methods of instruction may be the best way to teach scientists how to be ethical, there is still a need for formal instruction in ethics because informal instruction is not getting the job done (Hollander *et al.* 1995). There are several reasons why informal instruction is not working adequately. Modern science is a very large and complex social institution. A typical laboratory may include dozens or even hundreds of senior and junior researchers, postdoctoral fellows and graduate students. There are too many people in most research settings to rely solely on informal instruction to transmit ethical knowledge, to insure that research standards are upheld, or to discuss important ethical concerns. Furthermore, science education at the undergraduate level is often conducted on a massive scale; introductory science classes at state universities may be filled with hundreds of students. Once again, size works against informal instruction, since students in large classes do not get enough of an opportunity to discuss ethical issues. Finally, not all scientists do a good job of modeling ethical conduct. If science students witness scientists behaving unethically, then they are less likely to learn how to behave ethically.

To illustrate the relevance of ethics to science, I will discuss several recent cases of scientific research that have generated ethical questions and controversies.

The Baltimore Affair

In one of the most highly publicized cases of alleged scientific misconduct in recent memory, which has become known as the "Baltimore Affair," a paper co-authored by Nobel Prize winning scientist David Baltimore was suspected of containing fraudulent data. During the Summer of 1991, the *New York Times* gave this story front page coverage. This scandal embarrassed the organizations that sponsored the research, including the NIH and the Whitehead Institute, tarnished Baltimore's reputation, attracted the attention of Congress, and even involved the Secret Service.[2] The paper, which appeared in the 25 April 1986 issue of the journal *Cell*, listed six authors. Baltimore supervised the research, although he did not perform the experiments. The paper claimed that experiments showed that the insertion of a foreign gene into a mouse can induce the mouse's genes to produce antibodies mimicking those of the foreign gene. If this claim were true, it would suggest that one could control the immune system by using foreign genes to make it produce antibodies. So far, this research has not been confirmed by other scientists. The experiments were conducted at the Whitehead Institute, a lab associated with the Massachusetts Institute of Technology (MIT) and Tufts University, and they were funded by the NIH.

Margot O'Toole, a postdoctoral student working at the Whitehead Institute at that time, was under the supervision of one of the paper's authors, Thereza Imanishi-Kari. O'Toole grew suspicious of this research when she found seventeen pages of Imanishi-Kari's notes that contradicted the findings of the paper. She failed in an attempt to repeat some of the experiments and she suspected that many of the experiments described in the paper had either not been done or had not yielded the results stated in the paper. O'Toole blew the whistle on this research by informing review boards at MIT and Tufts about her suspicions, and these boards investigated the research. These initial investigations found some errors in the work, but they did not conclude that the research was questionable. When O'Toole's one year term as a postdoctoral student expired, she had difficulty finding work for quite some time and she became known as a troublemaker.

However, the NIH's Office of Research Integrity (ORI) followed up these initial investigations and Congress also learned about this scientific scandal. Representative John Dingell of Michigan and his staff at the House Oversight and Investigations Committee held two hearings on this case and ordered the Secret Service to assist the investigation. The earlier inquiries had not examined Imanishi-Kari's notebooks but the Congressional investigation did. This investigation found that dates in the notebooks had been altered, results had been written in different inks on different pieces of paper, and that much of the suspected research was not done when Imanishi-Kari said it had been done. The investigators concluded that Imanishi-Kari probably put together the notebooks after questions were raised about the research. In its final report on the case, the ORI concluded in 1994 that Imanishi-Kari had fabricated and falsified experimental data and results. After that report was issued, Tufts University asked Imanishi-Kari to take a leave of absence.

However, Imanishi-Kari maintained her innocence throughout this whole episode, and she was exonerated on 21 June 1996 after a research integrity appeals panel from the Department of Health and Human Services concluded that much of the evidence against her was either unreliable, uncorroborated, or inconsistent. The panel also criticized the ORI for investigating and handling the case in an irresponsible manner. Tufts University reinstated Imanishi-Kari shortly after the panel found her not guilty. In her own defense, Imanishi-Kari admits that her laboratory notebooks were not always well organized or up to date, and that she put together loose papers into one laboratory notebook when she was accused of misconduct. She maintains that she never intended to deceive investigators or the scientific community. She admits to poor record keeping, but she asserts that she never fabricated or falsified data. However, the panel's findings angered some scientists, who believe that Imanishi-Kari did fabricate or falsify data or that the NIH mishandled the case. Throughout the case, many scientists objected to governmental and bureaucratic intrusion into the investigation and adjudication of scientific misconduct. Scientists, according to many, should be able to police themselves.

Although Baltimore had not been accused of committing fraud, he resigned his presidency of Rockefeller University in December 1992, due to his involvement in the affair that bears his name. He has defended Imanishi-Kari throughout this entire episode, and he has compared investigations of alleged fraud to scientific witch hunts. In order to remove the errors contained in the paper, Baltimore and his co-authors issued a correction of their work that appeared in the journal *Cell*. Baltimore has asserted that many of the discrepancies in the records were due to sloppiness, not fraud, and he admits that he did not seek independent verification of the experimental results.

The Baltimore affair raises many important ethical questions. Should Baltimore have paid closer attention to the research that was being done under his supervision? If he could not adequately supervise the research, should he have been listed as an author? Should O'Toole have been given more protection for her whistle blowing? Should the initial investigators have conducted a more thorough and careful inquiry? Should people outside of science be allowed to investigate and adjudicate cases of scientific misconduct? Should fraud cases be decided on scientific or legal standards of evidence? Did politicians, scientists and the media "rush to judgment"? Assuming that Imanishi-Kari did not fabricate or falsify data, could her poor record keeping be viewed as irresponsible or unethical? How could one prove the allegations of fraud that were made in this case?

Cloning Research

On 13 October 1993 Jerry Hall, Robert Stillman, and three colleagues presented a paper at a meeting of the American Fertility Society that sent shock waves throughout the world. In their paper they described experiments in which they cloned human embryos. They had no idea at the time that they would soon find themselves in a storm of controversy. The story was splashed throughout the front pages of newspapers the world over and made the cover of *Time Magazine* and other periodicals. Journalists and commentators dredged up visions of baby farming, races of Hitlers, Einsteins, eugenics programs, and various *Brave New World* scenarios (Elmer-Dewitt 1993, Kolata 1993). Public officials from around the world condemned the research as horrifying and unscrupulous, and US President William Clinton ordered a ban on the use of federal funds to create human embryos for scientific purposes. In an attempt to alleviate some of the public's fears, Hall and Stillman appeared on the television shows "Nightline," "Good Morning America," and "Larry King Live." They tried to wash their hands of the moral implications of their research by portraying themselves simply as detached scientists interested only in knowledge.

If we take a closer look at this case, we can see that much of this uproar is based on a misunderstanding of the research done by Hall and Stillman and their colleagues. The embryos cloned by Hall and Stillman were made from nonviable embryos that were the product of fertilizing eggs with more than one sperm. An embryo fertilized with more than one sperm is nonviable – it cannot become a baby or adult human being. The nonviable embryos were put in a specially prepared fluid where they divided into eight-celled embryos. The eight-celled embryos were divided into single cells and began dividing again. Since all of the cells from eight-celled embryos are genetically identical, this process yielded eight clones per embryo.

Although this research is significant, many of the horrifying scenarios discussed in the public remain in the realm of science fiction. First, the embryos are not viable, so the process cannot yield an adult human being. The process might be modified so that it could produce an adult human being, but at its current state of development, it cannot. Second, it is not yet possible genetically to manipulate embryos to design human beings. Any manipulations we attempt at this point in time are likely to produce nonviable embryos or massively defective children. We simply do not know enough about human genetics and embryology to create human beings with specific characteristics. Finally, the clones produced by this process are not copied from adult cells. Thus, this research was not at all like the cloning depicted in the movies *The Boys from Brazil* or *Jurassic Park* (Caplan 1993).

While the public reaction to cloning experiments has been, for the most part, negative, the researchers received high praise at the American Fertility Society meetings; the paper presented by Hall and Stillman was awarded the General Program Prize. Fertility researchers touted the potential benefits of this work for couples that have difficulty conceiving. If a couple can only produce a few fertile eggs, they can increase their chances of conceiving if these few eggs are cloned to make many eggs.

On 23 February 1997 a similar public outcry occurred when Scottish scientists announced that they had cloned a sheep, named "Dolly," from adult cells (Kolata 1997). The lamb was born in July 1996, but these scientists kept this knowledge a secret for over six months while they monitored Dolly's development and waited for the journal *Nature* to review their findings. This was the first time that viable, mammalian offspring had been produced from adult mammalian cells. Ian Wilmut, an embryologist at the Roslin Institute in Edinburgh, and his colleagues cultivated cells from a ewe's udder in the laboratory, removed the nuclei from those cells, and used an electric current to fuse these nuclei to enucleated sheep eggs (eggs with their nuclei removed). They then implanted the eggs in ewe uteruses to develop. Only nineteen out of 277 embryos created in this fashion were viable, and only one out of these was born (Wilmut *et al.* 1997). Shortly after this startling announcement, scientists in Oregon revealed that they had successfully cloned rhesus monkeys from embryonic cells.

The cloning of animals could have some important applications for agricultural, pharmaceutical, and biotechnological industries. If this cloning technology is conjoined with gene therapy techniques, it could be used to make low-fat chickens, pigs that can serve as organ donors, super lactating cows, and animals that produce human hormones, vitamins, or other medically important compounds. Wilmut conducted his research in order to develop a process for turning sheep into drug factories. His work was supported, in part, by PPL Therapeutics PLC, a company that plans to sell drugs that can be extracted from sheep milk. The media spread the news of the sheep cloning and "Dolly" appeared all over magazine covers and the internet.

Many people found this research both shocking and horrifying because it is not far from the cloning of an adult human being. A *TIME*/CNN poll of 1,005 adults in the US showed that 93 percent of those surveyed think the cloning of human beings is a bad idea, and 66 percent said it was a bad idea even to clone animals (Lederer 1997). Soon public officials reacted to the news. President Clinton asked a federal bioethics commission to review the legal and ethical implications of cloning, and he also issued an executive order prohibiting the use of federal funds to sponsor research on the cloning of human beings (Clinton 1997). In his executive order, President Clinton warned that cloning threatens the uniqueness and sacredness of human life, and that it raises profound moral and religious questions. President Clinton acknowledged that many private companies will still have an interest in cloning mammals, but he urged corporations to observe a voluntary moratorium on cloning research on human beings. In some countries, such as Great Britain, cloning human beings is illegal. It is not illegal in the US as of the writing of this book, although legislation is pending. In Scotland, the British government announced that its Ministry of Agriculture would no longer sponsor Wilmut's cloning research. His $411,000 was cut in half in April 1997 and will be terminated in April 1998.

Questions about cloning abound. What are the social or biological consequences of this research? What are the agricultural or medical applications of cloning animals? Does the cloning of people threaten the dignity, uniqueness, or the sacredness of human life? Should research on human or animal cloning be stopped? Do scientists have a right to pursue any kind of research they deem significant regardless of its moral or social implications? How can we balance scientific freedom of thought and expression against moral and political values? If the US government refuses to fund human cloning studies, can this research be carried out in the US through private funding? What role, if any, does the media's and the public's misunderstanding of the research play in this global uproar?

The Debate over Cold Fusion

Reporters throughout the world covered the story of two electrochemists, Stanley Pons, Chairman of the Chemistry Department at the University of Utah, and Martin Fleischmann, a professor at Southampton University, who announced in a press conference on 23 March 1989 that they had discovered how to produce fusion at room temperature (Huizenga 1992). They claimed to have produced nuclear fusion using equipment available to most high school students. Their press release, however, was general in nature and contained virtually no technical information on how to reproduce their experiments. Most fusion scientists and physicists doubted Pons and Fleischmann's extraordinary claims, but the media were not as skeptical. Journalists hailed this wonderful discovery and their coverage of cold fusion raised many expectations.

According to standard theories of nuclear fusion, which are backed by many well-established experimental results, fusion can only occur at extremely high temperatures and pressures commonly found in the interiors of stars. Conventional, "hot" fusion research, which focuses on generating these extreme conditions in a laboratory setting, has made slow but steady progress for the last few decades. However, hot fusion technologies may not be available until the twenty-first century. Pons and Fleischmann's experiment contradicted fusion orthodoxy because it claimed to produce fusion at normal temperatures and pressures. Their experiment consisted of two palladium electrodes in a solution of lithium deuteroxide (LiOD) in heavy water (D_2O). Pons and Fleischmann claimed that when an electric current ran between the two electrodes, it decomposed the heavy water into deuterium gas (D_2), oxygen gas (O_2), and that it forced large amounts of deuterium (D) into the negatively charged electrode (the cathode). The cathode's unique structure, they claimed, would allow deuterium atoms to pack closely enough together to fuse into tritium (T), yielding heat and neutrons. Pons and Fleischmann claimed to have observed an extraordinary amount of heat that could not be produced by ordinary chemical means, as well as small amounts of tritium and neutrons (Fleischmann and Pons 1989).

Upon learning about these fantastic experiments, laboratories across the world rushed to repeat them. Many laboratories obtained results that contradicted Pons and Fleishmann's findings; some obtained results that either supported cold fusion or were inconclusive. Many scientists had a difficult time even understanding the experiment because Pons and Fleischmann did not describe it in enough detail. After several years of inconclusive or contradictory results, most fusion scientists believe that Pons and Fleischmann's research was based on careless errors, sloppiness, or self-deception. Pons and Fleischmann believed that they had produced fusion, but the phenomena they produced probably resulted from a misunderstanding or misinterpretation of ordinary electrochemical reactions.

If Pons and Fleischmann had described their experiments in more detail, then we might now know whether there is anything at all to cold fusion. But the two scientists had financial incentives for being vague: if other people can repeat their experiments, then they (and the University of Utah) could lose their chance to obtain patents for cold fusion. Since cold fusion would be a new power source, if successful it would generate fantastic wealth for those who own patent rights. But one cannot patent an invention without perfecting it and describing how it works.

Money also played an important role in two other significant aspects of this case. First, a veil of secrecy shrouded Pons and Fleischmann's work before the press conference and afterwards. The two scientists worked largely in isolation from the rest of mainstream fusion researchers. They made their public announcement before they had sought expert opinion on cold fusion, and most physicists outside the University of Utah were not even aware of their research before the press conference. The secrecy was deemed necessary by Pons and Fleischmann and officials at the University of Utah in order to secure patents for the research. Second, Pons and Fleischmann announced their results at a press conference instead of at a scientific meeting or in a scientific journal because they were concerned with securing patents and receiving proper credit. This public announcement circumvented the normal scientific review process and allowed the research to become public before it was thoroughly checked by other scientists.

This case raises many different ethical questions. Should Pons and Fleischmann have communicated their results via a press conference? Should they have worked more closely with other scientists? Should they have described their experiments in more detail? Should Pons and Fleischmann (as well as officials at the University of Utah) have been less concerned with money and prestige and more concerned with rigor and truth? Is cold fusion a pseudo-phenomenon resulting from self-deception or is it something worth investigating further? Is the sloppiness of this research tantamount to scientific negligence?

The three cases I have just described raise a number of interesting issues about the ethics of scientific research and they can supply a wealth of stimulating conversation. Indeed, since I believe that case studies provide one of the best ways of thinking about ethical improprieties and issues, I will discuss many real cases in this book, and I will include fifty hypothetical (but realistic) cases in an appendix. But ethics should be more than just a gut reaction to various situations, and a philosophical study should do more than simply allow us to chat informally about cases. We need to be able to understand the questions and problems that cases raise and the general principles, values, and concerns they exemplify. In short, we need to develop a general framework for thinking about the ethics of science. Such a framework will allow us to understand the important questions, problems, and concerns even if we cannot reach a consensus on some of the more vexing issues.

In the next three chapters, I will develop a conceptual framework for understanding the ethics of scientific research, which will include a discussion of the nature of ethics, the nature of science, and the relationship between science and ethics. It will also serve as a basis for justifying some principles of ethics in science, for discussing conflicts between scientific norms and broader, social norms, for applying science's ethical principals to practical decisions, and for thinking about questions pertaining to the ethics of science. The next four chapters will apply this framework to some important ethical dilemmas and issues in science.

A few words of caution are in order. Many of the issues discussed in the next chapters are controversial and the framework I develop is not likely to satisfy all readers. Fortunately, I do not have to construct an impenetrable treatise in order to discuss the issues and topics that are the subject of this book. As a philosopher, I am more interested in asking the right questions and in understanding the important issues than in providing absolute answers. I will, however, do more than ask questions in this book; I will also defend some answers. I only maintain that my views are reasonable and comprehensive, not that they are uncontroversial or should be accepted by all readers.

Although my arguments draw on case studies and other empirical sources, the book as a whole approaches its topic from a philosophical perspective. A number of studies take a sociological or psychological perspective on research ethics: they seek to describe ethical and unethical conduct in science and its causes. While these studies are essential to our understanding of ethics in science, a philosophical approach can offer some valuable insights. Indeed, before we can estimate the frequency of ethical or unethical behavior in science or its causes, we must first have a clear understanding of the nature of research ethics, what constitutes ethical or unethical behavior in science, and so on.

I hope that this book will serve as a useful tool for educating scientists and science students about the ethics of research, that it will enable scientists and the public to acquire a better understanding of the importance of ethics in science, and that it will convince other scholars who study science that the ethics of research is a subject worthy of further analysis, investigation, and discussion.

CHAPTER 2
Ethical Theory and Applications

I f we want to understand ethics in science, the three most fundamental questions to ask are "what is ethics?," "what is science?," and "how are science and ethics related?" People have proposed many different answers to these questions and I do not pretend to have the only defensible ones. Nevertheless, I believe that my answers are reasonable and defensible. I will discuss these fundamental questions in the order I have presented them.

Ethics, Law, Politics, and Religion

In order to answer the first question, we need to distinguish between ethics as a *subject matter* and ethics as a *field of study* (or moral philosophy). Ethics are standards of conduct (or social norms) that prescribe behavior. Standards of conduct do not describe our actual behavior, since people often violate widely accepted standards. For example, most people in the United States accept the idea that one ought to tell the truth, yet many people lie all of the time. Even though people lie all the time, we indicate our endorsement of honesty as a standard of conduct by defending honesty in public, by teaching our children to be honest, and by expressing our disapproval of lying (Gibbard 1986).

Ethicists (or moral philosophers) study standards of conduct. Ethics as a field of study is a normative discipline whose main goals are prescriptive and evaluative rather than descriptive and explanatory (Pojman 1995). Social scientists offer descriptive and explanatory accounts of standards of conduct; ethicists criticize and evaluate those standards (Rest 1986). While the sociologist attempts to understand how often people commit suicide in the United States, the ethicist tries to determine whether suicide can be rationally justified. The economist attempts to understand the economic impact of gambling on a community, but the ethicist assesses the morality of gambling. To help clarify the distinction between descriptive and prescriptive accounts of conduct, I shall use the phrases "standards of conduct" or "social norms" in a prescriptive sense, and I shall use "social mores," "customs," or "conventions" in a descriptive sense.

In thinking about standards of conduct, it will be useful to distinguish between *ethics* and *morality*. Morality consists of a society's most general standards. These standards apply to all people in society regardless of their professional or institutional roles (Pojman 1995). Moral standards distinguish between right and wrong, good and bad, virtue and vice, justice and injustice. Many writers maintain that moral duties and obligations override other ones: if I have a moral duty not to lie, then I should not lie even if my employment requires me to lie. Moral standards include those rules that most people learn in childhood, e.g. "don't lie, cheat, steal, harm other people, etc." Ethics are not general standards of conduct but the standards of a particular profession, occupation, institution, or group within society. The word "ethics," when used in this way, usually serves as a modifier for another word, e.g. business ethics, medical ethics, sports ethics, military ethics, Muslim ethics, etc.

Professional ethics are standards of conduct that apply to people who occupy a professional occupation or role (Bayles 1988). A person who enters a profession acquires ethical obligations because society trusts them to provide valuable goods and services that cannot be provided unless their conduct conforms to certain standards. Professionals who fail to live up to their ethical obligations betray this trust. For instance, physicians have a special duty to maintain confidentiality that goes way beyond their moral duties to respect privacy. A physician who breaks confidentiality compromises her ability to provide a valuable service and she betrays society's (and the patient's) trust. Professional standards studied by ethicists include medical ethics, legal ethics, mass media ethics, and engineering ethics, to name but a few. I shall discuss professional ethics in science in more detail in the next chapter.

Not all standards of conduct are what we would call "ethics," however. Hence, it is important to distinguish between ethics and other social norms, such as law, politics, and religion. There are several reasons why ethics is not law. First, some actions that are illegal may not be unethical. Speeding is illegal, but one might have an ethical obligation to break the speed limit in order to transport someone to a hospital in an emergency. Second, some actions that are unethical may not be illegal. Most people would agree that lying is unethical but lying is only illegal under certain conditions, e.g. lying on an income tax return, lying when giving sworn testimony, etc. Third, laws can be unethical or immoral (Hart 1961). The United States had laws permitting slavery in the 1800s but most people today would say that those laws were unethical or immoral. Although we have moral and ethical obligations to obey the law, civil disobedience can be justified when immoral or unethical laws exist. Since we can appeal to morality and ethics to justify or criticize laws, many writers maintain that the main function of a legal system is to enforce a society's moral and ethical consensus (Hart 1961).

Fourth, we use different kinds of mechanisms to express, teach, inculcate, and enforce laws and ethics (Hart 1961). Laws are expressed publicly in statutes, penal codes, court rulings, government regulations, and so forth. Although ethics and morals are sometimes made explicit in religious texts, professional codes of conduct, or philosophical writings, many ethical and moral standards are implicit. Laws are also often expressed in highly technical and complex jargon, and we often need specially trained people – lawyers and judges – to interpret them. Ethics and morals, on the other hand, tend to be less technical and complex. Finally, we use the coercive power of government to enforce laws. People who break certain laws can be fined, imprisoned, or executed. People who violate ethical or moral standards do not face these kinds of punishments unless their actions also violate laws. Often we "punish" people who disobey moral or ethical obligations by simply expressing our disapproval or by condemning the behavior. Since this book addresses the ethics of science, it will not explore legal issues in science in any depth, although it will raise some questions about laws and public policies relating to science.

Some standards of conduct are best viewed as political rather than ethical or moral in nature. For example, the principle of "one person, one vote" is an important rule for organizing voting precincts and apportioning elected representatives. The difference between this standard and an ethical or moral norm is that this political maxim focuses on the conduct of groups or social institutions, whereas ethical and moral standards focus on the conduct of individuals. Political standards take a macro-perspective on human affairs; ethical and moral standards adopt a micro-perspective. Politics as a subject of study, on this view, includes those disciplines that take a macro-perspective on human conduct, e.g. political science and political philosophy. However, the distinction between ethics and politics is not absolute since many actions, institutions, and situations can be evaluated from an ethical or political point of view (Rawls 1971). For example, abortion raises moral issues concerning the status of the fetus and a mother's right to self-determination, and it also raises political issues concerning the state's authority to intrude in personal decisions. Since the distinction between ethics and politics is not absolute, this book will explore political issues in science even though it will focus primarily on ethical questions.

Finally, it is important to distinguish between ethics and religion. It is true that all of the world's main religions prescribe standards of conduct. The Bible, the Koran, the Upanishads and the Tao Teh King all provide moral guidance and each of these books contains an ethic. But ethical standards of conduct do not need to be based on a particular religion or its sacred scriptures; ethical standards can be justified and defined without reference to any particular religious institutions, theologies, or texts. Christians, Muslims, Hindus, Buddhists, Jews, as well as different sects within these religions can all agree on some common moral principles despite religious and theological differences (Pojman 1995). Moreover, atheists can act morally and accept moral maxims as well; ethics can be secular. The difference between ethics *simpliciter* and a particular religiously-based ethics is that religions provide justifications, definitions, and interpretations of standards of conduct. Religious institutions, texts, and theologies can be very useful in teaching ethics and in motivating ethical conduct. Indeed, religions probably play a key role in the moral education of most of the people in the world. Religion can supplement and complement ethics, even though ethics need not be tied to any particular religion or its teachings. If we think of ethics as a modifier, then it makes sense to speak of Christian ethics, Muslim ethics, Hindu ethics, and so on, even though ethics need not be tied to any of these terms.

Moral Theory

Moral philosophy includes the sub-disciplines normative ethics, applied ethics, and meta-ethics (Frankena 1973). *Normative ethics* is the study of moral standards, principles, concepts, values, and theories. *Applied ethics* is the study of ethical dilemmas, choices, and standards in various occupations, professions, and concrete situations and the application of moral theories and concepts in particular contexts (Fox and DeMarco 1990). We have already mentioned several areas of applied ethics in the previous section, namely medical ethics, business ethics, etc. *Meta-ethics* studies the nature and justification of moral standards, values, principles, and theories and the meaning of moral concepts and terms. Two of the most important questions in meta-ethics are "is morality objective?" and "why should we obey moral obligations?" I will not spend too much time discussing these deeper questions in this book, since they take us far beyond the scope of our present discussion.[1] However, I will introduce readers to meta-ethical issues that have some bearing on ethics in science.

In order to get a better understanding of ethical theory and its applications, it will be useful to introduce several key concepts of moral philosophy. Each person in society gets exposed to a *commonsense morality*. This morality consists of a wide variety of standards of conduct, duties, obligations, values and principles that come from disparate sources, such as parents, teachers, peers, religious leaders, professionals, literature, music, the media, and so forth (Pojman 1995). Ethicists call these standards a "commonsense" morality because they are the norms that most people learn and practice without any explicit theorizing or deeper analysis. Some of these commonsense morals include principles like "do unto others as you would have them do unto you," "keep your promises," "be fair," "always do your best," and so on. Some of these commonsense values include happiness, honesty, justice, charity, courage, integrity, community, love, knowledge, and freedom.

A *moral theory*, on the other hand, attempts to provide a justification or foundation for commonsense morality. Moral theories describe, unify, explicate, and criticize commonly accepted morals (Fox and DeMarco 1990). Moral theories start with a database of commonsense moral convictions, but they can go beyond commonsense by drawing on findings from psychology, sociology, biology, economics, and other sciences. Once we have developed a moral theory, we can use that theory to challenge some of our commonsense moral convictions; these convictions can be revised in light of deeper reflections and analysis. Thus, commonsense morality can change in response to critical reflection and need not be taken at face value. For example, the interpretation of the commonsense maxim "spare the rod and spoil the child" has changed as a result of psychological research and deeper reflection on the ethics of disciplining children. In the 1800s this maxim implied that parents and teachers were justified in whipping, beating, and hitting their children for insubordination. Today, research in child development and moral discussions have led us to take a very different view of corporal punishment. Conduct that was perfectly acceptable in the 1800s would now be viewed as child abuse. After using moral theories to change commonsense morality, we can then revise those theories so that they cohere with this new database. This process of revising commonsense morality in light of theory and vice versa can continue indefinitely, and is known as the method of wide reflective equilibrium (Rawls 1971). Most ethicists believe that this method provides the best way of justifying moral theories.

Philosophers and theologians have defended a wide variety of moral theories, each with its own particular slant on morality. Some theories emphasize individual rights and dignity; others emphasize the common good. Some theories are secular; others are religious. Some theories focus on obligations and duties; others focus on virtues and character. Some theories establish moral ideals; others settle for practical principles. Some theories assess consequences in judging actions; others assess motives. Some theories are human-centered; others place human beings in a larger ecological framework. Rather than take the reader through the labyrinth of moral theories that scholars have constructed and refined over the last few centuries, I will provide brief summaries of some of the most influential ones. I will state the basic assumptions these theories make but I will offer no deeper analysis or criticism.[2]

The *divine command theory* holds that the rightness or wrongness of an act depends on God's commands: an act is right if it conforms to God's will; an act is wrong if it goes against God's will. Many of the world's most popular religions hold some version of this theory in that they base their morals on God's commands. As I mentioned earlier, I believe that it is possible to develop ethical standards that do not depend on particular religions or theologies, but the divine command theory denies this claim. While I think the theory can provide some insight into moral choices and standards, I will not rely on this theory in my analysis of the ethics of science, since I am attempting to develop a secular account of ethics. The remaining theories I consider provide ethics with secular foundations.

Utilitarianism holds that we should act in such a way that we produce the greatest balance of good/bad consequences (or utility) for all people in the long run (Mill 1979). There are two main types of utilitarianism, *act-utilitarianism*, which holds that individual actions should maximize utility, and *rule-utilitarianism*, which holds that actions should be based on a system of rules that maximize utility. According to popular caricatures of utilitarianism, this view implies that the ends justify the means and that the good of the many outweighs the good of the few. However, sophisticated versions of this theory can eschew or buffer these implications (Pojman 1995).

According to a view developed by the German Enlightenment philosopher Immanuel Kant (1981), one should always treat rational beings as having intrinsic value or worth, not as mere instruments or objects having only extrinsic value. Kantianism also holds that moral standards should be universalizeable: moral principles are rules that would be followed by all rational beings with a good will. (A person with a good will is motivated by the desire to do her duty for duty's sake.) For Kant, actions must be done for the right reasons in order to be worthy of moral praise. Kantianism implies that individuals should not be sacrificed for the common good, that we have moral duties that do not depend on the consequences of our actions, and that motives matter in assessing the morality of human conduct.

The *natural rights theory*, like Kantianism, emphasizes the importance of individual rights and freedoms. According to this view, all people have

natural rights to life, liberty, and property, and everyone is morally permitted to do anything they wish provided that their actions do not violate
the rights of other people (Nozick 1974). Moral rights, on this view, can be
thought of as like trump cards in that legitimate rights claims can be used
to criticize any actions that would violate those rights. Rights are usually
understood in a negative way: people have rights not to have things done
to them but they do not have rights to have things done for them. Thus,
the right to life implies a right to be killed but not a right to be saved from
dying. This view is sometimes characterized as a "minimal morality"
because it holds that we have no moral duties to help other people; we
acquire obligations to help others through agreements or by initiating
special relationships, such as husband–wife or parent–child.

Natural law theories hold that morality is founded on human nature: if
an action has a basis in our natural instincts, emotions, or social relations,
then it is right; if an action goes against our natural instincts, emotions, or
social relations, then it is wrong. Natural law theories also maintain that
we should strive to produce or achieve natural goods and eliminate or
avoid natural evils (Pojman 1995). Natural goods include life, health, and
happiness.

Social contract theorists propose that morality consists of a set of rules
that we agree are important to regulate society; it is a kind of social contract we make in order to live together in a society. In justifying moral
rules, social contract theorists imagine people as existing in a state of
nature prior to the formation of society. In order to live well, people must
cooperate; and in order to cooperate, they need some rules for conduct.
These rules are the rules of morality, politics, and the law (Pojman 1995).

Virtue approaches to ethics have a long history dating back to Aristotle
(1984), and they have been revived in recent years after a prolonged hiatus
from the philosophical scene. According to the virtue approach, the central
question in morality is not "what ought I to do?" but "what kind of a
person should I be?" Our main task in life is to develop certain traits of
character known as moral virtues. Some of these virtues might include
honesty, integrity, courage, humility, sincerity, kindness, wisdom, tem-
perance, and so on. One develops these virtues in the same way that one
develops other character traits, i.e. through repetition and practice. Becoming a virtuous person is thus like becoming a good basketball player or
musician. Most virtue theories imply that the virtuous person will follow
moral rules and principles as they develop their characters, but character,
not duty or obligation, defines ethical conduct.

The *ethics of care*, a theory inspired by feminist approaches to morality,
rejects traditional approaches to ethics on the grounds that they place too
much emphasis on duties, rights, and justice. Such theories are too
abstract, legalistic, and uncaring, according to this view. As an alternative,

the ethics of care holds that our main task in life is to love and care for ourselves and other people. We should cultivate loving and caring relationships in our conduct instead of relying on abstract concepts and principles (Gilligan 1982). In some ways, the ethics of care provides a modern rendition of Jesus' instruction to love your neighbor as you love yourself, and his critique of the Pharisees' legalistic morality.

One final type of theory worth mentioning has been inspired by the environmentalist movement. The *deep ecology* approach to morality is unlike all of the other approaches to ethics in that it is not human-centered. Human-centered moral theories frame important questions about nature in terms of human interests, rights, obligations, and so on. Thus, many writers maintain that pollution is undesirable only because polluted environments can harm people or prevent them from realizing various goods. Deep ecologists hold that human-centered ethics cannot adequately deal with moral issues involving other species, the land, ecosystems, the atmosphere, and oceans, since there are values in nature that are independent of human interests or rights (Naess 1989). Thus, an ecosystem is worth preserving because it has intrinsic, moral value, not because we happen to value it for its economic or social uses. Animals have rights, according to some writers, because they also have intrinsic moral worth and are not mere instruments for the promotion of human interests (Regan 1983).

As you can see, scholars have developed many different moral theories. These different approaches reflect some of the different insights and tensions that we find in our thinking about human beings, society, and nature and they are based on different insights into the nature of morality. Is one of these theories the correct approach to morality? Since we can use the method of wide reflective equilibrium to test moral theories, any theory worth its salt needs to adapt to the evidence provided by science and reflections on common sense. Thus, although these theories look very different at first glance, they often end up supporting similar standards and values after we use wide reflective equilibrium to revise them. The upshot of this is that most theories have similar practical implications.

Since there are a wide variety of moral theories that yield similar results, the most reasonable approach to moral theorizing, I believe, is to accept some kind of pluralism. According to pluralism, there are a number of basic moral standards (or first principles) that can conflict with each other (Ross 1930). Each of these standards has some *prima facie* justification from commonsense morality and most of these standards are supported by different moral theories. Thus, utilitarians, Kantians, and social contract theorists can all agree that we should not harm other people, that we should not lie, and so forth. Since these principles have a broad base of support, they are usually less controversial than the particular moral theories that support them (Beauchamp and Childress 1994).

Many philosophers who study applied ethics prefer to work with general, ethical principles rather than moral theories because one can use principles to support an ethical decision or a social policy without defending an entire (possibly controversial) moral theory (Fox and DeMarco 1990). Another reason for employing general principles is that they are easier to understand, to teach, and learn than moral theories. Finally, since principles are expressed in very general terms, they can be applied to a variety of cases and interpreted in different ways. This kind of flexibility allows one to apply principles to diverse cases without ignoring important details. Some of these basic moral principles are as follows (Fox and DeMarco 1990):

> *Nonmalificence:* Do not harm yourself or other people.
> *Beneficence:* Help yourself and other people.
> *Autonomy:* Allow rational individuals to make free, informed choices.
> *Justice:* Treat people fairly; treat equals equally, unequals, unequally.
> *Utility:* Maximize the ratio of benefits to harms for all people.
> *Fidelity:* Keep your promises and agreements.
> *Honesty:* Do not lie, defraud, deceive, or mislead.
> *Privacy:* Respect personal privacy and confidentiality.

Moral philosophers interpret and elaborate these principles by spelling out concepts like "harm," "benefit," "fairness," "rational," and "deception," but I will not undertake that task here. For our purposes, we need to recognize that some set of moral principles can be applied to a wide variety of moral choices.

These principles should be viewed as guidelines for conduct rather than hard and fast rules. We should follow these principles in our conduct but exceptions can be made when they conflict with each other or with other standards. When two principles conflict we may decide to follow one principle instead of another. For example, when asked to give our opinion of someone's cooking we may decide to be less than completely honest in order to avoid harming that person. Since conflicts among various principles and standards can arise, we must frequently exercise our moral judgment in deciding how we should act.[3] In order to exercise our judgment, we need to understand the particular features of a given situation. Thus, there is an important sense in which ethics are situational: although some general, ethical principles should guide our conduct, we need to base our decisions and actions on the facts and values inherent in particular situations. The next section outlines an approach to moral judgment and reasoning.

Moral Choices

We make choices every waking moment of our lives. Some of these choices are trivial; others are profound. Some choices are informed by personal preferences, tastes, or mere whimsy. Others are based on standards of conduct. Standards of conduct can regulate our actions by providing guidance for many of the choices we face in living. For example, a principle of honesty would obligate a person to tell the truth when faced with the choice of lying about their golf score or telling the truth. It is not easy to follow standards of conduct all of the time since they often conflict with each other or with our personal interests. For example, a person who could win a great deal of money by lying about their golf score would face a conflict between their interest in money and the obligation to tell the truth. People often violate accepted ethical or moral standards for personal gain, but we usually label such actions as immoral and selfish and we disapprove of such conduct.

But a different kind of situation arises when standards of conduct appear to conflict with each other. People often must choose not between ethics (or morality) and self-interest but between different moral, ethical, legal, political, religious, or institutional obligations. In these circumstances, the key question is not "should I do the right thing?," but "what is the right thing to do?" These problematic choices are known as ethical (or moral) dilemmas. Thus, an ethical dilemma is a situation in which a person can choose between at least two different actions, each of which seem to be well supported by some standard of conduct (Fox and DeMarco 1990). These choices may be between the lesser of two evils or the greater of two goods. Sometimes these choices involve two different ethical standards. For example, suppose a person has made a promise to a drug company to keep its trade secrets, but she discovers that the company has falsified and fabricated some of the data it has provided to the Food and Drug Administration (FDA) on a new drug it has been testing. She faces a conflict between a duty to prevent harms to the public and duties of fidelity and loyalty to the company. Sometimes these choices involve conflict between ethics and the law. For example, a driver who is trying to get someone to the hospital in an emergency situation faces the choice between breaking the speed limit and preventing harm to someone. I believe that most people, including scientists, face ethical dilemmas on a daily basis as they attempt to balance their various obligations and commitments.

So how does one "solve" an ethical dilemma? A solution to an ethical dilemma would be a decision or choice about what one ought to do. A fairly simple method for making any kind of choice also applies to ethical choices. This method is a kind of practical reasoning that proceeds as follows (Fox and DeMarco 1990):

> *Step 1:* Frame a set of questions.
> *Step 2:* Gather information.
> *Step 3:* Explore different options.
> *Step 4:* Evaluate options.
> *Step 5:* Make a decision.
> *Step 6:* Take action.

Posing a set of questions is usually the first step in any decision. A question can be as simple as "should I do X or not do X?" Once questions have been raised, one can gather information about the relevant facts and circumstances. Obviously, we can paralyze our decision-making abilities by expending too much time and effort gathering information, so we need to also decide which information is relevant. Since not having enough information can also result in poor decisions, it is often better to err in favor of too much information than in favor of too little. After one has gathered information, one also needs to explore different options. What are the different courses of action one can take? This step often requires some imagination and open-mindedness because often we fail to explore all of our options, and this causes us to overlook attractive alternatives. Sometimes we can even avoid dilemmas altogether by fulfilling conflicting obligations at different times.

The fourth step is often the most difficult of all the steps, since it requires us to assess different choices in light of our various obligations and the information we have at our disposal. In evaluating these options it is important to ask these questions in the following order: are any of these different actions required or forbidden by the law? Are any of these actions required or forbidden by special (institutional or professional) ethical standards? Do moral principles have some bearing on these different actions? Although I accept a pluralistic approach to morality, and I believe that people who face difficult moral choices need to balance competing standards, these different norms can be ranked (or prioritized) according to the following rule of thumb: other things being equal, moral obligations take precedence over ethical obligations, which take precedence over legal ones. Since all industrial societies depend on the rule of law, we have a moral obligation to obey the law even though breaking the law can be justified in some cases. Laws should be broken only when they require us to do something patently unethical or immoral or when civil disobedience is justified. Since socially valued professions and institutions can function only when people who occupy professional or institutional roles adhere to professional or institutional standards of conduct, we have a moral obligation to follow special ethical standards. However, professional or institutional standards can be violated if they require us to do something illegal or patently immoral.[4] The key point here is that the burden of proof lies on someone who would violate the law or special ethical standards, since these standards have a sound foundation. In an ideal case, a "best" decision will emerge as a result of considering how various standards – legal, ethical, and moral – apply to a given situation. After reasoning through an assessment of the various alternatives, the next step is to make a decision and then take action.

Sometimes it will not be difficult to make a decision as a preponderance of evidence will favor one option over another. However, sometimes two or more options will still appear to be equally good (or bad) after we have conducted a thorough evaluation. If we encounter this difficulty, we can go back to some of the earlier steps in this process. After evaluating our options, we may discover than we need some more information or that there is another option than we did not consider in our initial assessment. After going back to earlier steps, we can proceed to later ones, and then go back again. Thus, although I have portrayed this method as proceeding in a linear fashion, it often proceeds cyclically.

An example of a difficult decision will help illustrate this method. A professor is about to turn in her final grades for the semester when a student comes to her asking about his final grade in her course. She tells him that he will receive a C, and he begs her to change the grade to a B. He explains that he needs to receive a B in the course in order to continue his scholarship at the university. He tells the professor that he will do extra work in order to get a higher grade. The question the professor asks might be "should I allow the student to do extra work for a higher grade?" The information-gathering part of the professor's decision might involve reviewing the student's grades for the semester and determining whether she made any mistakes in grading. It might also involve looking at the overall grade distribution to see how close the student's grade of C is to other students' B grades. Her choices might be: (a) change the grade, provided the student does extra work; (b) change the grade with no conditions; (c) don't change the grade. In evaluating her decision, she would consider her different obligations. As a professor, she has an obligation to grade fairly, and a grade change might be unfair to the other students; the student does not deserve a better grade. She also has an obligation, as a professor, to try to help her students, and one might argue that the best way to help this student is to change his grade, since he will have to drop out of school if he loses his scholarship. On the other hand, one might also argue that the student needs to learn some lessons about academic responsibility, hard work, studying, and so forth, and that he can only learn these lessons by getting the C grade. Upon further reflection, the professor decides to gather more information and she asks more questions. She discovers that the student has approached his other professors with the same story and that none of them have agreed to change his grades. The professor decides not to change the student's grades because (1) she has an obligation to be fair; and (2) although she has an obligation to help the student, it is not at all clear that changing his grade (under any conditions) is the best way to help him.

This example seems to be an "easy" case because one solution emerges as the "best" way of solving the dilemma. But sometimes several different solutions can still seem to be just as good, even after we have conducted a thorough evaluation; and there may not be a single, optimal solution (Whitbeck 1995a). Moral decisions thus resemble engineering design problems: just as there may be more than one right way to build a bridge, there may also be more than one right way to solve a moral dilemma. None of this implies, however, that "anything goes" when it comes to solving ethical dilemmas, since some decisions are clearly wrong or unacceptable and some may be better than others with respect to specific standards. A bridge design that does not result in a stable structure would be unacceptable, and we can evaluate different designs with respect to cost-efficiency, reliability, durability, and other criteria. Likewise, a moral choice that violated most commonly held moral principles would not be acceptable, and we can evaluate different choices in terms of their adherence to beneficence, justice, autonomy, and other moral and ethical standards.

The possibility of multiple solutions also suggests that there can be some justification for allowing non-rational factors to influence moral decision-making. When reasoning yields several equally good solutions, and we need to act on one solution, we can appeal to other methods, such as intuition, emotion, or chance. Sometimes a gut feeling may be the final arbiter in a difficult dilemma. This does not mean, of course, that reasoning should not play an important role in decision-making, since the earlier stages of difficult decisions should involve reasoning. It would be foolish to rely on a gut feeling before gathering information or evaluating options. On the other hand, it would be imprudent to fail to make a decision due to one's inability to find a single, optimal solution to a dilemma. Reasoning can be counterproductive when it prevents us from taking effective action.

Before reaching a decision, the following questions can be useful in helping us evaluate our decision process: "Could I justify this decision to a public audience?," "Can I live with this decision?," "Can I rely on anyone else's experience or expertise to help me make this decision?" The first question addresses a concern about public accountability. Sometimes people act unethically or simply make poor decisions because they do not believe that their choices or actions will become public. But we often must justify or explain our choices and take responsibility for our actions. This is especially true in a professional setting, where clients and the public demand accountability (Bayles 1988). Focusing on accountability does not guarantee a result that will please everyone, since some people may still disagree with a decision. However, a person who can defend her decision to other people will stand a better chance of making a good choice than a person who cannot.

The second question addresses a concern about personal integrity. Part of living a good life is being proud of one's conduct and character. We often feel shame when we realize that we have made poor choices, that we have acted unwisely, or that we are not acting like the kind person we would like to be. Good choices, actions, and character traits shine like jewels in our lives and give us a sense of pride in our conduct. Good character results from and manifests itself in our deliberations about difficult moral choices. The final question is simply a reminder that we can and should seek advice when faced with difficult choices. It is likely that we know someone who has faced a very similar dilemma and that we can benefit from their wisdom and experience. Of course, we must take responsibility for any decision that we make – we should not let other people make choices that really belong to us – but it is often helpful to know that we are not alone. Scientists can rely on peers or mentors when making difficult ethical choices.

Relativism

Before wrapping up this thumbnail sketch of moral philosophy, I need to address a concern that plagues all discussions of ethics and morality. The concern is that the standards I discuss in this book may be nothing more than the social customs or conventions of a particular society or culture. What is right or wrong, ethical or unethical is relative to a particular society or culture. Hence, any claims I make about the ethics of science will apply only to those cultures or societies that happen to accept the values and standards I discuss here. Worries about relativism arose in my earlier discussions of the application of moral principles and ethical dilemmas. Although I do not have the space to explore this topic in detail, it is important to say a few words about relativism to help clarify discussions of science and ethics.

To focus the issues, I will distinguish between three different types of relativism:

(1) *Legal relativism* (LR): legal standards are relative to a given nation or society.
(2) *Special ethical relativism* (SER): special ethical standards are relative to a particular social institution or profession.
(3) *General ethical relativism* (GER) (or moral relativism): all standards of conduct are relative to a particular society or culture.

LR would seem to be the least controversial of the three views. A nation's sovereignty depends on its ability to make and enforce its own laws. When US citizens make laws, these laws do not apply to other countries and vice versa. Various nations can agree on international laws and treaties, but even these laws would only apply to nations that enter these agreements. If laws are relative to particular nations and their agreements, our obligation to obey the law is therefore also relative to a particular nation (or its agreements with other nations): when in Rome, obey Roman law. Since moral or ethical considerations may justify breaking the law in some cases, we can appeal to these standards in criticizing a nation's laws, however.

SER also seems like a reasonable position, so long as we understand that special ethical standards must still answer to the law and morality. For example, it seems clear that physicians and lawyers can and should obey different ethical standards, since their professions have different goals and provide different goods and services. Although some standards may hold in both professions, e.g. legal and medical ethics both include a duty to maintain confidentiality, lawyers and physicians should obey the standards of their own professions (Bayles 1988). When practicing medicine, follow medical ethics; when practicing law, follow legal ethics. However, standards of medical or legal ethics should not require physicians or lawyers to violate the law on a routine basis nor should they require physicians or lawyers to do things that are patently immoral. To see this point more clearly, consider some hypothetical standards of conduct in a street gang – "Gang Ethics." "Ethical" conduct in a gang might include assault, theft, arson, vandalism, murder, racketeering, and other illegal and immoral activities. Could we treat "Gang Ethics" as a professional standard akin to medical ethics? The answer is clearly "no," since these norms would violate legal and moral standards. We could call gang standards of conduct "social norms" but not "ethical norms."

This brings us to GER, the most controversial of the three different versions of relativism. Hundreds of years ago, most people in the Western world would have rejected GER as heresy, since morality was viewed as based on God's commands, which do not vary across cultures. Just as there is one, true God, there is also one, true morality, according to this view. People who do not recognize these moral standards are uncivilized, immoral, or irreligious. But things have changed in the last few hundred years, and probably more people in the Western world believe in moral relativism today than at any previous time in history. Several factors can help explain this rise in the belief in moral relativism (Pojman 1995):

(1)   *A decline in religion*: People are less religious today and therefore less apt to believe in an absolute morality based on God's will.

(2)   *A reaction to the abuses of colonialism*: During the colonial era (and before) Western settlers and explorers conquered and converted the "uncivilized" people they found in the Americas, Africa, and the Pacific Islands. These abuses destroyed cultures and exploited indigenous peoples in the name of Western religion and morality.

(3)   *Multiculturalism*: People have become more aware of cultural diversity as a result of immigration, global communication, and empirical data from anthropology.

(4)   *Science*: Many people today view science as the sole arbiter of truth and distrust disciplines, such as moral philosophy, that do not have the same level of objectivity. Further, many widely accepted scientific ideas, such as Darwin's theory of evolution, undermine the belief in objective, moral standards (Dennett 1995).

(5)   *Philosophy*: Many philosophers during the last century have challenged the objectivity of ethics and have defended versions of moral relativism. Some of them, such as Nietzsche and Sartre, have had an impact on Western literature and culture.

It is not my aim in this chapter to give a thorough critique of moral relativism – that task would require at least a whole book in itself. However, I will provide the reader with a brief assessment of this view and its implications for science and ethics.

One of the main arguments for moral relativism is the fact of cultural diversity (Benedict 1946). This fact is a descriptive thesis: different societies have different customs, mores and conventions. Anthropologists note that some cultures worship cows while others eat them; some cultures accept polygamy while others require monogamy; some cultures approve of female circumcision while others abhor this custom; some cultures practice cannibalism while others condemn the eating of human flesh, and so on. The second main argument for moral relativism is the fact of moral disagreement. This fact is also a descriptive claim: many people within a country and across national boundaries disagree about moral issues, such as abortion, euthanasia, capital punishment, human rights, and so forth. From these descriptive claims, those who defend GER draw a prescriptive conclusion: moral standards are relative to a particular society or culture (Pojman 1990). Relativists find additional support for their view in its implications for moral tolerance: if we understand that moral standards are relative to a particular society, then we will tolerate each society's values and standards. We will not pass judgment on other cultures or try to convert them to the "correct" way of living or thinking.

The two facts cited in the last paragraph are virtually beyond dispute, but do they support moral relativism? Critics of moral relativism attempt to debunk these facts in the following ways. First, cultural diversity may not be as great as appears at first glance. Anthropologists have also provided us with some evidence that many cultures have some standards in common. For instance, nearly all cultures have prohibitions against murder, assault, theft, rape, dishonesty, and incest (Pojman 1990). Cultures disagree about who belongs to the moral community, however. A culture might condone killing someone from a different moral community, e.g. someone from a different tribe or ethnic group, yet it might condemn killing someone from within the moral community. Although some moral standards exhibit a great deal of variation, such as standards pertaining to sexual practices, marriage, and personal liberties, one might argue that there are some basic standards held by all societies. We can refer to these standards as a core morality. There may even be a plausible scientific explanation for a core morality: the core morality consists of those standards which are necessary for the survival of any society (Pojman 1990). Without some common standards, societies would dissolve. We may even find that some of these core moral standards have a strong basis in common instincts and emotions, and that these traits have an evolutionary basis (Alexander 1987).

Furthermore, in many cases moral diversity can be explained away by appealing to economic conditions or background beliefs. For instance, people in the US abhor infanticide but people from other countries do not. Many of the cultures that do not abhor infanticide are far worse off economically than the US and often simply cannot afford to feed defective or unwanted infants. In the US, however, people have more than enough resources to care for defective or unwanted infants. If these countries that accept infanticide had more resources, it is likely that they would not condone this practice. In the US people eat cows; in India people worship them. These different attitudes result, in part, from different metaphysical beliefs about cows: most people in the US regard cows as unintelligent animals; most people in India regard cows as reincarnated people.

Second, people may share some common moral standards even if they disagree about controversial cases and issues. People who disagree about the morality of abortion may nevertheless agree that killing is wrong and that women should be granted the freedom to control their own bodies. At the center of this dispute is the question of the fetus's membership in the moral community – do fetuses have the rights we typically assign to newborn infants? Critics of moral relativism usually attempt to explain how moral disputes can arise even if most people accept a core morality (Pojman 1990).

Critics also point out that the relativist's inferences from descriptive claims about social customs to prescriptive ones about standards of conduct commit the naturalistic fallacy. According to most logicians, it is a fallacy to infer an "ought" from an "is" or a "value" from a "fact." From the fact that many people do smoke cigarettes, we cannot infer that many people should smoke cigarettes. So, it is a fallacy to infer moral relativism from cultural diversity. From the fact that different cultures have different social customs, we cannot infer that they should have those customs (Frankena 1973).

Finally, critics also attack the relativist's appeal to tolerance by arguing that relativism does not imply tolerance (Pojman 1990). Suppose tolerance is a social custom in society S1 but not in society S2. It follows, if we accept relativism, that people in S1 should be tolerant but people in S2 have no obligation to be tolerant. Therefore, if people in S2 attempt to destroy or change the customs of S1, the people of S1 have no grounds for appeal, since the obligation to be tolerant applies only if you live in a tolerant society. This seems like a very unsatisfactory defense of moral tolerance, but it follows from moral relativism's assumptions. To provide tolerance with a more substantial foundation, one needs to hold that at least one moral standard, tolerance for other cultures, applies to all cultures. The irony here is that a thorough and complete relativism undercuts one of the values relativists usually defend, tolerance.

The alternative to moral relativism is some form of moral objectivism. For the purposes of this discussion, we can distinguish between two versions of objectivism, strong and weak (Pojman 1990). Strong objectivism, also know as *absolutism*, holds that (1) there are some universal moral standards, and (2) these standards have no exceptions; they are hard and fast rules. Weak objectivism holds (1) but denies (2): moral standards, though universal, are guidelines to conduct, not absolute rules. The weaker version of objectivism would appear to be more plausible than the stronger version, since weaker versions are better at accommodating the facts of cultural diversity and moral disagreement. Moral differences and disputes can arise because different societies interpret and apply universal stand-ards in different ways; general principles have various exceptions. Of all the moral theories that I discussed in the section headed Moral Theory, the pluralistic approach fits best with weak objectivism (Pojman 1990).

Although I think moral objectivism is highly plausible, it has its own difficulties. The main problem for the objectivist is to provide an objective basis for morality. How can some ethical standards apply across cultures? What is the foundation for these universal moral values or principles? There are three traditional answers to this request for an objective founda-tion for morality:

(1) *Naturalism.* Morality is based on human biology, psychology, sociology, and so on.
(2) *Rationalism.* Morality is based on reason itself; moral standards are the rules that any rational, moral agent would accept.
(3) *Supernaturalism.* Morality is based on God's will.

Each of these approaches generates its own problems. Naturalists must face the naturalistic fallacy and they need to explain how their doctrine does not simply make morality relative to the human species and its needs and goals; rationalists owe us a non-circular, informative, and practical account of rationality; and supernaturalists need to justify belief in the existence of God and explain the relation between morality and God's commands. I will not probe these meta-ethical problems and issues in more depth here.[5]

As promised, I will bring this discussion back to our main topic, the ethics in science. What implications, if any, do various versions of relativ-ism have for ethical conduct in science? First, let's consider legal relativ-ism. If we apply this view to science, it holds that scientists should follow the laws of the nation in which their research takes place (or the laws that pertain to their research). This is a reasonable view that most scientists probably accept. (Some interesting legal questions arise when research spans over different nations, of course.) Aside from the moral legitimacy of laws, scientists also have some good practical reasons for obeying the law: scientists who violate the law can get into trouble with local author-ities and the public at large. Although scientists may still violate laws under extraordinary conditions, they still have a general duty to conform to local laws.

Special ethical relativism also makes sense in science, provided that science's ethics conform to laws and commonly accepted moral standards. As professionals, scientists should follow the standards of their profession, not the standards of other, non-scientific professions. Although account-ants and lawyers practice secrecy as a part of their profession, secrecy is generally frowned upon in science, except in some circumstances. When it comes to secrecy and openness, scientists should follow scientific ethics, not legal ethics. Thus, unless they have moral reasons for violating their professional standards, scientists should adhere to those standards. When practicing science, do as the scientists do.

This brings us to the last version of relativism, moral relativism. If scientists give priority to legal and special ethical standards, then concerns about moral relativism will usually play only a small role in scientific conduct. It should matter little to scientists whether honesty is valued in different cultures across the world; their main concern should be that honesty is valued in science. As long as scientists stay within their professional roles in science and do not interact with society at large, concerns about moral relativism should not be a major issue. However, since scientists must often interact with society at large, vexing moral questions arise in science, and it is these questions that summon the specter of moral relativism. Thus, moral relativism can be a real issue for scientists when they decide how to treat human subjects in a different country, how to share intellectual property rights across cultures, whether to conduct research on cloning human embryos, how to discuss research on homosexuality with the public, and so on.

CHAPTER 3
Science as a Profession

In the previous chapter I distinguished between ethics and morality, and I claimed that professions have their own ethical standards. If we view science as a profession, then people who occupy the professional role "scientist" should adhere to professional standards as well as moral ones (Shrader-Frechette 1994). A professional standard of conduct can be justified insofar as it enables that profession to provide people with valuable goods and services. Professional standards function as a quality control mechanism for a profession's goods and services and they help maintain the public's trust in the profession (Bayles 1988). Moral and legal standards can and should play a role in guiding professional conduct in that professional standards should not require people to violate the law or commonly accepted standards of morality. Moral norms can also provide guidance for professionals when their ethical standards conflict with each other or with other standards of conduct. Finally, professionals are sometimes justified in violating their special standards of conduct for moral reasons. In this chapter I will apply this way of thinking about professional ethics to science. To achieve this task, I will need to explain why science should be viewed as profession and explore the nature of science's goals and norms.

Science:
From Avocation
to Profession

What is science? Science is first and foremost a social institution (Merton 1973, Hull 1988, Longino 1990). Like other social institutions, science depends on the cooperation and coordination of different people to achieve common goals within a larger social environment. Science is a society that operates within society. Many different aspects of scientific research require the cooperation and coordination of different people, such as experimentation, testing, data analysis, writing research papers and grant proposals, refereeing papers and proposals, staffing research projects, and educating future scientists (Grinnell 1992). Many parts of research also bring scientists into direct contact with society at large, such as reporting results to the media, expert testimony, research on human and animals subjects, government funding of research, and so on.

But science is more than a social institution; it is also a profession (Fuchs 1992, Shrader-Frechette 1994). Not every social institution is a profession. Since a social institution is roughly any cooperative, social activity that generates obligations and social roles, social institutions include activities as diverse as baseball, the Stock Market, the US Marines, and marriage. There are many criteria that distinguish professions from other social institutions, but I will discuss only seven central ones below. These criteria should not be viewed as necessary and sufficient conditions for being a profession: that is, we might regard an institution as a profession even if it does not meet all of these criteria, and an institution might meet all of these criteria and yet not be regarded as a profession. Nevertheless, the criteria are useful in describing some common characteristics of professions. I shall now discuss how these criteria pertain to science.

(1) Professions generally enable people to obtain socially valued goals (or goods and services) and professionals have obligations to insure that these goals are obtained (Bayles 1988, Jennings *et al.* 1987). Science helps people obtain a variety of socially valued goals, such as knowledge and power.

(2) Professions have implicit or explicit standards of competence and conduct that govern professional activities, which help to insure that professionals perform as expected and that the entire profession maintains quality and integrity (Bayles 1988). Incompetent or unethical members of a profession betray the public's trust and deliver goods and services of questionable quality, and when professionals produce goods and services of poor quality, people can be harmed. Bad science can produce adverse social consequences, and science has its own standards of competence and conduct.

(3) Professionals usually go through a long period of formal and informal education and training before being admitted into the profession (Fuchs 1992). The education and training is necessary to insure that people meet the standards of the profession.

Scientists go through a long period of education and training which includes undergraduate and graduate education as well as postdoctoral work (Fuchs 1992). Although scientists do not have to pass professional examinations, it is virtually impossible to be employed as a scientist without mastering a wide body of knowledge as well as various techniques and methods. Most research scientists also have advanced degrees, such as a Ph.D. or MD.

(4) Professions have governing bodies for insuring that professional standards are upheld. Although science's governing bodies are not as powerful or formal as the governing bodies one finds in the other professions, science has its own, informal governing bodies, such as the NSF, NIH, AAAS, NAS, and other scientific organizations (Fuchs 1992). The editorial staffs of various scientific journals can also function as governing bodies insofar as they administer and enforce standards of competence and conduct (LaFollette 1992).

(5) Professions are careers (or vocations). People who occupy professional roles earn money for doing what they do, but a career is more than a way to earn a living: people who have a career usually identify with the goals of that career and draw self-esteem from their vocation. Although science may have been nothing more than a hobby or avocation at one time, it is now a career (PSRCR 1992, Grinnell 1992). Indeed, some writers have argued that the rampant careerism we find in science today is at least partly responsible for some of the unethical conduct that occurs in science (Broad and Wade 1993, PSRCR 1992).

(6) Professionals are granted certain privileges in order to provide their goods and services. With these privileges also come responsibilities and trust: people grant professionals certain privileges because they trust that professionals will provide their goods and services in a responsible, ethical way (Bayles 1988). Scientists are also granted certain privileges. For instance, archeologists are allowed to explore construction sites, psychologists are allowed to have access to controlled substances, and physicists are allowed access to plutonium and other fissionable materials. Special privileges also imply responsibilities and trust: we trust that scientists who receive government funding will not waste it, that psychologists who study the effects of cocaine on rats will not sell this drug on the black market, and so forth.

(7) Professionals are often recognized as intellectual authorities

within their domain of expertise (Bayles 1988). Just as lawyers are regarded as having special knowledge, judgment, and expertise about the law, scientists are viewed as having special knowledge, judgment, and expertise about the phenomena they study (Shrader-Frechette 1994). In today's society, intellectual authorities provide us with most of the knowledge we learn in school and they play a key role in shaping public policy (Hardwig 1994).

Should science be viewed as a profession, given what I have said about professions in general? I believe it should, though I recognize that some people may disagree with this claim. Science has not always been a profession, but it has become more like a profession since the Renaissance (Fuchs 1992). Many of the great figures in the history of science were not what we would call professional scientists, of course. According to the criteria listed above, we should view Aristotle, Copernicus, and Galileo as amateur scientists not because they were incompetent but because science was not a profession during their eras. However, by the time Darwin published his *Origin of Species*, science was clearly a profession and not merely a social institution. What important events happened between 1450 and 1850 that led to the professionalization of science? Although I cannot discuss them all here, some important events include: the development of a scientific method, the establishment of scientific societies and scientific journals, the growth of universities and university-based research, the emphasis of science education at all levels, the employment of scientists in industrial and military research, the technological applications of science, and public recognition of science's power, authority, and prestige (Meadows 1992, Fuchs 1992). However, science is less professional than some other social institutions, such as medicine or law. For instance, science does not have licensing boards and many sciences lack formal codes of conduct.

In my discussion of science as a profession I should note that the phrase "scientific profession" is an abstract, general expression I use to refer to the many different scientific professions, such as molecular biology, developmental psychology, immunology, biochemistry, astronomy, entomology, etc. Although there are important differences between various scientific professions, there are also some important similarities. These similarities consist, in part, of professional standards and goals common to many different sciences. While it is important to be aware of differences, we must not lose sight of the similarities. This book will focus on the similarities, and I will therefore often use the term "science" to refer to that which is common to all scientific professions.

Many scientists may object to my portrayal of science as a profession on the grounds that this view of science does not reflect the importance of amateur science, creativity, freedom, collegiality, and other aspects of sci-ence that do not fit the professional model. Moreover, many would argue that science could suffer irreparable damage if it becomes even more like a profession than it already is. The most serious threat posed by the pro-fessionalization of science, one might argue, would be harm to scientific creativity and freedom. Making science into a profession could reduce scientists to technocrats and place too many restrictions on how science is practiced. Science should not be governed by rigid rules, licensing boards, and other control mechanisms that we find in professions like medicine or law (Feyerabend 1975).

In response to these objections, I do not claim that science fits the pro-fessional model perfectly; I only claim that it fits the model well enough for us to regard it as a profession, and that it fits the model better now than it did a few centuries ago. I am also concerned about the potential damage to science that could result from further professionalization. However, given science's tremendous impact on society and its social responsi-bilities, completely unprofessionalized science poses grave risks for social values (Shrader-Frechette 1994). We need some standards of quality con-trol for scientific research, and virtually any standards will take science down the road toward professionalism. Perhaps we can reach some reason-able compromise concerning the degree of professionalization that science ought to achieve by reminding ourselves of the importance of creativity and intellectual freedom in science.

The Goals
of Science

Like other professions, science provides socially valued goods and services. Science scholars refer to these goods and services as the aims or goals of science (Longino 1990). We can define an aim or goal as an end result or outcome sought (but not necessarily always achieved) by individuals or groups. A profession's aims play a key role in defining the profession and in justifying its standards of conduct.

In thinking about the aims of science, we need to distinguish between the aims of traditional, academic science (or science *simpliciter*) and the aims of science practiced in non-academic settings, e.g. industrial or mili-tary science, since scientists who work in non-academic settings often must operate under constraints and standards that we do not normally associate with academic science. For example, secrecy is important in mili-tary and industrial science while openness is supposed to reign in academic science. For the purposes of discussion, I shall treat science *simpliciter* as a general category that includes industrial and military science as sub-categories. Thus, the difference between military science and science *simpliciter* is that military science is science practiced in a military setting.

So what is the aim of science? Since scientists attempt to achieve a wide variety of results, no single goal constitutes the sole aim of science (Resnik 1996b). We can divide these aims into two categories, epistemic goals and practical goals. Science's epistemic goals, i.e. those activities that advance human knowledge, include giving an accurate description of nature, developing explanatory theories and hypotheses, making reliable predictions, eliminating errors and biases, teaching science to the next generation of scientists, and informing the public about scientific ideas and facts. Science's practical goals include solving problems in engineering, medicine, economics, agriculture, and other areas of applied research. Solutions to practical problems can promote human health and happiness, technological power, the control of nature, and other practical goals. Particular scientific professions may have different interpretations of these general goals and emphasize some goals over others. For instance, quantum physicists seek knowledge about sub-atomic particles and fields while cytologists seek knowledge about cells. Astronomers may place more of an emphasis on the search for knowledge for its own sake than on the achievement of practical goals, while medical sciences, such as immunology and endocrinology, may have a more practical orientation. Even though there are some important differences among the various scientific professions with regard to their goals, these differences do not prevent us from discussing scientific goals in general.

For the purposes of this book, I shall understand "scientific knowledge" as justified, true belief about the world.[1] Since scientists must acquire true beliefs in order to obtain knowledge, truth constitutes a key part of science's epistemic aims. Since a large part of ignorance consists in holding false beliefs, science also aims to eliminate false beliefs (and statements) as part of its quest to overcome ignorance. This view implies that scientists seek to acquire true beliefs and to eliminate false ones (Goldman 1986, 1992).

I shall also interpret "scientific truth" in an old-fashioned, common-sense way: a scientific belief is true if and only if it provides an accurate representation of a fact about the world (reality). Some non-scientific beliefs may need not give an accurate representation of the world in order to be true. For instance, the truth of the belief that "Santa Claus wears a red coat" does not depend on its ability to portray the world accurately; the belief will count as true in the context of myths and folk-tales about Santa Claus. But the truth of the belief that "carbon atoms have six protons" does depend on the belief's ability to portray accurately a fact about the world: if carbon really does have six protons, then the belief is true; if it does not, then the belief is false. This view implies that scientific truths are objective because they are based on facts about the world that are independent of human interests, values, ideologies, and biases (Kitcher 1993). Since scientific knowledge consists in justified, true beliefs, scientific knowledge is also objective; it is not socially constructed belief.[2]

Although science seeks true beliefs (statements, hypotheses, theories) about the world, some truths are more valuable (or worthy of discovery) than others (Kitcher 1993). Many scientists would like to acquire true beliefs about the causes of HIV or life on other planets, but not many scientists would waste their time trying to find out how many pens are in Singapore. Clearly, psychological, social, and political factors can play a role in determining the value of true beliefs. Sometimes scientists seek to obtain truths in order to achieve various social or personal goals: a scientist may want to know the causes of HIV in order to find a cure for this disease. Sometimes scientists seek to obtain truths in order to develop a more complete understanding of the world: scientists are interested in learning whether life exists elsewhere because this knowledge would have profound implications for our understanding of life and its origins. However, none of these reflections on the value of scientific knowledge implies that this knowledge is not objective, since scientific knowledge, whether valuable or useless, must still provide us with accurate beliefs about the world.

Finally, I should also mention that the notion of "justification" also plays an important role in defining scientific knowledge. In science, justification consists in providing reasons and evidence for regarding a belief (or hypothesis or theory) as true. Although we may accept or reject non-scientific beliefs for practical reasons, we should accept scientific beliefs if we have reasons to regard them as true and reject scientific beliefs if we have reasons to regard them as false (Goldman 1986). Scientists have developed a process for justifying beliefs known as the scientific method, which I will discuss shortly. The scientific method provides scientists with reasons for accepting or rejecting beliefs, hypotheses, or theories (Newton-Smith 1981).

Before concluding the discussion of science's goals, we should note that it is important to distinguish between science's goals and scientists' goals, since some confusions about the goals of science can arise if we fail to make this distinction (Kitcher 1993). Science's goals are the aims of scientific professions; scientists' goals are the goals held by individual scientists. Although these individual goals often coincide with the goals of the scientific profession – scientists practice science in order to acquire knowledge, solve practical problems, and so forth – scientists may have goals that are not science's goals. For instance, individuals practice science in order to obtain money, employment, power, or prestige yet we would not claim that these goals are science's goals. We do not view these various goals held by individual scientists as the goals of the scientific profession because these goals do not distinguish science from other professions nor do they play an important role in justifying science's standards of conduct. We distinguish between different professions, in part, by appealing to the goals of different professions; a profession's goals help us to define that profession. If we focused on the goals held by various individuals, then we would not be able to distinguish between science and business, law, medicine, and many other professions. Individuals in almost any profession seek money, power, employment, social status, or prestige, but not all professions seek objective knowledge. Furthermore, goals pursued by individuals should play no significant role in justifying scientific standards of conduct. We do not justify honesty in science on the grounds that honesty helps scientists gain money, prestige, or power. Honesty is justified because it contributes to the advancement of knowledge, not because it brings scientists money, prestige, or power. Indeed, if money, prestige or power constituted some of science's ultimate aims, we would not expect scientists to be honest.

Thus, we have the sketch of an answer to one of our key questions, i.e. "what is science?" Science is a profession in which individuals cooperate together in order to advance human knowledge, eliminate ignorance, and solve practical problems.

The Contemporary Research Environment

In order to fill out this sketch of the scientific enterprise, we need to have a better understanding of the contemporary research environment. A research environment is a social institution that sponsors, enables, or fosters scientific research. In the United States and other Western nations, science is practiced in very different environments. These social institutions that foster research have their own goals, values, and standards that may or may not conform to scientific values and standards. The main types of social institutions that support research are universities (or colleges or other educational institutions), national laboratories, such as Oak Ridge National Laboratory, mission-oriented laboratories, such as the Center for Disease Control, businesses, such as Glaxo, and the military. These different social institutions place various conditions on the process of research, which can lead to ethical dilemmas and improprieties (PSRCR 1992).

The social institution familiar to most readers is the university (or academic institution). Most universities have three distinct missions: (1) to educate students, (2) to contribute to the advancement of knowledge, and (3) to serve the public. Universities have their own rules, regulations, and governing bodies (administrations) designed to carry out these objectives, and people who work for a university are governed by its institutional standards of conduct. Even though universities have rules, regulations, and governing bodies, most of these institutions still embody the Enlightenment ideal of a community of independent scholars (Markie 1994). Professors can design courses, choose research topics, advise students, and perform various other duties without a great deal of supervision from the university's higher authorities. Most universities still serve as bastions for intellectual freedom, openness, and the pursuit of knowledge for its own sake.

Thus, university-based scientists have obligations to both the university and to the scientific profession; they occupy the roles "professor" and "scientist." Often these different sets of obligations coincide. For instance, as an employee of a university, a person may have obligations to both teach and to conduct research, and as a scientist she has the same obligations. But sometimes these different obligations conflict. Suppose a university requires a scientist to serve on committees and teach two courses a semester and these duties take away valuable time from her research. She may find it difficult to do research, and she may be forced to choose between institutional and professional obligations or between different institutional and professional obligations (Markie 1994).

The research group forms the most basic unit of all scientific research, and most scientific professions are composed of dozens (or even hundreds) of different research groups (Grinnell 1992). Research groups typically have a hierarchical structure: a senior researcher oversees the group; she (or he) often functions as the director of a laboratory at which the research is conducted. At a university, the director of a research group may have the title "professor." Subordinates (or junior researchers) include research assistants and associates, who may have the titles "associate professor" or "assistant professor" at a university. Postdoctoral students, graduate students, undergraduate students and technical assistants occupy the lower rungs of the ladder. Postdoctoral students assist professors with research and conduct their own research. Technical assistants help out with many of the technical aspects of research, although they do not usually help develop hypotheses or write papers. They often do not have advanced degrees and they usually do not aspire to be independent researchers. Graduate students (and sometimes undergraduate students) may assist professors in teaching classes, in conducting research, or both. Although they are usually assigned the more menial tasks of the research group, students also do some of their own research and often work closely with professors (Grinnell 1992).

Since nearly all scientists receive most of their education and training in academic settings, research groups at universities form the backbone science. Scientists may leave these research groups to work in business, the military, or elsewhere, but they usually spend the initial parts of their careers in universities or other educational institutions. Most scientists learn the various traditions, methods, and values of their practices in academic research groups (Hull 1988, Grinnell 1992).

Research groups may be as small as a dozen scientists or as large as several hundred. They may pursue several different problems at the same time or they may focus on just one problem. Research groups have grown bigger in recent years with the advent of large, government-funded science projects, or "big science." Those professions that require expensive, sophisticated instruments, such as particle physics, or those professions that require the close cooperation of many different people, such as molecular genetics, tend to have larger research groups; other professions, such as ecology and cognitive psychology, tend to have smaller research groups. The increased size of research groups in recent years may contribute to some ethical improprieties in science, since it is more difficult to supervise, coordinate, and control a large group than a small one (Weinberg 1967).

Research groups also carry out most other aspects of the research process, such as the recruitment, hiring, training, and education of new scientists, peer review, and so forth. By working within the group, a person learns how to do scientific research and she receives the proper training and instruction necessary to be a good scientist. The Ph.D. is usually the final right of passage in the professionalization of scientists. After scientists have become fully professionalized, they may join new research groups or form their own.

Mentors play an important role in the education and training of future scientists (PSRCR 1992). Mentors are scientists who provide students with experience and know-how that goes beyond what students can learn in a lecture or textbook. They show students how to do good research, how to teach, how to write research papers, how to obtain funding, and how to survive in academia. Mentoring involves close, one-on-one supervision and instruction between a scientist and her students. The mentor–mentee relationship provides a way to initiate new scientists and pass on scientific standards and traditions. Mentors often help their students obtain employment in science by writing letters of recommendation, helping mentees prepare for interviews, helping mentees prepare curriculum vitaes, and so on. A student may have more than one mentor and a student's mentor need not be her Ph.D. or thesis advisor, although advisors usually play a key role in mentoring. Although professors usually serve as mentors, graduate and postdoctoral students can mentor undergraduate students.

Research groups operate out of work stations known as laboratories. Laboratories may vary in size, location, instrumentation, cost, and other features depending on the nature of the research. For instance, the Stanford Linear Accelerator (SLAC) near San Francisco spans dozens of square miles, employs hundreds of people, is located off campus, and costs tens of millions of dollars to fund (Traweek 1988). The chemistry laboratories at the University of Wyoming, on the other hand, are located in a single building, employ only a few dozen people, are located on campus, and do not cost tens of millions of dollars a year to fund. Although some non-experimental sciences do not have sophisticated equipment, buildings, and so on, we can still speak of their work sites as laboratories. Thus, a statistician's lab may consist of nothing more than a few offices, storage areas, seminar rooms, and a computer room. An anthropologist's lab may consist of a village where she studies a particular culture. Even though these work stations do not resemble the laboratories we see in popular films, we can still refer to them as laboratories (Latour and Woolgar 1979).

Although some research groups can function as independent, knowledge producers stationed at one location, most research groups require the cooperation of other groups and are stationed at different locations (Fuchs 1992). Some research groups also conduct interdisciplinary research, which requires the cooperation of scientists in different professions. For instance, research on the genetics of Alzheimer's disease brings together geneticists, biochemists, neurobiologists, cognitive psychologists, and physicians. Thus, scientific collaboration is often important not only within but among research groups (Committee on the Conduct of Science 1994).

While most scientists hired by universities receive a salary for their work, they usually must acquire financial support for research from federally funded organizations, such as the NSF, the National Research Council (NRC), the DOE, or the NIH. Funding pays for the cost of materials and equipment, the salaries of assistants or postdoctoral students, the publication of results, the use of buildings and vehicles, travel expenses, and so forth.

Nearly all scientists who work at universities face the pressure to obtain funding for their research and to publish papers (PSRCR 1992). These pressures exist because universities make hiring, tenure and promotion decisions based in large part on research productivity, and most universities cannot afford to fully fund research projects. Competition for funding has become more intense in recent years as the scientific profession has increased in size despite significant cutbacks in the federal government's funding of research (Martino 1992). Although most universities stress the importance of teaching in tenure and promotion decisions, the phrase "publish or perish" is an academic reality for scientists (and for philosophers). University tenure committees, for example, often evaluate a person's research efforts by focusing primarily on the number of publications the person has produced or the number of grants she has obtained. Most students have heard stories of scientists (or philosophers) who were good teachers but were not granted tenure because they did not have enough publications or grants. In order to counteract the "publish or perish" syndrome, some universities now limit the number of publications used to evaluate scholars and some have tried to put more emphasis on activities not related to research (PSRCR 1992).

Communication and Science's Peer Review System

During the early stages of Western science, communication among scientists was quite limited. Scientists read the books that were available, talked to each other at universities, and met for informal discussions. The development of the printing press in the 1400s helped to enhance scientific communication by allowing scientists to publish their findings and distribute them to a wide audience. The growth of universities from 1400 to 1700 also contributed to communication by bringing scientists together to share ideas and by promoting scientific education. By the 1600s, scientists also communicated their ideas through letters, since the postal services had become more expeditious by this time (Ziman 1984).

The English philosopher Francis Bacon recognized the importance of communication in the development of science. In *The New Instrument* Bacon argued for the development of a scientific method based on observation and experiment, logic, public criticism and discussion, skepticism, and the rejection of false idols and dogmas (Bacon 1985). Bacon also argued that science is a powerful tool that should be used for the benefit of the human condition. In *The New Atlantis* he advanced the idea that scientists should form their own associations to discuss data, hypotheses, and theories (Bacon 1985). In 1662 Bacon's dreams started to materialize with the founding of the Royal Society of London, the world's first scientific association. The Royal Society held regular meetings to discuss ideas and theories and it published the world's first scientific journal, *The Philosophical Transactions of the Royal Society of London*, which is still published today. Four years after the founding of the Royal Society, King Louis XIV established the French Royal Academy of Sciences in Paris. Within the next two hundred years, there were scientific societies throughout Europe and in the United States. The first scientific societies encompassed many different areas of science, and more specialized societies appeared in the 1800s, such as the Geological Society of London (1807), the Royal Astronomical Society of London (1820), and Zoological Society of London (1826). Today, virtually every scientific profession has one or more scientific associations (Ziman 1984).

The Royal Society published its *Philosophical Transactions* to enhance scientific communication, criticism, and the exchange of ideas. It included papers that described experiments, some that proposed theories, and others that discussed philosophical and conceptual aspects of science. Many of the early scientific journals were published by scientific societies (and many still are) and some journals were published by private companies (and many still are). These early journals were different from modern journals in that they had very little quality control (LaFollette 1992). The journals often published ideas that were highly speculative and unconfirmed. Some of the early journals also published works of fiction as well as the writings and ramblings of amateur scientists.

The editors of scientific journals began to recognize the need for some type of quality control and their efforts spawned the modern peer review system. Peer review emerged in the 1800s but did not become widespread until the middle of the twentieth century. The peer review system functions as a quality control mechanism by distinguishing between high and low quality papers, and editors attempt to publish only papers of high quality. Quality judgments are based on various standards of argumentation and evidence, methodology, and writing. Thus, the peer review system provides a way of legitimizing scientific knowledge, since a published paper is supposed to meet certain methodological standards (Armstrong 1997). The peer review system strives to provide fair (unbiased), careful, and honest evaluation of scientific research. It also can only operate effectively when authors trust that their manuscripts will be handled in a responsible, objective, and fair fashion.

A typical peer-reviewed journal operates as follows. An editor receives manuscripts from authors. She will make an initial judgment as to whether a paper is good enough to merit further review. If it does, then she will send it to some experts in the field. The experts, known as reviewers (or referees), may belong to the journal's editorial board or they may not. A reviewer that does not belong to a journal's editorial board is known as an outside referee. Reviewers generally charge no fee for the services they perform; they regard their important role in the advancement of knowledge as reward enough for their efforts. Although there are no universal criteria for evaluating manuscripts, reviewers are typically asked to answer the following questions: (1) Is the subject of the manuscript within the journal's scope?; (2) Are the manuscript's conclusions and interpretations well supported by the data/evidence?; (3) Does the paper represent a new and original contribution? In science, most journals use a single-blind review system: although the reviewers and editors know the identities and institutional affiliations of the authors, the authors do not know the identities and affiliations of the reviewers. Some journals use a double-blind system in which reviewers do not know the identities or affiliations of authors (LaFollette 1992).

After the reviewers have read a paper, they will offer one of four types of assessments: (a) publish the paper with no revisions; (b) publish the paper with minor revisions; (c) publish the paper with major revisions; (d) do not publish the paper. The reviewers usually also offer some comments about the paper and suggestions for revision. After receiving the reviewers' reports, the editor will decide to act on their recommendations or send the paper out to other reviewers. An editor may send a paper out again if she finds that the referees do not agree about its merits. Some papers are read by only the editor and one reviewer, while others are read by many people. After some time, the editor will inform the person who submitted the paper whether it has been rejected, accepted, accepted with minor revisions, or accepted with major revisions. The time from submission of a manuscript to its publication ranges from a few months to two years (LaFollette 1992).

The number of scientific journals has exploded during this century. Even a very narrow sub-field may be served by hundreds of journals. Since it is nearly impossible for scientists to read even a significant fraction of the papers pertaining to their fields of expertise, scientists rely on computerized abstracting systems that allow people to use a computer to search for topics in the scientific literature. Due to the vast number of articles and journals, it is estimated that very few scientific articles are even read (LaFollette 1992).

Contemporary scientists communicate with each other in many different ways, including presentations at meetings, regular mail, electronic mail, and the publication of books. However, publication in scientific journals constitutes one of the most important methods of scientific communication. In the last decade, electronic publication has emerged as another important form of scientific communication. In electronic publication, journals are transmitted and stored electronically, eliminating the need to publish journals on paper. Also, pages on the worldwide web constitute a form of electronic publication. Electronic publication could significantly alter scientific communication by making it faster, cheaper, and bigger. These changes could also have important impacts on the ethics of publication and on the quality of published papers (LaFollette, 1992).

The peer review system plays a key role in funding decisions as well as in confirmation, and many scientists believe that this system allows science to be self-correcting (Committee on the Conduct of Science 1994, Kiang 1995). The peer review system, according to many scientists, encourages honesty, objectivity, and truthfulness; it eliminates errors and biases; and it prevents the publication of research that does not meet certain standards of quality. If an author submits a paper that includes errors, inaccuracies, logical fallacies, unacceptable assumptions, flaws in the interpretation of data, or questionable methods, then referees and editors will discover these problems and the paper will not be published. If a poor paper gets published, then other scientists will be able to spot these problems by repeating experiments or reanalyzing data, and they can contact the authors or challenge them in print. Authors can also print retractions or corrections to address problems in their published work. The peer review system insures that eventually the truth will win out and errors will be eliminated.

Unfortunately, the peer review system does not always function in this manner. Indeed, a growing body of research suggests that there are many flaws in the peer review system. Many errors and other problems slip past referees, editors, and other scientists. Since scientists usually do not have the time, the desire, or the funding to repeat experiments and reanalyze data, mistaken, biased, inaccurate, and even fraudulent research often goes unchallenged (Chubin and Hackett 1990, Kiang 1995, Armstrong 1997). The peer review system is better than having no quality control mechanism for scientific research, of course, but the stark truth is that it often does not operate as advertised. This fact has important implications for the ethics of scientific research, which we will discuss in due course.

Before concluding these remarks on scientific communication, I should also mention something about communication between scientists and the public. Once again, this type of communication has undergone some significant changes over the years. Before the Renaissance, the public had very little direct knowledge of scientific achievements, and communication proceeded very slowly, mostly by word of mouth. With the advent of the printing press, scientific books became readily available to the public and newspapers emerged. Newspapers provided the public with information about new inventions and discoveries and continue to do so today. During the Enlightenment, writers such as Voltaire and Diderot wrote books about science for the general public. These books, known as popularizations, also remain an important avenue of communication between scientists and the public. As science became more of a force in society, writers of drama and fiction, such as Goethe and Mary Shelly, began to depict scientists in their works and discuss scientific ideas. This fascination with science led to the emergence of science fiction during the late 1800s, a new literary genre. During this century, the public learns about science through public education, newspapers, magazines, books, radio, and television. Also, magazines that provide popular accounts of science, such as *Scientific American* and *Discover*, have emerged. Science reporting has also become an integral part of journalism, and the print and broadcast media now assign reporters to cover science and technology (Nelkin 1995).

The Scientific Method

As I mentioned earlier, methodological standards play an important role in governing scientific conduct and in defining the aims of science. Indeed, many writers argue that science's methods are what distinguish it from other areas of inquiry and debate, such as philosophy, literature, religion, and pseudo science (Popper 1959, Kitcher 1983, Laudan 1990). Science may be characterized either as a profession that pursues objective knowledge or as a profession that develops knowledge according to a method that promotes objectivity. Thus, objectivity can enter into our understanding of science either as a product (objective knowledge) or as a process (objective methodology). Earlier I claimed that what makes knowledge objective is its relation to facts that are independent of human interests, theories, and biases. If we think of objectivity in this way, then objective methods are methods that tend to promote the acquisition of objective knowledge. Objective methods are instruments for acquiring truth and for avoiding error (Goldman 1992).

Although most students learn something about scientific methods in high school science classes, methodological standards can be very technical, complex, and discipline-specific. Thus, it is important to distinguish between general, methodological standards – the scientific method – and discipline-specific norms (Kantorovich 1993). General methodological standards are principles that govern inquiry in any scientific discipline; discipline-specific standards are principles that apply to inquiry in a particular profession, given its goals, theories, traditions, and techniques. For example, the general principle "repeat your experiments" applies to any science that performs experiments, but the principle "prevent contamination of virus strains" applies only to those disciplines that conduct research on viruses. In any case, all methodological standards play a similar role in inquiry: scientific methods guide scientists in research by providing a systematic, objective way of obtaining knowledge and avoiding ignorance.

What we today now know as "the scientific method" did not arise overnight or by accident (Cromer 1993). In the West, debates about how to obtain knowledge trace their origins to ancient Greece, where Plato and Aristotle discussed the roles of contemplation, observation, deduction, and induction in the acquisition of knowledge. Plato argued that we can only acquire real knowledge by contemplating eternal, immutable, non-physical forms. Since nature changes constantly, information we obtain from the senses produces ignorance but not genuine knowledge. Aristotle, on the other hand, believed that we can acquire knowledge by observing the natural world since forms can be immanent in nature. Aristotle claimed that induction and deduction play an important role in science. We can use induction to develop qualitative generalizations from our observations of nature, and we can use deduction to derive additional consequences from these generalizations, i.e. explanations and predictions. While Plato made important contributions to philosophy and politics, most historians of science credit Aristotle with developing some of the cornerstones of the scientific method (Dijksterhuis 1986, Cromer 1993). Aristotelian ideas about knowledge and method contributed to the Golden Age of Hellenic Science from 300 BC to 200 AD. During this era, Archimedes, Aristarchus, Euclid, Theophrastus, Hipparchus, Hero, and Ptolemy made important advances in mechanics, engineering, mathematics, zoology, astronomy, optics, and geography.

During the medieval period, the Western world made few advances in the development of scientific thinking, although Islamic scientists, such as Ibn al-Haitham (Alhazen) and Muhammad Ibn Musa al-Khwarizmi batanni, maintained and extended the Aristotelian tradition. By the late Middle Ages (1200 AD), the Western world had emerged from its Dark Ages as Robert Grosseteste, Roger Bacon, Albertus Magnus, and William of Ockham called upon people to observe nature, to use logic and reason in thinking about problems, and to question authority and common opinion. By the time Nicholas Copernicus proposed a heliocentric astronomical theory in *The Revolutions of the Heavenly Bodies* in 1542, the seeds of the scientific method had already germinated and the Scientific Revolution had begun.

During the Scientific Revolution, scientists and philosophers paid careful attention to the method used in the developing sciences of physics, astronomy, chemistry, physiology, and anatomy. It became clear to many writers that science needed a clearly defined, systematic, reliable way of obtaining knowledge so that people could form beliefs that were not based on ignorance, authority, or superstition. Francis Bacon, René Descartes, Galileo, Isaac Newton, Paracelsus, Vesalius, Robert Hooke, Robert Boyle, and William Harvey all made important contributions to the development of the scientific method. This new way of thinking differed from Aristotelian science in that it emphasized the development of quantitative (mathematical) generalizations and hypotheses and the rigorous testing of generalizations and hypotheses through repeated observations and controlled experiments. Scientists and philosophers during this era also emphasized the importance of skepticism, logic, and precision in inquiry, and they developed special instruments, such as the microscope and telescope, for making observations. By the end of the eighteenth century, Western thinkers had developed a framework for doing science. However, during the 1800s mathematicians, scientists, and philosophers developed one very important pillar in the scientific method, namely statistics. Statistical techniques now play a key role in the description, analysis, and interpretation of data, even though some of the great figures in science, e.g. Copernicus and Galileo, did not use statistics (Porter 1986).

The scientific method, as we now know it, can be described a series of steps:

Step 1: Ask a question or pose a research problem based on initial data and background knowledge.
Step 2: Develop a working hypothesis.
Step 3: Make predictions from the hypothesis and background knowledge.
Step 4: Test hypothesis; collect additional data.
Step 5: Analyze data.
Step 6: Interpret data.
Step 7: Confirm or Disconfirm Hypothesis.
Step 8: Disseminate results.

I should note that these stages represent a rather simplified, schematic account of the research process. Sometimes the stages occur concurrently or in a slightly different order, and often scientific research feeds back through the various stages (Kantorovich 1993). The scientific method can be described as a series of sequential steps, but it usually proceeds in a non-linear fashion.

Students are probably familiar with many informal rules of scientific methodology. I state but a few of them here:

(1)   Seek clarity and precision when formulating hypotheses and describing experiments.
(2)   Hypotheses should be simple, testable, plausible, and consistent with the data.

(3) Wherever possible, use controlled, repeatable experiments to study phenomena.

(4) Use the most reliable instruments available in gathering data; understand and evaluate errors that are due to your instruments.

(5) Carefully record and save all data.

(6) Be critical, rigorous, and skeptical: do not accept any theory or idea without good reason, and subject your own ideas and theories to careful scrutiny.

(7) Avoid self-deception, bias, and careless errors in all aspects of research.

(8) Use appropriate statistical methods in describing and analyzing data.

Many books have been written on scientific methodology, and I see no need to explore this topic in any more depth here.[3] However, I think it is important to include at least a brief discussion of the scientific method in this book since ethical and methodological standards in science are closely connected. A scientist who fabricates data, for example, violates ethical and methodological standards in science (Resnik 1996b). In subsequent chapters we shall see how the account of science defended in this chapter provides a rationale for many of the ethical standards that apply to scientific research. Indeed, one flaw I see in relativistic approaches to science is that they cannot give an adequate account of science's ethical standards. To wit, if science is simply a social construct, then why should we care about the fabrication of data? If there is no difference between telling a story and defending an hypothesis, then why should fraud, bias, self-deception, or error matter in science? The idea that science is a quest for objective knowledge ought to guide our thinking about ethics in science.[4]

CHAPTER 4
Standards of Ethical Conduct in Science

In the last chapter I argued that science's ethical standards are based on the goals of the scientific profession, which include the quest for knowledge, the elimination of ignorance, and the solution of practical problems. Many of the standards of conduct in science also have a moral foundation. For example, fabricating data is unethical in science because it is a form of lying, which is morally wrong, and because data fabrication promulgates errors and destroys the atmosphere of trust that plays a key role in science. Scientists should practice social responsibility in order to satisfy moral obligations and to secure the public's support for science. Thus, ethical standards in science have two conceptual foundations, morality and science. Ethical conduct in science should not violate commonly accepted moral standards and it should promote the advancement of scientific goals. In this chapter I will defend twelve principles of ethics in science, which apply to different aspects of the research process. After discussing these principles, I will make some additional remarks to clarify my approach to ethics in science. The principles are as follows.

Honesty

Scientists should not fabricate, falsify, or misrepresent data or results. They should be objective, unbiased, and truthful in all aspects of the research process.

This principle is science's most important rule because if this principle is not followed, it will be impossible to achieve science's goals. Neither the search for knowledge nor the solution of practical problems can go forward when dishonesty reigns. Honesty also promotes the cooperation and trust necessary for scientific research. Scientists need to be able to trust each other, but this trust breaks down when scientists are not honest (Committee on the Conduct of Science 1994, Whitbeck 1995b). Finally, honesty is justified on moral grounds: all people, including scientists, should be truthful.

In order to understand dishonesty in science, we need to distinguish between dishonesty and error (PSRCR 1992). Dishonesty and error produce similar consequences but they spring from different motives: a dishonest act always involves the intent to deceive an audience that expects to be told the truth.[1] Deception can occur when someone lies, withholds information, or misrepresents information. Dishonesty does not occur when the audience does not expect to be told the truth: novelists do not lie when they tell tall tales. It is important to define dishonesty in terms of motives because motives play a key role in our assessment of human conduct. If scientists were instruments or mechanical devices, then we would only expect them to be reliable: a thermostat can give an accurate or inaccurate reading but it cannot tell the truth or lie. Indeed, since scientists are human beings, we forgive honest errors and reserve our harshest judgments for lies and intentional deceptions.

Many kinds of dishonesty in science involve the production and analysis of data. Fabrication occurs when scientists make up data; falsification occurs when scientists alter data or results (PSRCR 1992). In the Baltimore affair, Imanishi-Kari was accused of fabricating or falsifying data in her research team's experiments on mice.[2] Misrepresentation occurs when scientists do not truthfully or objectively report data or results. The most common forms of misrepresentation are known as trimming, cooking, and fudging (Babbage 1970). Trimming occurs when scientists fail to report results that do not support their hypotheses. Fudging occurs when scientists try to make results appear to be better than they really are. Scientists "cook" the data when they design tests or experiments in order to obtain results they already have good reasons to suspect will be positive or when they avoid conducting tests that are likely to yield negative results.

Most scientists view fabrication and falsification as serious violations of scientific ethics, but there is some disagreement about the seriousness of misrepresentation because the line between misrepresentation of data and good methodology is sometimes ambiguous (Sergestrale 1990). Scientists sometimes have good reasons for eliminating or ignoring recalcitrant data; a certain amount of trimming can be a part of good scientific practice. For instance, some scholars have argued that Millikan trimmed data when he classified results as "good" or "bad" and only reported the "good" results in a paper discussing his oil drop experiments. (Millikan attempted to determine the charge of the electron by measuring the charge on drops of oil and using this measurement to calculate the minimum charge, the charge on an electron.) Others claim that Millikan had good reasons for distinguishing between "good" and "bad" results and for omitting the "bad" ones. Millikan understood his experiments and equipment and exercised his scientific judgment in evaluating his data (Committee on the Conduct of Science 1994).[3]

The same point also applies to fudging and cooking data. Today's scientists often need to use statistical methods to convert masses of disorganized, meaningless data into meaningful, organized numbers or figures. If scientists are justified in using various statistical techniques in analyzing, organizing, and presenting data, then scientists need to exercise judgment and discretion in choosing those techniques. Scientists who misuse statistics can be accused of fudging; those who do not are simply practicing good science.[4] It is even acceptable to design tests in order to get positive results, so long as one does not avoid tests that might yield negative ones. Since there are no explicit rules for trimming data sets, choosing statistical methods, or for designing tests or experiments, scientists must exercise their judgment in deciding how to collect and analyze data. The ability to make judgments about the proper treatment of data can be acquired through experience in the laboratory and by following examples of good science.

Since the line between accurate representation and misrepresenting is often not clear cut, how can we tell when someone is unethically representing data or results? Correct representation of data involves the exercise of scientific judgment. We could rely on the judgment of experienced scientists to determine whether an action counts as misrepresentation. However, since even experts may disagree, we will also need to appeal to the motives or intentions of scientists in order to determine whether they are behaving improperly (PSRCR 1992). If a scientist trims data with the intent of deceiving other people; then he is being dishonest; if he trims data with the intent of reporting results in a clear fashion, then he is not. If a scientist uses statistical techniques in order to give a clear and objective picture of the data, then she is acting ethically; if she uses statistics simply as a rhetorical device to deceive her audience, then she is acting unethically. Of course, it is not always easy to determine a person's intentions.

Although honesty is most important in the production, analysis, and reporting of data and results, honesty also applies to many other aspects of the research process. For instance, in writing research proposals, scientists sometimes stretch the truth in order to have a better chance of obtaining funding (Grinnell 1992). Scientists, engineers, and public relations officials greatly exaggerated the scientific and economic importance of the Super-Conducting Super-Collider in defending this expensive project before Congress (Slakey 1993).

Scientists who act dishonestly may sometimes have reasons for behaving this way. According to my definition, parody is a form of dishonesty, though it might not be unethical. Consider physicist Alan Sokal's (1996a, 1996b, 1996c) parody of cultural studies of science. In order to defend science from social constructivist critics, Sokal put together a paper that parodied their jargon, rhetoric, and reasoning. The paper contained numerous "red flags," such as errors in reasoning and unintelligible sentences, but the editors of *Social Text* published it. Sokal later revealed his "experiment" in *Lingua Franca*. His spoof challenged the judgment of the editors of *Social Text* as well as the intellectual standards of the entire field of cultural studies of science. Although many people laughed at the editors of *Social Text*, Sokal's quarrel was not with those editors or their journal. Sokal wrote his parody as a plea for reason, evidence, and logic. (Many people who work within the field known as cultural studies of science argue that reason, evidence, and logic play only a minimal role in scientific discovery, and they argue for the subjectivity of knowledge, truth and reality.) Were Sokal's actions unethical? Although dishonesty is usually unethical, one might argue that parody is not unethical when it is used to expose corruption and scandal in politics and the academy; satire is often the best way of revealing the truth (Rosen 1996). However, since even any lie can damage the integrity of the research process, honesty is the best policy in science and deviations from this standard require a special justification.

Carefulness

Scientists should avoid errors in research, especially in presenting results. They should minimize experimental, methodological, and human errors and avoid self-deception, bias, and conflicts of interest.

Carefulness, like honesty, promotes the goals of science in that errors can hinder the advancement of knowledge as much as outright lies. As we noted earlier, a lack of carefulness is not the same thing as dishonesty, since carelessness need not involve the intent to deceive. Carefulness also is important in promoting cooperation and trust among scientists and the efficient use of scientific resources (Whitbeck 1995b). When relying on someone else's work, scientists normally assume that the research is valid. This is an important assumption to make because it would be an incredible waste of time to check every piece of research one uses for errors. When errors plague the research process, scientists cannot make this important assumption, they cannot trust each other, and they must waste time and energy checking for errors.

Many scientists do not view error as a serious crime against science, even though errors are more prevalent than fraud. A scientist who publishes a paper containing numerous errors might be viewed as incompetent but not as unethical. However, even though carelessness is not as serious an offense as dishonesty, it is still very important to avoid carelessness, since errors can waste resources, erode trust, and result in disastrous social consequences. Errors in applied research, medicine, and engineering, can cause a great deal of harm. A miscalculation in a drug dosage can kill dozens of people, and a defect in a bridge design can kill hundreds. Thus, although some errors can be treated as honest mistakes or incompetence, serious and repeated errors can be viewed as a form of negligence (Resnik 1996b). The proper response to discovering an error in one's published or submitted work is to admit the mistake and publish a correction, erratum, or retraction (Committee on the Conduct of Science 1994).

In discussing carefulness, it is important to distinguish between different types of errors in the research process. Experimental errors are those errors relating to the use of scientific instruments in collecting data. Every instrument produces some noise, distortions, and false readings, though some instruments are more precise and reliable than others (Kyburg 1984). It is standard practice in all scientific disciplines to take these errors into account when reporting data and results. Methodological errors include errors relating to the interpretation and analysis of data by statistical methods or the use of theoretical assumptions and biases in inference. Most scientists learn that statistical methods can yield very deceptive results and it is always important to use the statistical techniques appropriate to an area of research. The use (or misuse) of theoretical assumptions and biases can also lead to errors. For instance, astronomers who accepted Copernicus' heliocentric system struggled for years to make it fit planetary observations because they assumed that all heavenly bodies must move in perfect circles (Meadows 1992).

Human errors are simply errors made by people in using instruments, in performing calculations, in recording data, in drawing inferences, in writing papers, and so forth. In Chapter 3 I mentioned that many scientists are under pressure to produce results in a timely fashion. Hasty research can lead to inattention, sloppiness, indiscretion, and other errors. In the case discussed in Chapter 1, Imanishi-Kari admitted to carelessness but not fraud.

A phenomenon dubbed self-deception in science is usually produced by a combination of human, methodological, and experimental errors (Broad and Wade 1993). In self-deception, scientists deceive themselves about the validity or significance of their results. Although scientists are taught to be critical, skeptical, and rigorous, they, like other human beings, often see what they want to see. A scientist who deceives herself may sincerely believe that an experiment confirms her hypothesis. The errors made by scientists are often subtle. Scientists may fail to see mistaken assumptions and biases in their own research, and they can fail to evaluate their work critically and objectively. The cold fusion experiments discussed in the first chapter could be viewed as a case of self-deception in science (Huizenga 1992).

Although errors and biases will always occur in science, the peer review system and the open discussion of ideas and results can minimize their effects and lead the scientific community toward the truth. Thus, although scientists make many errors, science can be self-correcting. However, in order for the mechanism of peer review to work, it is important that scientists do not circumvent this process. Research should be evaluated by other members of the scientific profession before it is applied or made public. One of the ethical problems with the cold fusion case is that the researchers did not allow their work to be evaluated by peers before they called a press conference. The importance of peer review in science ties in well with our next principle.

Openness

Scientists should share data, results, methods, ideas, techniques, and tools. They should allow other scientists to review their work and be open to criticism and new ideas.

The principle of openness promotes the advancement of knowledge by allowing scientists to review and criticize each other's work; science's peer review system depends on openness (Munthe and Welin 1996). Openness prevents science from becoming dogmatic, uncritical, and biased. Openness also contributes to the advancement of science by helping to build an atmosphere of cooperation and trust in science and by enabling scientists to use resources effectively (Bird and Houseman 1995). Knowledge can be obtained more effectively when scientists work together instead of in isolation, when they share data, research sites, and resources, when they build on previous research, and so forth. Another reason in favor of openness in science is that secrecy undermines the public's trust in science (Bok 1982). When scientific activities are not open and accessible, people can begin to suspect that scientists are dishonest or untrustworthy, and the scientific profession can suffer many adverse consequences when public support for science erodes. Finally, insofar as all people have a moral duty to help other people, and the sharing of data and resources constitutes a form of help, scientists have a general, moral obligation to avoid secrecy in addition to their scientific duties to be open.

Although openness is a very important principle of scientific conduct, exceptions to this rule can be justified in some situations. For instance, many scientists avoid openness in order to protect ongoing research (Grinnell 1992). In order to protect her reputation, a scientist may not wish to share her data or results before her experiments are complete or before she has had time to think about her work in some detail. A scientist may also not wish to share her data, ideas, or results in order to guarantee that she receives proper credit, recognition, and compensation for her work (Marshall 1997). Once a study is complete, however, the need to protect ongoing research no longer exists, and the results should become a matter of public record, especially if the study is supported by public funds.

All of these arguments in favor of limited secrecy assume that scientists are justified in wanting to receive credit, recognition, or compensation. One might even argue that this kind of self-interest in science plays a key role in the advancement of knowledge (Merton 1973, Hull 1988). Science thus involves a trade-off between self-interest and egoism and cooperation and trust. Indeed, since scientists are rewarded for making original contributions, and these contributions advance the goals of science, it is likely that science's reward system works like an "invisible hand" for the benefit of science: individual scientists may unwittingly contribute to the overall good of science by simply seeking to accomplish their own, personal goals, e.g. prestige and respect (Merton 1973).

Most scientists would agree, I think, that secrecy should be the exception rather than the rule in research. However, one might argue that scientists may sometimes have other obligations that override their obligations to science. For instance, scientists who work for private companies may be obligated to keep trade secrets (Bok 1982, Nelkin 1984), and scientists who do military research are obligated to protect classified information (Nelkin 1972, Bok 1982). Thus, openness, a scientific value, may conflict with business and military values. These issues raise many difficult questions, which I will return to later.

Freedom

Scientists should be free to conduct research on any problem or hypothesis. They should be allowed to pursue new ideas and criticize old ones.

Great battles in the history of science have been fought over this principle. The struggles of Galileo, Bruno, Vesalius and the Soviet geneticists all attest to the importance of freedom in science. The principle of freedom promotes the attainment of scientific goals in several ways. First, freedom plays an important role in the expansion of knowledge by allowing scientists to pursue new ideas and work on new problems. Second, intellectual freedom plays an important role in nurturing scientific creativity (Kantorovich 1993, Shadish and Fuller 1993). Scientific creativity stagnates in oppressive, authoritarian, overly structured environments. When societies attempt to limit scientific research or direct it in certain areas, they risk undermining science itself (Merton 1973). Third, freedom plays an important role in the validation of scientific knowledge by allowing scientists to criticize and challenge old ideas and assumptions. Freedom, like openness, helps science from becoming stagnant, dogmatic, and biased (Feyerabend 1975). For instance, during this century genetics in the Soviet Union stagnated because Soviet geneticists were not allowed to challenge Lysenko's ideas about heredity (Joravsky 1970). Finally, we should also note that morality provides a rationale for freedom in research: freedom of thought, expression, and action imply freedom in inquiry.

Although the principle of freedom is crucial to science, one might argue that minor restrictions on freedom can be justified under certain conditions. In order to understand limitations on scientific freedom, we should distinguish between restrictions on actions, restrictions on funding, restrictions on publication, and restrictions on thought and discussion. It is important to understand these distinctions because they have different moral and ethical ramifications. First, most types of research involve actions by scientists and these actions can be restricted in order to prevent scientists from harming people or violating their rights. Even the strongest defenders of autonomy recognize that my right to do as I please stops at your nose. Thus, there are sound moral reasons for not allowing scientists to perform research that harms human subjects or violates their rights to autonomy. Most scientists would not consider protocols for the use of human subjects in research to be a significant or worrisome restriction on scientific freedom.

Second, most scientific research requires a great deal of money that scientists obtain from government agencies, businesses, private foundations, universities, or the military (Dickson 1984). Agencies allocate their funds according to the demands of their constituencies: businesses fund research in order to generate profits, government agencies must answer to Congress and the public, and so on. Given these political and economic realities, it is frequently the case that funding decisions restrict research: unfunded research does not get done. For example, Congress's decision to terminate the Super Conducting Super Collider stopped many proposed experiments in high energy physics (Horgan 1994). Although these experiments may be conducted at some later time, Congress effectively put a great deal of research on "hold." Should we consider the failure to obtain funding for research to be a significant restriction on scientific freedom? Probably not. Although these funding decisions hamper research, scientists cannot legitimately claim to have a "blank check" to fund their pet projects. Funding is a privilege, not a right. Scientists who fail to obtain funding are still free to discuss their ideas or pursue funding at some later time. Although it is important for societies to fund scientific research in order to create an environment that nurtures scientific creativity, the failure to fund a particular scientific project does not cause significant damage to this environment.

On the other hand, some restrictions on research should be taken very seriously and can cause significant harm to science. During the height of Lysenkoism in the Soviet Union, scientists were not allowed to do research that would challenge Lysenko's views, they were not allowed to publish papers that challenged Lysenko, and they were not allowed to teach or even discuss views that contradicted Lysenkoism, such as Mendelian genetics. Since censorship, moratoriums, and other more severe limitations on the discussion of scientific ideas can have a detrimental effect on science and violate basic rights and liberties, we have good reasons for avoiding these kinds of restrictions on research. However, even these more serious limitations on science can be said to be justifiable under dire conditions. For example, one might argue that research can be censored to protect national security or that some kinds of research, such as studies on cloning human embryos, should be banned in order to prevent adverse social consequences. Thus, the issue of freedom of inquiry often requires scientists and society to balance the advancement of knowledge against other social goals (Cohen 1979).

Credit

Credit should be given where credit is due but not where it is not due.

I have already alluded to the principle of credit in discussing secrecy and openness in science. Although this principle does not directly promote the advancement of knowledge or science's practical aims, it is justified insofar as it motivates scientists to conduct research, it promotes cooperation and trust, and it insures that the competition for science's rewards will be fair (Hull 1988). Rewards in science include recognition, respect, prestige, money, and prizes. When a principle of credit does not operate in science, scientists may be less motivated to do research, and they may be reluctant to share information since they may be afraid that their ideas will be stolen. Credit also plays an important role in punishing scientists or allocating blame. If a piece of research is flawed, one needs to know who is responsible for it, so that the errors can be corrected or the person(s) can be punished. Thus, responsibility and credit should be viewed as two sides of the same coin: a person should be given credit for a piece of research only if they can take responsibility for it (Kennedy 1985). Finally, credit can be justified on moral grounds as well: standards of fairness imply that all people, including scientists, should be given just rewards for their contributions and efforts.

Plagiarism and honorary authorship represent two opposing types of unethical conduct in credit allocation. Plagiarism occurs when someone falsely represents another person's ideas as his own through irresponsible citation, attribution, or paraphrasing. Plagiarism embodies a failure to give credit where it is due. Plagiarism can also be viewed as a form of dishonesty, since plagiarizers make false or misleading statements pertaining to authorship (PSRCR 1992). On the other extreme, sometimes scientists grant honorary authorship to a person who has not made a significant contribution to a paper (LaFollette 1992). Honorary authorship may be granted in order to compensate a lab director or senior researcher, help a friend or colleague, or add some prestige to a paper. Honorary authorship is unethical because it grants credit where it is not due. Although most scientists agree that plagiarism and honorary authorship are unethical, there is less agreement once we move away from these two extremes. How much must a person contribute to a piece of research in order to receive credit? Should authors take credit for different sections of papers or different parts of a research process? I will examine these and other questions pertaining to credit allocation in Chapter 6.

Education

Scientists should educate prospective scientists and insure that they learn how to conduct good science. Scientists should educate and inform the public about science.

Education includes recruitment, formal instruction, training, and mentoring. A principle of education is important in science since the profession will grind to a halt if it cannot recruit, train, and educate new members. Recruitment is important in attracting new people to the scientific profession. Although formal science instruction also occurs in high school and lower grades, scientists do not usually become actively involved in this part of science education. However, scientists do have a duty to offer their suggestions and input into science education at these lower levels, and they have an obligation to educate people who intend to teach science at the K-12 level. Training is a type of informal instruction that involves imitation, practice, and apprenticeship. It involves the acquisition of various skills and an intuitive understanding of scientific practice. A well-trained scientist has tacit knowledge of her subject that extends far beyond what she can learn in textbooks or lectures (Kuhn 1970, 1977, Kitcher 1993). Scientists also have an obligation to support the effort to educate the general public through popular books, magazine articles, television appearances, and so on. This is an important part of science education as well, since the general public needs to gain an understanding of science. Since science depends on public support, science benefits when the public has a sound understanding of science and suffers when ignorance about science abounds.

Although education is important in science, different scientists may decide to participate in science education in different ways. Some scientists may focus on graduate education, others may focus on undergraduate education. Some scientists may mentor many students, others may not. Some scientists may become actively involved in recruitment, others may not. Some scientists may write popular works or make media appearances, others may not. Some scientists may decide completely to opt out of science education in order to pursue academic, military, or business research. As long as enough scientists are involved in education, the scientific community can afford the luxury of having some pure researchers.

Social Responsibility

Scientists should avoid causing harms to society and they should attempt to produce social benefits. Scientists should be responsible for the consequences of their research and they should inform the public about those consequences.

The general idea behind this principle is that scientists have a responsibility to society (Lakoff 1980, Shrader-Frechette 1994). Scientists should not conduct inquiry with the attitude that someone else can worry about the consequences of research or science's impact on society. Social responsibility implies that scientists have an obligation to conduct socially valuable research, to participate in public debates, to give expert testimony (if asked), to help make science policy, and to debunk junk science. Some scientists may reject the notion of social responsibility on the grounds that scientists should pursue knowledge for its own sake and should let politicians and the public deal with the social consequences of research. Responsibility for the social impacts of science falls on the media, politicians, and the public, not on scientists. Although this attitude has become less common in recent years, it still has a significant enough influence that it is worth refuting.

There are several reasons why scientists should take responsibility for the social impacts of research. First, although scientists cannot be held responsible for the unanticipated consequences of research, scientists can be held responsible for the consequences that can be anticipated. Second, scientists are also members of society who have moral duties toward other people, such as beneficence, nonmalifience, and utility. Third, scientists have professional duties to promote benefits and avoid harms. As professionals, scientists are expected to produce socially valuable goods and services and they are accorded a great deal of authority, responsibility, and trust. Social responsibility recognizes and honors this public trust (Shrader-Frechette 1994). Finally, social responsibility benefits science by increasing the public's support for science: socially responsible science promotes public support for science; socially irresponsible science undermines public support for science (Slakey 1993). By serving society, scientists can fight negative images of socially irresponsible scientists, e.g. Mengele, Frankenstein, and replace them with positive ones (Nelkin 1995).

However, although scientists have a duty to be socially responsible, this duty should be carried out with discretion. As we noted earlier, scientists should not disclose information prematurely; information should be validated by other scientists through the peer review process before it is disclosed publicly. When research is disclosed prematurely, two types of bad consequences may occur. First, people may be harmed. For instance, a person might try a new kind of treatment if scientists say that it works, even if it has not been thoroughly tested, and she might suffer harmful side effects from the treatment. Second, science's image can be harmed. When the public learns of an important discovery or cure that upon further inspection turns out to be a sham, they will be disposed to view scientists as incompetent or irresponsible. (The cold fusion debate serves as an unfortunate example of this effect.) Third, premature disclosure of scientific information can disrupt the process of credit allocation in science, but the general public is usually not qualified to assess priority disputes (Longino 1990). (A concern for priority probably helped to motivate the premature disclosure of cold fusion research.) Researchers who present their results to the public may receive undeserved recognition and credit if it turns out that some more conscientious researchers have reported the same results but have submitted their work to a scientific journal.

Finally, we should note that the principle of social responsibility is like the principle of education in that some scientists may (at times) decide to set aside social responsibilities in order to pursue other goals. Some scientists may wish to be less outspoken than others; some may choose careers that generate few results with social implications, and so forth. Social responsibility is a shared obligation that can be met by different scientists at different times.

Legality

In the process of research, scientists should obey the laws pertaining to their work.

As I argued in Chapter 2, all people, including scientists, have moral obligations to obey the law. Moreover, science may suffer great damage when scientists disobey the law: scientists may be arrested, equipment may be confiscated, funding may be denied, the public support for science may erode, and so forth. Laws pertain to many different aspects of research, including the use of hazardous and controlled substances, the use of human and animal subjects, the disposal of wastes, hiring practices, the appropriation of funds, and copyrights and patents (PSRCR 1992). Although scientists have strong moral and ethical duties to obey the law, this standard of conduct, like the other ones, can have exceptions. One might argue that sometimes scientists can break the law in order to gain important knowledge or benefit society. Throughout the history of science legal restrictions have impaired the advancement of knowledge. For instance, in Medieval Europe there were many legal restrictions on human dissections, and those who wanted to learn more about the human body had to conduct underground research. In Galileo's day, the Catholic Church imposed sanctions on teaching Copernicus' heliocentric astronomy. Although scientific civil disobedience can be justified in some instances, I should reiterate the point that burden of proof lies with those who would break the law (Fox and DeMarco 1990).

Opportunity

Scientists should not be unfairly denied the opportunity to use scientific resources or advance in the scientific profession.

A principle of opportunity can be justified on moral or political grounds: if all people in a society should not be unfairly denied opportunities, then scientists (as members of society) should also have these opportunities (Rawls 1971). This principle can also be justified on the grounds that it promotes scientific objectives. Opportunity is like a principle of openness writ large because it opens the scientific community to new people and ideas. In order to overcome biases and dogmas and achieve objective knowledge, science needs to examine and consider a diversity of hypotheses, ideas, approaches, and methods (Kuhn 1977, Longino 1990, Solomon 1994). Although people from similar backgrounds might generate this epistemological diversity, it is more likely that people from different backgrounds generate the diversity of opinions required for the advancement of knowledge. Objectivity is more likely to emerge from the clash of different cultures, personalities, and styles of thought than from the consensus of like minds.[6]

This principle supports several important science policies. A great deal of government money these days goes to large scientific projects and to prestigious labs (Martino 1992). Scientists who work on smaller projects or at less prestigious places can thus be denied research opportunities. While there are some legitimate reasons for putting lots of money into large projects at the expense of smaller ones and for funding prestigious labs, science funding policy should not be so large-scale or elitist that many deserving scientists are denied research opportunities. A principle of opportunity implies that in funding science it pays to spread the wealth around.

Second, although women and minorities have made significant advances into science's professional ranks, there still are very few women and minorities among the scientific elite, i.e. Nobel prize winners, members of the NAS, full professors, etc. Indeed, there is some evidence that a type of "old-boy-network" or "glass ceiling" exists in science when it comes to career advancement and prizes (Holloway 1993, Etzkowitz *et al.* 1994). Although there is nothing inherently wrong with relying on personal relationships to achieve career advancement, these relationships become a problem when they tend to exclude deserving people from a profession's upper echelons. A principle of opportunity implies that scientists should recruit, employ, and reward underrepresented groups, such as women and minorities.

Third, the principle of opportunity also implies a general prohibition against discrimination in science, since discrimination can unfairly violate a person's opportunities. Thus, scientists should not discriminate against colleagues or prospective colleagues on the basis of race, sex, national origin, nationality, age, or other characteristics not directly related to scientific competence (Merton 1973). This prohibition applies to a wide range of decisions scientists make in a professional context including hiring and promotion, admission, recruitment, resource allocation, and education. In addition to being unethical, many forms of discrimination are illegal. Although discrimination should be avoided in science, one might argue that some types of discrimination, e.g. preferential hiring, are justified in order to promote diversity in science or to correct for past injustices. I will address questions relating to affirmative action in Chapter 7.

Mutual Respect

Scientists should treat colleagues with respect.

Although this principle can be justified on moral grounds, it can also be justified in that it is important for achieving scientific objectives: the scientific community is built on cooperation and trust, which will break down when scientists do not respect one another (Whitbeck 1995b). Without mutual respect, the social fabric of science unravels, and the pursuit of scientific aims slows down. The principle implies that scientists should not harm one another, either physically or psychologically, that they should respect personal privacy, that they should not tamper with each other's experiments or results, and so forth. Although one might argue that some of the best scientists have not respected their colleagues (Hull 1988), the stereotype of the aggressive, mean-spirited, though highly successful scientist does not hold for science as a whole. While science can operate effectively when some people behave this way, I doubt whether it could operate effectively if all scientists behaved this way.

Efficiency

Scientists should use resources efficiently.

Since scientists have limited economic, human, and technological resources, they must use them wisely in order to achieve their aims. Although this principle seems somewhat trivial and obvious, it is still important in that many practices can be viewed as ethically questionable because they waste resources. Several practices related to publication can be viewed as unethical because they are inefficient. The "least publishable unit" is a phrase coined by William Broad (1981) that refers to the smallest piece of writing that can be published. Research that could probably be reported in one paper is sometimes divided up into three, four, or five papers. Additionally, scientists also sometimes use the same results for several different papers simply by making some minor changes in writing or presentation. Both of these practices can be regarded as unethical because they waste the scientific community's resources (Huth 1986). It is not difficult to understand why scientists engage in these wasteful activities, since tenure and promotion committees tend to stress quantity over quality in assessing publication records.

Respect for Subjects

Scientists should not violate rights or dignity when using human subjects in experiments. Scientists should treat non-human, animal subjects with appropriate respect and care when using them in experiments.

This principle can be justified on moral grounds. If we hold that human beings have inherent moral dignity and some basic rights, then scientists should not violate these rights and dignities when using human beings in experiments (Jonas 1969). If we hold that non-human animals also have some moral standing, then scientists should treat animal subjects with appropriate respect and care (LaFollette and Shanks 1996). Furthermore, since both of these principles reflect the public's concern for the ethical treatment of research subjects, they can be justified in that they help secure public support of science: scientists who fail to demonstrate proper respect for human and animal subjects may incur the public's wrath. Since many societies have laws protecting human and animal subjects, scientists also have legal obligations pertaining to research on humans and animals. This principle needs to be spelled out in more detail, of course, since it can be interpreted in different ways, depending on how we understand notions like "treat with respect and care," "human rights and dignity," and so forth. I will explore this principle in more depth when I discuss research on humans and animals in Chapter 7.

Concluding Remarks

Before winding up this chapter, I will make some concluding remarks concerning the standards of conduct described above.

Remark 1: Although I stressed this point earlier, it is important to reiterate the claim that these standards are prescriptions for conduct (or normative ideals); they do not attempt to describe the behavior of scientists. While these standards are normative, they are based on some empirical assumptions. Although most of the principles can be defended on moral grounds, their main rationale is that they benefit science; they are effective means of achieving scientific goals (Resnik 1996b). Thus, I have assumed that science works best when it conforms to these ideals. But we need further psychological, sociological, and historical research to verify these assumptions. It may turn out that some of the principles I have described are not effective means to scientific objectives, although I feel quite confident that the standards discussed in this chapter are not way off the mark.

Remark 2: Since empirical research should have some bearing on the justification of science's standards of conduct, we must face the possibility that different standards could be justified in different social circumstances. As recently as this century, a principle of non-discrimination would have seemed ridiculous to many scientists. Indeed, many scientists would have insisted on discriminating against women and minorities in order to keep them out of the scientific profession. During Stalin's rule a principle freedom may not have been very important in Soviet science. Since it is possible for inquiry to take place under different social, economic, and political conditions, the ethical standards I have defended might not apply to all sciences at all times; they might only apply to a particular kind of science practiced in modern, Western, capitalistic, democratic nations.

However, I would maintain that some of the principles I have discussed would still hold even under radically different social, economic, and political conditions. For instance, a principle of honesty should govern scientific research no matter where it occurs. Indeed, one might view this principle as one of the defining features of science: a profession (or social institution) that did not value honesty, objectivity and truthfulness should not even be viewed as scientific.

Although it not possible to lightly dismiss the specter of ethical relativism pertaining to scientific conduct, we can help allay these worries by realizing that science must be understood in context. The standards I have described here are based on some assumptions concerning science's social, political, and economic conditions, its institutions, traditions, and goals. These conditions give us a fairly reasonable portrait of contemporary, Western science. If we take this context as a starting place, then the standards I have described make a great deal of sense and the possibility of alternative norms does not pose a significant threat to the legitimacy of the principles discussed in this chapter.

Remark 3: Although it is clear that scientists have ethical obligations that are similar to the obligations that govern all people in society, scientists also have special obligations different from these other obligations. For instance, the obligation to be honest in scientific research is much stronger than the moral obligation to be honest in general. Most of us will admit that it is permissible to tell a small lie in order to prevent harm or to benefit someone. However, even a small lie in science can do a great deal of damage.

Remark 4: Some of the principles discussed above primarily apply to individuals while others apply primarily to social institutions. For instance, the principle of mutual respect applies primarily to individuals, while the principle of freedom applies primarily to social institutions, e.g. governments, funding agencies, universities, etc. Many of the principles, such as legality and openness, apply to both individuals and institutions.

Remark 5: Many of the principles also imply subsidiary principles and less general rules and maxims. For instance, the principles of honesty and efficiency imply that scientists should not mismanage funds; the principle of mutual respect implies that sexual harassment is unethical in science, and so on. All of these principles imply an obligation to teach and enforce ethical standards in science. Teaching and enforcement imply that scientists should protect people who blow the whistle on unethical or illegal conduct in science; that scientific societies, laboratories, and universities should have governing bodies to review cases of misconduct in science; that sanctions for misconduct may be imposed in some cases; and that scientists should sponsor workshops or seminars on ethical issues in science (Garte 1995).

Remark 6: These principles of conduct may sometimes conflict. For instance, the principle of openness may conflict with the principle of credit when a scientist must decide whether to allow other people to see her work or to keep it under wraps in order to protect her interests in not having her work stolen and in receiving proper credit for the research. When these conflicts arise, scientists can use something like the method of moral reasoning described in Chapter 2 to adjudicate among principles.

Remark 7: Since these principles are only *prima facie* rules for conduct, then one might wonder whether the principles are of any use at all. I have already touched on this point in the second chapter, but it is worth repeating here: ethical rules can offer us useful guidance even when they do not hold under all circumstances (Beauchamp and Childress 1994). Since conflicts are the exception rather than the rule, principles of scientific conduct can function quite well in guiding conduct under most circumstances. The rules are also useful in teaching students how to be good scientists.

Remark 8: Some of these principles are clearly more important than others. Most scientists would agree, I think, that the principle of honesty is science's most important ideal: it should almost always override other principles and it should almost always be followed. Some principles might be regarded as less important. For instance, most scientists would agree that scientists are sometimes justified in foregoing their educational responsibilities in order to conduct research.

Although I believe that some principles should be regarded as generally more important than others, I will not provide the reader with a ranking of the principles in terms of their priority because I do not believe that such a ranking is possible. Whether a given principle should override another principle (or principles) depends, in large part, on the details of the situation in which a conflict arises. In some circumstances a principle may be given high priority; in other circumstances it may be given a lower priority. Since there are so many different actual (and possible) cases where conflicts might arise, we simply cannot construct a ranking of the principles. Indeed, it would be misleading to construct such a ranking because this ranking would gloss over the important details of various cases.

Remark 9: Since I have stated the principles in very general terms, different sciences may interpret and apply them in different ways. These differences in interpretation and application will result, in large part, from differences in subject matters, methodological standards, research practices, and social conditions (Jardin 1986, Fuchs 1992). For instance, different sciences may interpret and apply the principle of honesty in different ways, depending on their subject matters and methodological standards. Some sciences, such as evolutionary biology, tolerate a great deal of speculation (Resnik 1991), while other sciences, such as biochemistry, do not. Presenting speculative research might be regarded as dishonest in biochemistry but not in evolutionary biology. Other important differences among the sciences may also lead to different interpretations and applications of the principles discussed above.

Reflecting on the differences among the various sciences also invites a certain degree of skepticism about the principles of research discussed above. If there are so many differences among the scientific professions that have important implications for ethical conduct, does it even make sense to discuss general standards of conduct for all sciences? My reply to this worry is that all sciences do have some things in common despite their differences. For instance, all sciences are professions dedicated to the advancement of knowledge and practical goals. These common features provide a basis for general standards of conduct for all sciences. It is worth developing and discussing these standards for the same reason why it is worth studying science (or any human endeavor) from a more general perspective. Just as methodological differences among the various sciences should not undermine an investigation of general principles of scientific method, so too the practical differences among the various sciences should not undermine an exploration of general principles of scientific conduct.

Another reason for seeking a general code of conduct for science is that scientists from different professions frequently interact with each other in the process of research; much research today is interdisciplinary and multi-disciplinary (Fuchs 1992). Furthermore, new scientific professions emerge from time to time, and members of these new professions may need some guidance when it comes to professional conduct. New professions do not yet have established codes of conduct, and a general code of scientific conduct could provide them with some guidance.

Remark 10: Readers familiar with the work of Robert Merton (1973) may recognize that my code resembles his norms of science in many ways. According to Merton, scientists accept the following norms: (1) communism (scientists share data and results); (2) universalism (political and social factors play no role in evaluating scientific ideas or individual scientists); (3) disinterestedness (scientists are interested in only the truth, not in personal or political agendas); (4) organized skepticism (scientists have high standards of rigor and proof and do not accept beliefs without good evidence).

This resemblance is not accidental: I have benefited from Merton's insights into science and I have modeled my code of scientific conduct on his norms of science. I even justify my code in the same way that Merton justifies his code: we both regard scientific norms as justified insofar as they are effective means to achieving scientific aims. However, my code is a bit different from Merton's. First, Merton's norms are more general and all-encompassing than my principles. Where Merton discusses the norm of communism, I discuss several different principles, such as openness, mutual respect, and education. Second, some of Merton's norms, such as organized skepticism, function both as principles of scientific methodology and as principles of scientific conduct; my code is intended to focus solely on scientific conduct. I should also mention at this point that many other writers have defended similar standards of conduct in science; I am not claiming that my ideas are entirely new or original. My presentation of these ideas may be in some way original, but that judgment is best left to critics.[7]

Remark 11: My final comment is that these standards of conduct also bear a strong resemblance to the codes of ethics that one finds in many sciences, such as physics, chemistry, psychology, and anthropology.[8] Since many sciences already have professional codes, one might wonder whether the standards of conduct I defend here serve any important purpose. I think there are several reasons why it is still useful to discuss ethical principles even when professional organizations have adopted codes of ethics. First, since many professional codes are shorter and less detailed than the principles I discuss here, these principles can provide students with a deeper and fuller understanding of ethical conduct in science. Second, since some professional codes are vague and unclear, these principles can help students clarify important concepts and ideas in the ethics of science. Third, since no professional code can tell a scientist how to behave in every situation, principles of scientific ethics can play an important role in guiding scientific conduct. Fourth, since not all scientists or science students know or understand their professional codes, these principles of ethical conduct can provide scientists with useful knowledge and information. Finally, since many sciences do not have professional codes of conduct, these principles can fill a normative void. Thus, principles of ethics can play a useful role in guiding conduct and in helping professionals think about ethical dilemmas. They can complement but not supplant codes of professional ethics (Beauchamp and Childress 1994).

CHAPTER 5
Objectivity in Research

In the previous chapter I defended and described some principles of ethical conduct in science. In the remaining chapters in this book, I will expand on this general discussion of ethical standards by exploring some of the ethical dilemmas, problems and questions that arise in the interpretation and application of these principles. This chapter focuses on the first three principles of scientific ethics: honesty, carefulness and openness. I group these standards together here because they all have important implications for the objectivity of inquiry. The need for objectivity in science applies to collecting, recording, analyzing, interpreting, sharing, and storing data, as well as other important procedures in science, such as publication practices and peer review.

Honesty in Research

In the previous chapter I argued that scientists should not fabricate, falsify, or misrepresent data or results. Most students of science do not have a hard time understanding what is meant by "fabrication" or "falsification" or why one should not fabricate or falsify data. However, it may be useful to say a few words about the different kinds of fabrication and falsification that can occur, since there are different ways that people can commit these cardinal sins of science.[1] For our purposes we can distinguish between dishonesty in collecting data and dishonesty in recording data. Dishonesty in the collecting of data occurs when scientists construct artifacts or forgeries that produce fabricated results. When this kind of dishonesty occurs, the entire experiment or test is a sham. Dishonesty in recording data occurs when scientists conduct legitimate tests or experiments but then dishonestly report the results by making them up (fabrication) or changing them (falsification). Thus, fabrication can occur in collecting or recording data, though falsification only occurs in recording data.

An infamous case of scientific misconduct illustrates how fabrication can occur in collecting data. During the early 1970s, William Summerlin conducted skin transplantation experiments on mice and eventually joined the prestigious Sloan Kettering Institute in New York. Organ and tissue transplantation in mammals is usually unsuccessful unless the donor and recipient are genetically identical, since mammalian immune systems are very adept at distinguishing between "self" and "non-self" cells and tissues. Every cell in a mammalian body contains histocompatibility antigens (HLA) on its surface. These proteins, known as antigens, have a complex, genetically coded structure. The immune system will attack cells that do not have an HLA structure that it recognizes as belonging to the self. If donor and recipient are not genetically identical, then transplanted organs or tissues will be attacked by the recipient's immune system unless the immune system is suppressed through various drugs (immuno-suppressants). Immuno-suppressants produce harmful side-effects by weakening the recipient's immune system. While these drugs may be effective in the short run, many organ transplantations that depend on immuno-suppression are ultimately unsuccessful. Summerlin hoped to offer a new method of organ and tissue transplantation that would overcome some of these difficulties. Summerlin's approach was based on the idea that if tissues are removed from a donor and cultured in a nutrient solution for a period of time, they may lose some of their HLA, making them less likely to be recognized as "non-self" by the recipient's immune system. Summerlin claimed that he used this approach successfully to graft skin from genetically unrelated mice. In his experiments, he grafted pieces of skin from black-haired mice on to white-haired mice.

However, it was discovered in March 1974 that Summerlin had used a black felt-tipped pen to color white mice and fabricate successful results. James Martin, a lab assistant, noticed that the black colored hair could be washed away with alcohol. Martin reported this discovery to a research fellow, who brought it to the attention of the vice-president of Sloan Kettering. Summerlin soon confessed and he was temporarily suspended until a peer review committee could investigate the incident. The committee concluded that Summerlin was guilty of misconduct and that there were some irregularities in his previous research. The committee recommended that Summerlin be given a leave of absence and that he correct the irregularities in his previous research. The committee also concluded that the lab director should be held partly responsible, since he supervised Summerlin's research and even co-authored some papers with

Summerlin. In his own defense, Summerlin claimed that he fabricated research results because he was under a great deal of personal and professional stress, which led to mental exhaustion (Hixson 1976).

We can easily see the dishonesty in this case, since artifacts constitute physical evidence for unethical conduct. Some of the most outrageous cases of misconduct involve sham experiments and hoaxes (Kohn 1986, Broad and Wade 1993). However, determining whether a scientist has dishonestly reported results is often more difficult. Consider, for example, the allegations presented against Imanishi-Kari. She was never accused of faking the experiment itself but she was accused of making up or changing results. In order to determine whether she dishonestly recorded results, investigators studied her laboratory notebooks to determine whether the results had been recorded in an appropriate fashion. Although the Secret Service concluded that the notebooks had been faked, further inquiries showed that their forensic evidence was inconclusive. Imanishi-Kari has been found "not guilty" and the world may never know the whole truth about this case. This case illustrates the importance of trust in collecting data. Since scientists, including science students, often record results in private, there may be no witnesses to an act of false reporting of data. Just as a professor may never know whether a student has faked his lab notebooks or lab report, scientists may never know whether their colleagues have reported results falsely. Hence, scientists must trust that data have been reported accurately (Whitbeck 1995b, Bird and Houseman 1995).

Misrepresentation of data occurs when scientists honestly collect and record data but dishonestly represent the data. Cases of misrepresentation are usually much less clear cut than cases of fabrication or falsification, and misrepresentation remains a controversial topic in scientific ethics. As I mentioned in the previous chapter, misrepresentation can occur through the misuse of statistics in science. There are many different ways that scientists can misuse statistics, but one of the most common forms of the abuse of statistics is when scientists exaggerate the significance of results (Bailar 1986). I will not discuss all the possible misuses of statistics here, since this discussion would require an entire course on statistical reasoning.[2] However, I will note that since statistical methods play an important role in the analysis and interpretation of data, it is often very difficult to know when someone crosses the line from using to misusing statistics. In order to use statistics properly, scientists need to acquire a great deal of knowledge, experience, and judgment in their chosen professions and have a solid grasp of statistical techniques.

This discussion of statistics also brings us back to the another point I stressed in the last chapter, namely that the distinction between "misrepresentation" and "good scientific judgment or acceptable practice" is vague. Millikan's oil drop experiments provide a good illustration of how the boundary between misrepresentation and good judgment in science can be murky. Although I mentioned this case briefly in the last chapter, I will include a fuller discussion here. Millikan won the Nobel Prize in 1923 for experiments conducted in 1910 to determine the electrical charge of the electron. The experiments were an improvement on work done by Regener. In Regener's experiment, water droplets were dropped between two charged plates. One could compare the rate of fall of the droplets in the presence of charged plates to their rates of fall without the plates to determine the charge's effect. This difference would reflect the amount of charge acquired by the water droplets, which could be used to calculate the value of the smallest possible charge, i.e. the charge of an electron. This experiment had one main difficulty, however: the water droplets evaporated too quickly. One of Millikan's graduate students, Harvey Fletcher, suggested that the experiment be performed with oil droplets, and Millikan switched from water drops to oil drops. Millikan graded his results from "best" to "fair" and wrote down some reasons for his assessments of the data in the margins of his laboratory notebooks. However, his 1913 paper on his oil drop experiments did not include these comments, nor did it include forty-nine out of 140 observations that were judged as only "fair" (Holton 1978, Franklin 1981). Millikan's paper reported no fractional charge on the oil droplets but exact multiples of charges, while other papers on the same experiments had reported fractional charges. The net effect of excluding forty-nine drops was that Millikan's paper was more elegant, clear, and convincing than other papers on the subject. If Millikan had included the recalcitrant data, he might not have won the Nobel Prize. (By the way, Millikan also did not acknowledge Fletcher's contributions to the paper, a point I will discuss later.)

There are some difficult questions we need to ask about Millikan's conduct. The first is "did Millikan commit some form of scientific dishonesty?" One might argue that he should have reported all of his results instead of excluding forty-nine of them. By excluding these observations, he crossed the line from acceptable practice to dishonesty (Holton 1978). Millikan's paper should have discussed all of his results and explained why he based his calculations on the ninety-one good results. Indeed, today's science students are taught that they should analyze recalcitrant data and give reasons for excluding "bad" results. On the other hand, Millikan practiced science during an era where standards of evidence and proof were not as rigorous as they are today. Millikan's conduct might be judged as "unethical" by today's standards but it would have been regarded as "acceptable" by the standards of his own time. Millikan was an established scientist who had a good understanding of his experimental apparatus, he had good scientific judgment, and he followed standard research practices (Franklin 1981).

In order to understand situations like the Millikan case, it is useful to remind ourselves that dishonesty occurs only when there is an intent to deceive an audience. Thus, in order to know whether Millikan misrepresented the data we must understand his motives and intentions. We also need to acknowledge that there is a difference between dishonesty and disagreement (PSRCR 1992). Scientists often disagree about research methods and practices, and it makes little sense to accuse someone of acting dishonestly when scientists lack agreement on research methods and practices. Dishonesty occurs when a scientist intentionally defies widely accepted research practices in order to deceive an audience; disagreement occurs when scientists lack an overall consensus on research practices.

Before concluding this section, I will mention some other kinds of dishonesty that occur in science. First, sometimes scientists include some misinformation in papers they submit to scientific journals (Grinnell 1992). For example, a manuscript might not accurately report the details of an experiment's design. A person who lacks the experiment's secrets will not be able to repeat it. Researchers who engage in this practice often do so in order to protect their claims to priority and intellectual property, since they fear that referees could steal their ideas. They also often print a correction after their papers are accepted and they have received proper credit for their work. (Researchers may not always print corrections, however.)

Second, scientists sometimes stretch the truth or even lie when applying for government grants, and they also engage in a fair amount of exaggeration and hyperbole when lobbying for big science projects, such as the Super Conducting Super Collider (Slakey 1993). In applying for grants, scientists often overestimate the significance of their research or its feasibility, they may omit some important details that might portray their research in a dim light, and they may describe work that they have already done but have not yet published. Some scientists may even fabricate, falsify, or misrepresent preliminary results or lie when reporting their results to the funding organizations. Finally, scientists often use their funding to conduct research not explicitly funded by the granting agency.

Are these other kinds of dishonesty unethical? It is easy to understand why someone might include some misinformation in a paper or lie on a grant application, since these behaviors can be viewed as responses to a competitive research environment. Although these problems in the research environment can explain these actions, they cannot justify them. Dishonesty in all of its forms is harmful to objective inquiry. Scientists who include misinformation in their papers hamper the peer review process and they may also promulgate errors. The proper response to the fear of having one's ideas stolen by a referee is to take steps to promote ethical refereeing and peer review. (I will discuss these topics in the next chapter.)

Scientists who lie on grant applications interfere with the objective evaluation of grants, since granting agencies need accurate and truthful information in order to assess research proposals. Moreover, this type of dishonesty in science can also lead to an unfair and wasteful distribution of resources. Distributions of funds by granting agencies are unfair if they reward people who lie or cleverly stretch the truth and they "punish" people who do not engage in these practices. Distributions are wasteful if they fund poor proposals that appear to be promising because a scientist has lied or stretched the truth. A certain amount of "selling" of science is acceptable, but not at the expense of seriously undermining the process of evaluating grant proposals.

Perhaps science as a whole would benefit if some changes were made in the process of evaluating grant proposals, since policies may encourage dishonesty. For instance, grants often stipulate that money is not to be used to conduct research unrelated to the proposal, but scientists often use grant money to perform research not directly related to the proposal, since they need some way of funding the research. Although granting agencies restrict the use of funds in order to insure accountability, perhaps they should allow more leeway so that scientists won't have to lie about their activities in order to conduct research not directly related to the proposal. Perhaps granting agencies should be less stringent in their evaluation of research as well. If the agencies were a bit less stringent in their evaluation of proposals, i.e. if they were more willing to fund research that is not progressing well or is based on very little experimental data, then scientists would not feel as compelled to lie to them in order to meet their standards.

Finally, I will also mention that there are various other ways that scientists may act dishonestly when they publish their research, such as plagiarism, misrepresentation of publication status, and so on (LaFollette 1992). Many scientists view plagiarism as a serious breach of scientific ethics on a par with fabrication or falsification. I will discuss plagiarism and other publications issues in more depth in the next chapter.

Misconduct in Science

Serious deviations from the principle of honesty in science have been labeled "misconduct in science" by several scientific agencies and institutions, including the NAS, the National Academy of Engineers (NAE), the Institute of Medicine (IM), and the NIH. The organizations have developed a definition of "misconduct in science" for the purposes of reporting, investigating, and adjudicating alleged violations of research ethics. In an influential report, the NAS, NAE, and IM defined misconduct as fabrication, falsification, or plagiarism in research. This definition focuses on some of the most egregious kinds of unethical behavior in science, but it does not include other infractions, such as the misrepresentation of data or misconduct unrelated to the research process (PSRCR 1992). The report recognizes that there are many types of ethically questionable practices that can occur in science, such as abusing statistical techniques, exploiting subordinates, or failing to keep adequate records, but these practices are not treated as misconduct. The report also discusses a third category, "other misconduct," which includes unacceptable behavior not unique to science, such as harassment of individuals, misuse of funds, violations of government regulations, and vandalism (PSRCR 1992).

I do not find these definitions particularly useful in thinking about or discussing ethical issues in scientific research, since they oversimplify complex problems, such as dishonesty and plagiarism. This approach assumes that there is a "clear demarcation" between misconduct in science and questionable research practices, but as we have already seen (and we will continue to see in this book), the line between unethical and ethical conduct in science is often murky. Although some ethical questions have clear, unambiguous answers, most of the interesting and important questions in ethics do not have simple or easy answers. If ethical questions in science could be understood in black and white terms, then there would be no need for writing a book on ethics in science or teaching ethics to science students. Scientists could memorize various ethical principles and follow them without any further reflection. According to the view I defend in this book, there are some general guidelines for ethical conduct in science, which scientists should follow, other things being equal. These guidelines are easy to learn, but they are difficult to apply. In order to apply these principles, scientists must reason about ethical problems and questions and exercise their scientific, practical, and moral judgment.

I also object to the report because it obfuscates other important ethical problems and issues in scientific ethics, such as harassment and vandalism, by insisting that these problems and issues are not unique to science and therefore do not come under the purview of misconduct in science. I agree that many ethical questions and problems that arise in ordinary life also arise in science. Scientists are human beings who live in human societies, and the ethical problems inherent in all human interactions will also affect those interactions involving scientific research. I argued in previous chapters that scientists, *qua* members of society, have moral duties as well as ethical ones: standards of conduct in science therefore include and embody professional as well as moral principles and values. If we follow this report's advice, then a principle of mutual respect would pertain only to "other misconduct." This classification implies that a scientist who vandalizes his peers' work has violated moral (and probably legal) standards but not scientific ones. I do not agree with this way of thinking about ethics in science, since it simplifies the complex web of professional, moral, and legal obligations in science to the point of banality.

Error and
Self-deception

As I have noted earlier, dishonesty is not the same thing as error or disagreement. Both dishonesty and error presuppose some kind of methodological agreement in that errors or deceptions can only occur when we have some agreement on what counts as valid, honest research. Although dishonesty and error can have similar results – they undermine the search for objective knowledge – they arise from different motives. Since error and dishonesty often produce similar results, we often cannot tell whether someone has acted dishonestly by merely examining their actions; we must also try to uncover their motives or intentions. Although it is notoriously difficult to determine a person's motives or intentions, we can use several sources of evidence to classify an action as dishonest and not simply erroneous. First, we can try to assess the accused scientist's character by talking to her students and colleagues. Second, we can examine the scientist's previous work to see if there is a pattern of deception that supports fraudulent intent. In Summerlin's case, it turned out that many of his published papers were based on fabricated data (Kohn 1986). Third, we should pay close attention to a person's response to allegations of fraud. The person who willingly admits their errors and does their best to correct them is different from the person who maintains the validity of their results, denies all allegations, and refuses to admit errors in the face of strong incriminating evidence.

In the previous chapter I discussed some reasons why it is important for scientists to avoid errors as well as some of the different kinds of errors. I would like to re-emphasize a point made earlier that standards relating to errors must be discipline-specific, since different disciplines aspire to different degrees of reliability, objectivity, and precision. Since methodological standards in social science may not apply to chemistry or vice versa, principles for assessing errors in social science may not apply to chemistry or vice versa. Since errors are more prevalent than dishonesty and can have a detrimental impact on the advancement of knowledge, scientists need to devote a great deal of time toward teaching their students how to avoid errors. Students of science need to learn how to recognize the different kinds of error, possible sources of error, the importance of avoiding error, and the proper way to respond to error (Committee on the Conduct of Science 1994). The proper response to error is to print a correction, erratum, retraction, or apology, if a paper has been published. Most scientific journals routinely publish corrections for previously published papers. Since most scientists make mistakes during their careers, scientists are willing to tolerate and excuse occasional honest mistakes, provided that these mistakes are corrected. However, the research community should not take a sanguine attitude toward scientists who continually make mistakes or who fail to admit or correct their mistakes, since these researchers should be regarded as careless or negligent. If an error occurs in research that has not been published, the proper response is to insure that any colleagues who are using the unpublished research learn about the error and correct the error in any manuscript submitted for publication.

Although many errors in science are straightforward and simple, many of the worst errors in science are subtle and complex. These are the errors that result from faulty assumptions, fallacies in reasoning, the misuse of statistics, poor experimental design, and other elaborate follies. Sometimes it takes many years to discover these mistakes and scientists may repeat them over and over again. One reason why it is often so difficult to eliminate these more subtle errors is that scientists, like other people, are gullible (Broad and Wade 1993). Although scientists attempt to be skeptical, rigorous, honest, critical, and objective, they may fail to see their own errors as a result of self-deception. Several cases illustrate these kinds of errors.

The debate over cold fusion, according to many writers, is a classic case of scientific self-deception (Huizenga 1992). Self-deception is usually a combination of carelessness and wishful thinking: researchers want so much for an hypothesis to be true that they do not subject it to rigorous testing or careful scrutiny. Pons and Fleischmann wanted to believe in cold fusion for obvious reasons: if they could perfect the process they would obtain a great deal of money, status, and prestige. But they failed to subject their experiments to rigorous tests and careful scrutiny. For example, one of the key "results" of their experiment was that they were getting more heat out of the system than they were putting into it. This heat was measured near the electrode where cold fusion was allegedly taking place. However, other scientists have analyzed the thermodynamics of cold fusion and have claimed that ordinary chemical reactions will cause heat build-up near this electrode if the solution is not mixed properly (Huizenga 1992). Thus, Pons and Fleischmann have been charged with failing to understand their experiment's design.

The examples discussed thus far suggest that only individual scientists or research teams succumb to self-deception, but the infamous N-Ray affair was a case where an entire community of scientists deceived themselves. During the late 1800s and early 1900s, scientists discovered some new forms of radiation, such as X-rays, radio waves, and cathode rays. As a result of these discoveries, many scientists became interested in new forms of radiation and a "scientific bandwagon" started rolling. N-rays were "discovered" in 1903 by the French physicist Rene Blondlot. These rays could be detected by an increase in brightness from an electric spark, which could only be observed by the naked eye. Soon other French physicists reported similar observations, and N-rays were also "discovered" in gases, magnetic fields, chemicals, and the human brain. Between 1903 and 1906, over 100 scientists wrote more than 300 papers on N-rays. Many of the scientists who studied N-rays, such as Jean Bacquerel, Gilbert Ballet, and Andre Broca, were highly respected men who made important contributions to science. Blondlot even received the French Academy of Sciences' Leconte Prize for his work on N-rays. However, an American physicist R.W. Wood demonstrated that N-rays were an illusion after he visited Blondlot's laboratory. In his "experiment" Blondlot said that he could "observe" the splitting of N-rays into different wavelengths upon passing through a prism. In a darkened room Blondlot claimed to observe this effect, even after Wood had removed the prism. N-rays turned out to be nothing more than an "observer effect."[3] Shortly after Wood's exposé the rest of the scientific community lost interest in N-rays, although French physicists continued to support Blondlot's work for several years. Although some historians consider the N-ray affair to be a case of pathological science, other historians argue that it more closely resembles ordinary science than some scientists might be willing to admit (Broad and Wade 1993). All scientists – even some of the most respected scientists – can succumb to various forms of self-deception during research. To prevent self-deception, scientists need a strong commitment to carefulness, skepticism, and rigor.

Before concluding this section I think we need to place self-deception in an historical perspective, since research methods may change over time and scientists may uncover previously unknown errors in reasoning. From our modern viewpoint, ancient Greek astronomers may have seemed self-deceived, since they believed that the planets had to move in perfect circles; and phrenologists may have seemed self-deceived, since they believed that head shapes determine intelligence and personality. Even some great scientists, such as Copernicus and Newton, could be considered self-deceived, since Copernicus believed that the planets move in perfect circles and Newton believed that the geometry of the universe is Euclidean. But it would be unfair and uncharitable to draw these conclusions. Scientists have to be judged according to the research practices that are accepted during their time. If we learn that those practices generate errors, then those practices can and should be changed, and scientists have an obligation to conduct research in light of these improvements. It is only when scientists make errors as a result of failing to conform to accepted practices that we may consider them self-deceived; being mistaken is not the same as being self-deceived. Even those scientists who believe a correct theory could still be self-deceived if their correct conclusions are based on unacceptable research practices. The difference between self-deception and intellectual integrity in research does not reduce to the difference between getting the wrong or right results. Scientists have intellectual integrity insofar as they strive to follow the highest standards of evidence and reasoning in their quest to obtain knowledge and avoid ignorance.

Bias in Research

In the past two decades, many scholars have argued that various types of biases have infected and continue to infect scientific research. Though biases often lead to errors, there are several reasons why it is useful to distinguish between biases and errors. First, biases are systematic flaws in research. Biases, like rotten apples, can spoil the whole research barrel. Errors might have isolated effects. For example, a Nissan speedometer would be biased if it always underreported a car's speed by 10 percent. A speedometer that merely makes errors might give inaccurate readings in specific circumstances, e.g. when the car is accelerating at a very high rate. For a striking example of biased research, consider the "science" of craniometry practiced during the 1800s (Gould 1981). The craniometrists believed that human head sizes and shapes determine personality traits and intelligence: people with ape-like heads or small craniums were believed to be intellectually inferior. This false assumption invalidated the entire field of craniometry.

Second, biases can be highly controversial; scientists can usually agree when research contains errors, but it is more difficult to reach agreement concerning biases. One person's bias may be another person's valid assumption or methodology. It can be difficult to detect biases in research because one often needs an independent source of evidence or criticism to detect a bias. For example, if you have want to know whether your Nissan speedometer is biased, you cannot check it against other Nissan speedometers; you need a measurement that is independent of your particular speedometer or its type. It is not always easy to achieve this independence in science, since institutional, political, and social factors can militate against it. It might happen that all scientists in a particular field, such as craniometry, accept the same research bias.

Third, since it is often so difficult to agree on when or whether research is biased, it may not be appropriate to regard biased research as unethical. Although all researchers should strive to avoid biases, it may not be useful to assign moral or ethical blame to a person or research group if their research is judged to be biased. The person who conducts biased research is more like the person who defends an hypothesis that is later proven wrong than the person who makes a mistake or attempts to deceive her audience. The craniometrists, as mistaken as they were, may have conducted careful, honest research. Craniometrists appeared to be doing good science.

Fourth, biases often result from political, social, and economic aspects of science. For example, feminist scholars have argued that some research on human evolution is biased insofar as it reflects patriarchal assumptions (Longino 1990).[4] Since craniometrists claimed that a study of craniums could show that some races were intellectually inferior, many writers have claimed that craniometry's biases resulted from racist assumptions (Gould 1981). A more in-depth discussion of the social, political, and economic aspects of science takes us beyond the present scope of this book.[5]

I would like to mention at this point, however, that freedom and openness in research can help science to eliminate some of its biases. Science is more likely to achieve objective, unbiased knowledge when scientists pursue different ideas and are open to criticism (Longino 1990). I will discuss openness in more depth shortly.

Conflicts
of Interest

Sometimes scientific objectivity can be compromised not by error, bias, self-deception, or dishonesty but by conflicts of interest. Before discussing conflicts of interest in science, I will give a brief explication of the notion of a conflict of interest. A conflict of interest occurs when a person's personal or financial interests conflict with their professional or institutional obligations. This conflict undermines or impairs their ability to make reliable, impartial, and objective decisions and judgments (Davis 1982). Impaired judgment is not the same as biased judgment, and a person who has a conflict of interest may make a variety of errors that are not slanted in any particular way. A person with impaired judgment is like an unreliable speedometer; sometimes it overestimates speed, sometimes it under-estimates it, and so on.

For example, a father who is asked to referee his daughter's basketball game has a conflict of interest: his relationship with his daughter, a personal interest, conflicts with his duty to be an impartial referee, an institutional obligation. One might expect the father to make too many calls in favor of his daughter's team, but he also might try to compensate for his impairment and make too many calls against his daughter's team. Since his judgment is impaired, his calls are unreliable and untrustworthy. A city council member making a zoning decision that would affect the value of his property – it would increase in value by $50,000 if a new zoning proposal is approved – has a conflict of interest because his economic interests conflict with his obligations to make objective decisions in government. Finally, a person who serves on a jury would have a conflict of interest if the defendant is a close, personal friend because her relationship with the defendant could prevent her from making a fair and impartial decision. It is important to understand that conflicts of interest do not automatically invalidate judgments or decisions, since a person with a conflict can still make correct judgments or decisions. The father who referees his daughter's basketball game could try his best to be impartial and he could make correct calls for the entire contest. The problem with his refereeing the game is that his judgment is not reliable, given his conflict.

We should also note there is a difference between a conflict of interest, a conflict of commitment, and an apparent conflict of interest (Davis 1982). A conflict of commitment occurs when a person has professional or institutional obligations that may conflict. For example, a university pharmacy professor who is also president of the state's board of pharmacy would have obligations to the university and the board that might conflict. The board could take a great deal of the professor's time and energy and prevent her from being an effective professor. An apparent conflict of interest occurs when it might appear to an outside observer that a person has a conflict of interest when she does not. For example, suppose a state legislator has a retirement fund that invests 1 percent of its funds in a coal company located in his state. It might appear to an outside observer that this legislator cannot make any decisions that affect the company because he has an economic interest in the company. On closer examination, however, it turns out that the legislator would derive a minimal and indirect economic benefit from decisions he makes that affect the company, since these decisions would not have a significant impact on the value of his retirement fund. Apparent conflicts of interest can become real, however, if a person's personal interests change. For instance, if the retirement fund changed its investments so that 40 percent of its funds were invested in the coal company, then the legislator's apparent conflict of interest would be a real conflict of interest.

This discussion raises the thorny question of how we distinguish between real and apparent conflicts of interest. How much money needs to be involved before a person has a conflict of interest? What kind of relationships or personal interests can affect our judgment? These are important, practical questions that I will not try to answer here. Even if we do not answer these questions here, we should note that they give us some reasons for taking apparent conflicts seriously, since the distinction between apparent and real conflicts may not be as clear cut as one might suppose. Since the difference between real and apparent conflicts is not absolute, perhaps it is most useful to think of the difference as a matter of degree. We could grade conflicts as follows: (a) egregious real conflicts of interest, (b) moderate real conflicts of interest, (c) suspicious apparent conflicts of interest, (d) innocuous apparent conflicts of interest. In this classification, an egregious conflict is a situation where a person's judgment is definitely compromised; a suspicious apparent conflict is a situation where we have reasons to believe that a real conflict may arise.

Since people in professional occupations are expected to make objective decisions on behalf of their clients, the profession, or society, people in the various professions should avoid conflicts of interest (Davis 1982, Steiner 1996). The proper response to an apparent or real conflict of interest is to first disclose the conflict to the people who should know about it. If the conflict is real and not merely apparent, then the next step is to avoid making or even influencing decisions that involve this conflict. For example, the city council member should disclose his conflict of interest, he should not vote on the proposed zoning change nor should he influence the vote. He should remove himself from any debate about the zoning. If the conflict is only an apparent conflict, then the parties who are affected by the conflict should monitor this conflict since it could become a real conflict. For example, the state legislator, his constituents, and other people in government should keep track of his retirement fund's investments. Some people may decide to avoid even apparent conflicts of interest in order to protect their public image, avoid ethical problems, and so on. In order to do this, one would need to disclose all conflicts and remove oneself from decisions where such conflicts arise. People who have a lot of money invested in different companies and funds sometimes decide to place their investments in a blind trust in order to avoid even apparent conflicts of interest. (A blind trust is a way of turning over management of your investments to an outside agency that will not let you know how or where your funds are invested.)

Since most people have economic or personal interests that can conflict with their professional or institutional obligations, it is virtually impossible to avoid apparent conflicts of interest. Only a hermit could avoid apparent conflicts. Sometimes it is also difficult to avoid real conflicts of interest. For example, suppose the six out of nine members of the city council declare a conflict of interest. Should all of these members remove themselves from this zoning decision? Probably not, since it would not be in the best interests of the people of the town to have this decision made by only three members of the council. The best thing to do in this situation is to declare conflicts and to strive to be objective.

Although conflicts of commitment can adversely affect professional responsibilities, they do not by their very nature affect professional judgment. Hence, professionals should manage conflicts of commitment though they need not avoid them. The appropriate course of action is to disclose the conflict of commitment to the relevant people and to make sure that the conflict does not compromise one's primary professional commitments and loyalties. For example, the pharmacy professor should let her department chair know about her position on the board, and she should step down from this position if it prevents her from fulfilling her obligations to the university.

When conflicts of interest occur in science, they can compromise the objectivity of scientific judgments and decisions, such as the analysis and interpretation of data, the evaluation of scientific papers and research proposals, and hiring and promotion decisions. A scientist whose judgment has been compromised by a conflict of interest could overestimate the significance of data, she could exclude recalcitrant data, she could fail to subject her work to critical scrutiny, and so on. A scientist who has a conflict of interest could still strive to be objective and could still make correct decisions and judgments. Nevertheless, we have reasons to suspect that her judgments and decisions are unreliable, if she has a conflict of interest. When a scientist makes a judgment that is affected by a real or apparent conflict of interest, other scientists who know about this conflict have reasons to scrutinize that judgment carefully.

A common kind of conflict of interest in science occurs when researchers stand to benefit financially from research results. These benefits might include salary increases, royalties on copyrights or patents, funding of additional research, shares of stock, dividends, and so on. All of these financial rewards can create apparent or real conflicts of interest in that they can compromise a scientist's ability to design experiments, conduct tests, or interpret data in an objective fashion. For a recent case, consider the Cleveland scientist, Michael Macknin, who had invested in a company that makes zinc throat lozenges. He bought stock in the company, Quigley Corporation, shortly after he obtained data showing that zinc lozenges can alleviate cold symptoms. The company's stock soared after Macknin published these results, and he profited $145,000 (Hilts 1997). In this case, it appears that Macknin only had a moderate conflict of interest, since he had some financial incentives for obtaining positive results and he was probably planning on buying stock in the company. If he had bought stock in the company before he conducted the research, he would have an egregious conflict of interest. The proper response to this conflict is to disclose it, which he did, and to monitor the conflict, which he and other parties should attempt to do.

If we apply my earlier analysis of conflicts of interest to science, it follows that scientists have an obligation to disclose conflicts of interest, including apparent conflicts. Although a conflict of interest might not undermine a paper or taint its results, other scientists (and the public) should know that the conflict exists. Even if Macknin's results are valid, other scientists may want to repeat his experiments or subject his work to further scrutiny, since they would have reasons to doubt the reliability of his judgments. Scientists who receive their funding from businesses should also disclose the source of their funding, since they could have financial incentives for obtaining profitable results. Many journals now require scientists to disclose sources of funding in order to deal with conflicts of interest (International Committee of Medical Journal Editors 1991).

Ideally, scientists, like other professionals, should avoid all conflicts of interest and they should monitor apparent conflicts. However, practical realities may prevent scientists from meeting these ideal standards. Research often yields financial rewards and it is often funded by business. Given these fiscal and economic realities, we can expect that conflicts of interest will often arise in science and that they may be unavoidable in many cases, e.g. when scientists work for industry or when they attempt to develop patentable inventions. If scientists avoided all conflicts of interest, then a great deal of research would never get done and many scientists would have to find employment elsewhere. Neither of these results would be in the best interests of society, business, or the scientific profession. Scientists should disclose all conflicts of interest (real or apparent), and they should avoid the most egregious ones. But moderate conflicts of interest can be tolerated in science, and apparent conflicts can be monitored. Science can tolerate some conflicts of interest since the scientific community can check and scrutinize the work of scientists who have conflicts. Peer review helps to insure that biases or errors that result from conflicts of interest can be corrected.

Many other kinds of conflicts of interest can arise in science besides the types discussed here. Some other situations where conflicts of interest can arise include peer review, government funding, hiring and promotion, and expert testimony. I will discuss these other situations in subsequent chapters.

Openness

We have already seen how many different problems can compromise the objectivity of scientific research. These range from dishonesty and deception to error, bias, self-deception, and conflicts of interest. Peer review provides the common solution to all of these problems because it enables the scientific community to weed out various forms of deception, to catch human and experimental errors, to prevent and discover self-deception and bias, and to control conflicts of interest (Munthe and Welin 1996). It is often said that "science is self-correcting." What this means is that peer review and other key elements of the scientific method insure that the deceptions, errors, and biases that frequently occur in science will be eliminated in the long run. Although the scientific method is not perfect, it is our most useful tool in the quest for objective knowledge. But this method can only work when scientists practice openness by sharing data, ideas, theories, and results. Openness in science also implies that scientists should disclose sources of funding and financial interests, and that they should be open to new ideas, new methods, and new people. Openness should prevail in scientific research because it promotes objective inquiry and because it contributes to cooperation and trust in science.

It may come as a surprise to some students to learn that openness did not always prevail in science. During the later Middle Ages and the Renaissance, scientists kept secrets in order to prevent their ideas from being stolen and to avoid religious persecution. In order to protect his ideas, Leonardo Da Vinci wrote notes in mirror-writing (Meadows 1992).

Mathematicians often wrote proofs in secret code during this time, and alchemists guarded their secret formulas and techniques (Goldstein 1980). During the debate over Copernican astronomy, many scientists did not make their heliocentric views public out of fear of persecution. During this century, Soviet scientists kept their discussions about Mendelian genetics secret in order to avoid political persecution. Several important changes have taken place over the last 500 years that have allowed scientists to share their ideas openly, such as the formation of scientific societies and journals, the establishment of governments that value freedom of expression, and the promulgation of intellectual property laws. Since many of the same conditions and pressures that encouraged secrecy in science 500 years ago still prevail today, scientists should not take this current climate of openness for granted. Science could very easily become highly secretive once again if scientists do not safeguard openness.

Although today's scientists are not likely to keep secrets in order to avoid religious or political persecution, there are some powerful threats to openness, such as rampant careerism and economic self-interest. Some of the most difficult questions relating to openness also arise in the context of military and industrial research, since scientists who work under these circumstances are often required to keep secrets (Bok 1982). I will discuss these questions in more depth later on in the book. For our present purposes, it will be useful to ask if secrecy is ever justified in academic science.

In the previous chapter I argued that scientists are sometimes justified in keeping secrets in order to protect ongoing research. This seems like a good reason to allow for a limited form of secrecy in science. Consider Charles Darwin's reluctance to publish his theory of evolution by natural selection. Darwin's idea germinated while he served as the ship's naturalist on the five-year voyage of the HMS Beagle. From 1836 to 1859, he gathered more evidence for his theory and refined its basic concepts and principles. In 1842 Darwin wrote an essay on natural selection, which he showed only to Joseph Hooker. In 1856, Charles Lyell advised Darwin to write a book on the subject. But what prompted Darwin to finish the work was a letter from Alfred Wallace announcing his own theory of natural selection. The two men agreed to present their ideas together at a meeting of the Linnean Society, although Darwin was listed as the sole author of the *Origin of Species*. It is not difficult to understand why Darwin took so long to publish his work or why he kept it secret: he wanted to make sure that he could present a solid and convincing case for evolution. He knew that his theory would be subjected to a great deal of scientific and religious criticism, and he wanted to give it a good chance of succeeding (Meadows 1992). It is also likely that Darwin took a long time to publicize his research in order to protect his reputation and his ideas.

Although Darwin offers us an example of someone who had good reasons to guard his research carefully, today few scientists follow his example. In the current research environment you would be hard pressed to find a scientist sitting on a hypothesis for a few years, to say nothing of waiting more than two decades to publish an idea. Though Darwin erred almost on the side of hesitancy, today's scientists often err on the side of urgency. The "rush to publish" plays a large role in the propagation of errors, biases, and deceptions and other threats to the integrity and quality of research (LaFollette 1992). The cold fusion case provides an unfortunate example of this phenomenon: driven by a desire for priority, prestige, and money, the scientists publicized their work before it had been validated by peers.

There are several other reasons for secrecy in science in addition to the need to protect ongoing research. First, scientists are justified in not revealing the names and institutional affiliations of reviewers or authors in order to insure that peer review is candid and objective. This practice, which I will discuss later in the book, is known as blind review. Second, scientists are justified in suppressing the names, addresses, and other personal identifiers of human subjects in order to protect their privacy. (I will also discuss research on human subjects in Chapter 7.) Third, scientists may be justified in sharing ideas with only a limited audience, such as a group of specialists in a particular field; not all scientific theories need to be reported in the popular press in order to satisfy the demands of openness. I will also discuss various aspects of the relationship between science and the media later on in the book.

The final reason for secrecy I will discuss in this section concerns the issue of sharing scientific information among nations. From the scientific viewpoint, it would seem that international scientific collaboration and cooperation should not only be permitted but strongly encouraged (Wallerstein 1984). If collaboration and cooperation in science contribute to the advancement of knowledge, then international collaboration and cooperation should also promote this goal. This is especially true when science undertakes large-scale, multi-billion dollar projects that cannot be fully funded (or used) by any one nation, such as the high-energy physics laboratory, Conseil European pour la Recherche Nucleaire (CERN) in Geneva, Switzerland. Scientists from many different nations conduct experiments at this lab, and many different nations help to fund it (Horgan 1994). Although international collaboration and cooperation is especially important in "big science," it is also should be encouraged in "little science."

While openness implies both unilateral and multilateral sharing of information, one might argue that moral or political goals sometimes justify restrictions on international cooperation in science. These restrictions would be limits on openness that extend beyond restrictions on classified, military information. For instance, during the height of the Cold War, there was virtually no scientific collaboration or cooperation between the United States and the Soviet Union. These restrictions on openness applied to many kinds of research that had little to do with nuclear weapons, such as computing technology, mathematics, physics, engineering, medicine, and chemistry. Both countries discouraged or even banned cooperation in order to gain a scientific and technological edge in the Cold War. Although the Cold War is over, one might argue that similar restrictions on international cooperation can be justified for political reasons. The United States could limit international scientific collaboration and cooperation in order to prevent renegade nations or terrorists from acquiring more scientific knowledge and technological power. If knowledge is power, then some nations may attempt to control knowledge in order to achieve political goals (Dickson 1984). These larger political issues take us beyond the scope of this book, however. While I will not attempt to criticize the United States' past or current foreign policies, I will observe that these policies can have an important impact on the flow of scientific and technical information (Nelkin 1984).

Data Management

Questions about data management in science have a direct bearing on questions about openness, since in order to share data one must store it and make it accessible to others (PSRCR 1992). Data can be stored in many different forms, e.g. on paper, computer diskettes, tapes, microfilm, slides, videotape, and so on. Data should also be well organized in order to insure easy access and transmission: a library is of little use if no one can find or read its books. It is important to store data for several reasons. First, scientists need to store data in order to check their own work. Sometimes scientists want to take another look at the hard data or reanalyze it. Second, data should be stored so that critics and reviewers can scrutinize or verify research. The data serves as proof that the research was indeed done as it has been described. If someone wants to question the validity of a study, or even decide whether it is fraudulent, they need access to the data. Third, data should be stored so that other scientists can use the original data in their own research. Since original data often contain more information than can be gleaned from published data, those who want to benefit from previous research will often want access to original data. Finally, data are scientific resources that scientists should not mismanage or waste.[6] All of these reasons for storing data and making it accessible promote the objectivity of inquiry and cooperation and trust among scientists.

Although it is fairly obvious that data should be stored, it is not at all clear how it should be stored, for how long, or who should have access to it. Since laboratory space is limited, most scientists need to minimize the amount of space they devote to the storage of data. NASA has accumulated so much data from planetary exploration during the last two decades that it has vast storerooms of data that have not even been analyzed or interpreted. It is likely to take many years for planetary scientists to sort through all of the data from missions to Saturn, Jupiter, and Neptune. No matter how scientists decide to store data, they should be responsible for taking care of it and keeping it from being lost due to decay, contamination, or other difficulties. However, economic considerations also have an impact on data storage, since there are significant costs associated with data management. Laboratories often need to keep and maintain obsolete machines that are designed to read outmoded forms of data storage, such as computer tapes. Although it is sometimes possible to transfer data to new mediums, the transferring of data incurs its own costs. In an ideal world, scientists would have enough space and money to keep data forever. But limitations in economic and other resources require scientists to balance the goal of storing data against the goal of making efficient use their resources. Although scientists usually strive to keep data as long as possible, data are sometimes destroyed after only a few years in order to save space and money (PSRCR 1992). Many factors enter into decisions about data storage, and each decision to destroy or keep data needs to be made on its own merits. I mention some of the basic issues here, but the practical questions are best left to professional scientists.

Although academic scientists have an obligation to save data, scientists who conduct research on human subjects may have an obligation to destroy data after a period of time (American Psychological Association 1990). The reason for destroying data about human subjects is that researchers have an obligation to protect confidentiality, and one of the best ways of keeping information secret is to destroy it.

Finally, I should mention that some ethical questions can arise when scientists decide who should have access to data. The people who might reasonably request access to data include collaborators, colleagues in the same research group or laboratory, scientists working within the same field, scientists working in different fields, and representatives from funding agencies. Others who may request access to data include government officials, the press, scholars in non-scientific disciplines, and laypeople. Although openness implies unlimited access to data, there are some reasons for limiting access to data that do not undermine openness (Marshall 1997). For instance, scientists may be concerned that nonexperts will accidentally destroy data, that rivals will steal data, that enemies will intentionally destroy data, or that other scientists or laypeople will misinterpret data. Data access may sometimes be denied for political reasons. All of these reasons for denying access to data suggest that data can be viewed as a kind of intellectual property. Although this property should be shared, scientists and other parties may legitimately claim a right to control its use. Just as a scientist has a right to control access to her laboratory, she also has a right to control access to her data. In making data access decisions, scientists need to balance the ethic of openness against other concerns and values, such as carefulness, prudence, fairness, respect for political interests, and accountability.

CHAPTER 6
Ethical Issues in Scientific Publication

This chapter examines some of the ethical issues and problems that arise when scientists publish results from their laboratory work. Since one meaning of "publish" is to "to make publicly known," this chapter will discuss the various ways that scientists make their results publicly known. These include publication in scientific journals and academic presses, as well as internet publication and publication in popular presses and the media. This chapter will follow a pattern laid out in the previous one: it will apply some of the ethical standards defended in Chapter 4 to practical problems in science.

Objectivity
in Publication

In the previous chapter I argued that scientists should not fabricate, falsify, or misrepresent data or results and that they should avoid errors and biases in collecting, recording, analyzing, and interpreting data. These imperatives also apply to all of the parties who play a role in scientific publication, i.e. authors, editors, and reviewers. Thus, papers, books, or other works that are submitted for publication should be honestly, objectively, and carefully written, reviewed, edited, and published.

In order to promote objective peer review, authors have an obligation to write papers clearly, carefully, and objectively. Since this is not a book on scientific writing, I will not explore objectivity in writing in any depth here.[1] However, it is worth noting that even if an author follows all of the guidelines given in various science writing books, she still needs to make sure that the paper is accurate and that it discloses relevant information, since reviewers and editors cannot make sound judgments if they lack pertinent information or if some of the information they receive is inaccurate. Information that should be accurately reported includes data, materials and methods, names and institutional affiliations of authors, references, acknowledgments, permissions, and the paper's publication status. In addition to these pieces of information, authors should also disclose sources of funding as well as any financial interests that could generate a conflict of interest. An author's obligations do not end after the paper has been accepted for publication or appears in print, however. If an author discovers that her work contains an error, inaccuracy, or omission, she has an obligation to report this problem to the editors. The author may then be allowed to print an erratum, addendum, or retraction, depending on the nature of the mistake.

If peer review is to function properly, then it must be done carefully, critically, and objectively. Since editors and reviewers serve as science's quality control mechanism, they have an obligation to read papers carefully, critically, and thoroughly. They should detect and report any errors, omissions, inaccuracies, experimental design flaws, misinterpretations, and logical, methodological, or statistical fallacies. If reviewers and editors find that a paper falls short of acceptable scientific standards, then editors should inform the authors about its errors, inaccuracies, fallacies, or other errors. If they suspect that a paper is fraudulent, then they should inform the proper authorities (LaFollette 1992). Although reviewers and editors cannot be the sole guardians of scientific quality and integrity, they should do their part to help to prevent fraud and error. Scientific journals should assist the battle against fraud and error by printing retractions, corrections, and apologies from scientists who commit fraud or make errors, and by clearly stating their standards of scientific integrity in their statements on information for contributors (Armstrong 1997).

Editors and reviewers also have an obligation to insure that peer review is itself unbiased, since biases in peer review can undermine the quest for objective knowledge (Chubin and Hackett 1990). This goal is not always easy to achieve, since editors and reviewers are human beings and their biases and interests can infect and affect this process. For example, reviewers may sometimes have personal or professional interests that undermine their ability to serve as unbiased reviewers. Reviewers may unwittingly (or wittingly) attempt to suppress theories they dislike and they may attempt to prevent rival researchers or laboratories from publishing. Sometimes reviewers have personal vendettas against particular scientists or schools of thought (Hull 1988). Reviewers who act on behalf of these interests may reject a manuscript without good reason or they may delay its publication as long as possible. Editors may also engage in this type of biased review. Indeed, editors can wield even more power than reviewers because they have more control over the editorial process. If an editor does not like a manuscript or its authors, then she can send it to reviewers who she believes will give it a negative review, or she can simply disregard any positive reports from reviewers.

Although it is difficult to estimate the frequency of biased peer review, some evidence suggests that it occurs.[2] When peer review is biased, science's methods of criticism, confirmation, and debate cannot function properly. Dysfunctional review generates distrust among scientists and prevents scientists from challenging old ideas or proposing new ones. Since the health of science depends on careful and unbiased peer review, many journals take specific steps to promote fair, objective peer review. Many journals use secrecy to promote unbiased reviewing. Most journals in the sciences practice single-blind review: authors do not know the names or institutional affiliations of referees, but referees know the names and institutional affiliations of authors (LaFollette 1992). According to some, single-blind promotes objectivity and fairness in peer review because it allows reviewers to evaluate manuscripts without fearing repercussions from the authors. Some journals practice double-blind peer review: neither authors nor referees know each other's names or institutional affiliations. According to some, double-blind peer review is even more effective at promoting objectivity and fairness because it prevents referees from using information about the authors' names or institutional affiliations as a basis for giving either favorable or unfavorable reviews. Ideally, reviewers should make their judgments based on content, not on context, and blind review (double or single) seeks to promote this goal.

However, some writers object to double-blind review on the grounds that reviewers can almost always determine the authors of various papers based on their citations, their ideas, and other aspects of content. This is especially true in some very small, tight-knit fields where virtually all the top researchers know what their colleagues are doing. Double-blind review is a sham that deceives authors into believing that their identities are being kept secret. Some writers object to single-blind review on the grounds that it simply serves as a shield for dishonest and unfair reviewers and prevents them from being held accountable for unethical conduct (LaFollette 1992).

Some writers argue that the best way to promote fair, honest, and effective reviewing is to make the whole process completely open (LaFollette 1992). Completely open peer review would be like a presentation at a scientific meeting: when a person gives a presentation, the audience knows her identity and she can determine the identity of people who criticize her work. Some journals, such as *Behavioral and Brain Sciences* (BBS), allow for open peer review (Armstrong 1997). In many BBS issues an author writes a lead article that is followed by a half dozen or so signed critiques. Electronic publishing also offers some opportunities for open review, since papers can be put on web-pages and critics can add their comments to the web-page or join an electronic discussion.

While I think these issues require further study, I am not sure I would favor complete openness in peer review. I think that reviewers need some protection in order to do their job. The social pressures that reviewers face can lead to dishonest and unfair reviews. If reviewers choose to reveal their identities, then they may do so, but they should be given some anonymity. On the other hand, something does need to be done to hold reviewers accountable for their conduct. Perhaps the burden of holding reviewers accountable for their conduct should rest with editors. Editors could promote unbiased review by listing the names of reviewers at the end of the year without saying who reviewed each manuscript, or by making the names of reviewers available to authors under exceptional circumstances. In any case, editors should work closely with reviewers in promoting unbiased review and they should take actions that are required to promote objectivity.

Another solution to the problem of biased review is to circumvent the normal peer review process by inviting authors to submit articles for publication. This technique may be useful if an area of research is so controversial or innovative that it will be difficult to achieve fair or unbiased peer review (Armstrong 1997). According to many historians of science, scientists often strongly resist novel or controversial ideas (Barber 1961). I agree that editors should sometimes circumvent normal peer review in order to publish innovative or controversial research, but this policy should be the exception rather than the rule, since circumventing peer review entirely would undermine the integrity and quality of published research.

Although the last few paragraphs may give the reader the impression that I think peer review suffers from many problems, I do not believe that this is the case. Most of the people I know who review scientific papers or grant proposals take their jobs very seriously. They regard manuscript reviewing as an honor and an important service to the profession. However, since even sincere people can make mistakes or succumb to biases, it is important to take steps to insure the integrity of peer review. In any case, science scholars should study the peer review process in more depth.

Before closing this section, I would like to discuss several other responsibilities that editors and reviewers have. First, editors and reviewers should avoid conflicts of interest in peer review. These conflicts will usually be personal rather than financial in nature. For example, a person's Ph.D. advisor should not serve as a reviewer for that person's papers or grant proposals, as she would have a conflict of interest. Since sometimes there are only a few experts in a given field who know each other's work quite well and often compete, it may not always be possible to avoid conflicts of interest in peer review, but such conflicts should be avoided wherever possible.

Second, editors and reviewers have a duty to help authors improve their work; many authors learn a great deal from comments they receive from editors and reviewers. Although peer review's main purposes is to control the quality of scientific publications, it also serves an educational function. Careful, constructive criticism can help authors improve their work; careless, trivial, or destructive comments (or no comments at all) offer little help.

Third, reviewers and editors have an obligation to treat authors with dignity and respect, but this does not always happen. Some reviewers' comments contain insults, personal attacks, and other disparaging remarks (LaFollette 1992). Personal attacks violate science's principle of mutual respect and they have no place in peer review. They are unethical, unprofessional, and they undermine trust among authors, editors, and reviewers. Criticism should focus on an author's ideas, her methods, or her arguments, not on the author herself. If a reviewer's report contains personal attacks, editors have an obligation to censor these attacks from the report in order to prevent harm to author(s). The editors may also consider not asking the reviewer to assess manuscripts again.

The obligation to treat authors with dignity and respect also implies a duty to return manuscripts in a timely fashion (LaFollette 1992). Reviewers and editors who fail to meet this obligation can harm authors by preventing them from securing priority or establishing their publication records. A person's career may literally hang in the balance while they await an editorial decision. A tardy review process can also contribute to the breakdown of trust among authors, editors, and reviewers, since authors expect that peer review will be punctual and effective.

Fourth, editors and reviewers should protect the confidentiality of manuscripts that are under review and they should not steal the ideas, theories, and hypotheses that they review. Editors and reviewers have a unique opportunity to learn about new ideas and methods. Unscrupulous editors and reviewers could easily take advantage of this privilege to profit from the creativity and hard work of their colleagues. While it's often impossible to prove that a reviewer has stolen an idea, or to estimate the frequency of this type of theft, there is some evidence that it occurs (Chubin and Hackett 1990). Scientists who abuse their editorial power in this fashion not only violate science's principle of credit, they also threaten the climate of trust implicit in publication: when authors submit their manuscripts for publication, they trust that their ideas will not be stolen. If authors lack this trust, then they will not submit papers for publication or they will submit papers that contain misinformation in order to prevent their ideas from being stolen (Grinnell 1992). Needless to say, intellectual theft by reviewers or editors also threatens the objectivity, reliability, and integrity of peer review.

Finally, since editors have the final say over whether an article will be published, they bear the responsibility of making fair, informed, and objective decisions. This responsibility usually implies that editors should evaluate the peer review process itself; editors should understand the various biases and problems inherent in peer review and they should take steps to improve peer review. Editors should adjudicate between conflicting opinions when reviewers do not agree about a manuscript, they should assist authors in improving their manuscripts or in understanding a reviewer's comments, and they should be willing to experiment with different approaches to peer review (Armstrong 1997).

Other Publication Issues

There are several other important issues in publication that deserve our attention. In this section I will address some questions concerning content, style, and quantity of publication. Concerning content, we can distinguish between three types of publications: (1) peer-reviewed original research; (2) peer-reviewed research designed to repeat old experiments; (3) review articles. Most of the articles published in scientific journals summarize original research (LaFollette 1992). A piece of original research may offer a novel solution to an old problem, solve new problems, explore new territories, or develop new models, methods or techniques. Obviously, original research benefits the scientific profession in many ways and is necessary for the advancement of knowledge. Accordingly, science's reward system emphasizes originality: tenure and review committees stress original research, Ph.D. students are supposed to do some type of original research, and journals prefer to publish original research (Gaston 1973).

However, other types of publications also play an important role in science. It is important to repeat old experiments because science is supposed to be self-correcting. Unfortunately, scientists rarely repeat experiments and very few articles published in scientific journals describe attempts to repeat old experiments (Kiang 1995). It is usually the case that journals only publish articles that repeat previous work if the research is controversial. If journals rarely publish work that repeats previous experiments, and scientists are rewarded for publishing original research, then the failure to publish unoriginal work can encourage scientists to not repeat experiments. In order to combat this problem, journals should be more willing to publish articles than repeat previous work.

Since it is becoming increasingly difficult for scientists to keep up with the research in their fields of study, it is also important to write and publish review articles. A review article is an article that summarizes current research in a given field of study, and it is usually written by one of the top scientists in that area of research. A review article may also develop an overall perspective on the field of research and discuss some of the outstanding, unsolved problems in the field. Given the immense volume of scientific research in any given field, review articles play an important role in helping scientists keep track of all this information (LaFollette 1992). Unfortunately, tenure committees often do not think much of review articles and most journals rarely publish them. In order to combat this problem, scientists should be rewarded for writing review articles and journals should make more of an effort to publish them (Armstrong 1997).

The issue of how much to publish has become an important concern in the information age, and it is an issue for both authors and the scientific publishing community. From the authors' perspective, the pressure to publish in order to get tenure, funding, and other scientific rewards encourages authors to publish as much as possible (LaFollette 1992). This pressure may also drive some scientists to publish many papers of low quality in order to build up their publication records (Huth 1986). Although low quality papers do not do great damage to the scientific profession, scientists should seek to publish papers only of the highest quality. The scientific community benefits more when scientists take their time to polish and refine papers than when they rush papers into print.

The pressure to publish can also lead some authors to divide their research into "the least publishable unit" (Broad 1981). Although this practice can certainly help to benefit individual scientists by padding their publication records, it may not benefit science as a whole. First, it wastes scientific resources by multiplying the number of manuscripts that need to be edited, refereed, and published beyond what is needed to communicate information. Second, it also distorts science's reward system by giving scientists more publications than they genuinely deserve. Publication records should reflect one's research efforts, not one's mastery of the publication game (Huth 1986).

Editors can take two different approaches to the issue of how much to publish, the democratic approach and the elitist approach. Editors who adopt the first approach believe that they should publish as much material as possible in order to provide a free and open forum for the exchange of ideas and to make sure that great discoveries or results are not overlooked.

The good papers, like cream, will eventually rise to the top, and the bad papers will sink into obscurity. Moreover, when a paper is rejected, there is always a chance that some new or important idea will be missed. This is especially true since innovative or controversial papers often attract negative comments from referees due to their theoretical biases against new ideas. On the other hand, editors who adopt the second approach fear that publishing too much will have at least two negative impacts: (1) invalid or sloppy research will be published; (2) scientists will be unable to sift through the large volume of literature to find papers that are worth reading. Thus, some editors and publications have very high standards and only publish papers that meet these standards. Currently, both democratic and elitist journals exist and I see no reason why we should alter the status quo. Elitist journals serve an important function by permitting scientists who do not have time to keep up with the huge volume of literature to read only some of the best papers in their field. Democratic journals play an important role in allowing for the free and open communication of ideas.

The use of electronic forms of publication may provide the scientific community with a way to pursue both of these approaches successfully, since large quantities of information can be published electronically at a relatively low cost. However, publication on web-pages creates some serious issues relating to quality control. Since virtually anyone can publish material on the world-wide web, those who search the web for scientific information have no guarantee that the information they receive is reliable or valid. The world-wide web contains a great deal of useful information but it also contains a great deal of misinformation, junk science, opinion, advertising, and so on. In order to allow web browsers to know that the research they read is accurate and valid, those who publish on web-pages may need to provide some mechanism for peer reviewing and rating the web. Different scientific organizations could put their "stamp of approval" on some web pages in order to let readers know the research is valid and accurate.

Credit Where
Credit is Due

In Chapter 4 I discussed science's principle of credit, which instructs scientists to give credit where credit is due but not where it is not due. There are many ways of giving credit to a person in a scientific publication: one can list a person as a co-author, cite a person in the paper or discuss their work, or mention a person in an acknowledgments section. The worst form of failure to give credit is plagiarism. In the last chapter I characterized plagiarism as a type of dishonesty, but it can also be regarded as a type of intellectual theft.[3] There are many different ways to plagiarize another person's work. These range from copying another person's paper word-for-word to using another person's ideas or phrases without proper attribution. Earlier, I mentioned that reviewers can be tempted to steal ideas from the unpublished papers they read. Ideas can also be stolen when scientists share unpublished work with colleagues or when they discuss science informally.

While it is difficult to estimate the incidence of plagiarism in science, scientific organizations investigate a significant number of alleged cases of plagiarism each year. Although there are many documented cases of plagiarism in science, it is likely that much of the plagiarism that occurs in science is unintentional.[4] Many people, especially undergraduate students, unintentionally plagiarize because they do not know how to attribute or cite sources appropriately. Some people make mistakes because they do not remember where their ideas have come from. Other people make mistakes when researching, writing, and editing papers and books. Someone who does not do an adequate survey of the literature may fail to realize that another person has already done the very research she has undertaken. In order to avoid these kinds of errors, scientists need to make sure they do a thorough search of the literature before undertaking research (Grinnell 1992). Unintentional plagiarism, whether due to ignorance or carelessness, can be viewed as error rather than dishonesty or theft because it does not result from an intent to deceive an audience or steal an idea. Scientists who plagiarize unintentionally should take appropriate steps to correct their errors, and science educators should teach their students how to cite sources properly (Markie 1994).

Sometimes two (or more) scientists may happen to have the same idea at the same time by accident. This phenomena, known as co-discovery, happens frequently in science. Co-discovery is not plagiarism, even though co-discoverers often accuse each other of intellectual theft. Two famous cases include Darwin and Wallace's co-discovery of the theory of natural selection and Newton and Leibniz's co-discovery (or co-invention) of calculus. However, scientists often dispute claims of co-discovery in an effort to secure priority, and priority disputes also occur on a regular basis in science (Merton 1973).[5] When co-discovery occurs and scientists settle any outstanding priority disputes, the principle of credit implies that both discoverers receive credit for making the discovery. For example, once Darwin realized that Wallace had also come up with a theory of natural selection, the two scientists agreed to announce the theory in concert.

Although most scientists can agree that intentional plagiarism is unethical, unintentional plagiarism should be avoided, and priority disputes should be settled, there is less agreement about other issues concerning the allocation of credit in science. Questions about authorship practices have generated a great deal of discussion and debate. The general rule of thumb in science concerning authorship is that a person should be listed as an author if she makes a significant contribution to a publication. However, the concept of "significant contribution" varies across different scientific fields, and there are at present no uniform standards for granting authorship. A person could be listed as an author for designing an experiment, collecting or analyzing data, developing a concept or hypothesis, writing a grant, presenting results at a scientific meeting, directing a laboratory, giving scientific or technical advice, or drafting or editing a manuscript (Rose and Fisher 1995). Although authorship questions are not as momentous as other ethical issues in scientific research, they can be very important to scientists who raise them, since authorship provides scientists with recognition and respect and plays a key role in career advancement.

In order to answer the question, "when should a person be listed as an author?," it is important to understand the role that authorship plays in scientific research and publication. Authorship plays two distinct, though complementary roles. As we have already seen, authorship is a way of giving scientists credit for their contributions, but the flipside of credit is responsibility. An author of a scientific work should be prepared to take responsibility for its content. It is important to assign responsibility in case the work contains errors or deceptions. The scientific community needs to have a way of assigning responsibility for research in order to correct errors or investigate allegations of misconduct. It is a sad reflection on current authorship practices that some people listed as authors cannot or will not take responsibility for a paper's methods or results. In many documented cases of scientific misconduct, several co-authors denied knowing anything about the misconduct and were shocked to find out that a paper they had co-authored contained errors or deceptions (LaFollette 1992). Those who receive the benefits of credit should be willing to bear the burdens of responsibility. A final reason why co-authorship should not be taken lightly is that awarding undeserved authorship cheapens science's authorship practices. If anyone can be listed as a co-author for almost any reason, then it no longer means anything to list someone as a co-author.

These considerations suggest the following rule of thumb for authorship: an author of a scientific work is a person who makes a significant contribution to the work and can take responsibility for its content (Resnik, forthcoming). Responsibility could be parceled in various ways, and authors need not take responsibility for all parts of a work in order to be listed as authors. For example, several authors could contribute to a book by writing (and taking responsibility for) different chapters; several people could co-author a paper even though different individuals take responsibility for different sections of the paper.

What about people who contribute to a scientific work but cannot take responsibility for all or part of its content? Current scientific practices allow for other contributors to be recognized in an acknowledgments section. However, one problem with this method of assigning credit is that it usually does not provide adequate recognition for people who make these significant contributions. Being listed in an acknowledgments section counts for very little in hiring, tenure, and promotion decisions, nor does it add much to one's status or prestige in the scientific community. This gap between authorship and other forms of acknowledgment is so wide that it creates a pressure to list people as authors who do not merit this kind of recognition. People succumb to this pressure in order to give their colleagues, students, or supervisors some form of recognition.

For example, the practice of "honorary" authorship is a way of providing recognition to a person beyond a mention in an acknowledgments section. Lab directors or senior researchers are sometimes listed as honorary authors of papers even when they have not contributed to the research (LaFollette 1992). Sometimes scientists grant honorary authorship to renowned researchers to recognize their contributions to the field or to give a paper some extra status and thereby increase its chances of being read. "Gift" authorship occurs when authorship is awarded as a gift. For example, sometimes people are listed as authors in order give them some extra publications for the purposes of tenure, promotion, or other rewards (LaFollette 1992). Some scientists even establish reciprocal agreements to increase their apparent productivity (Huth 1986). These ethically questionable authorship practices may be partly responsible for the overall increase in the rate of co-authorship in the various sciences (Drenth 1996). On my view of credit allocation, none of these practices are ethical in science.

The problem of recognizing contributions to scientific works takes on a new dimension when many people contribute in an important way to research, and it is especially acute in sciences that have large laboratories and research teams. In one case, over 200 people were listed as authors on a physics paper (LaFollette 1992). Papers with many co-authors completely obscure responsibility, credit, and authorship in scientific publication.

I should also mention that sometimes people who should be listed as authors are not listed or given any form of recognition. For example, Millikan did not acknowledge Fletcher's contributions to his paper on the charge of the electron. Millikan failed to give credit to Fletcher although he did not plagiarize Fletcher's work. One might argue that Fletcher deserved some form of acknowledgment in the paper, perhaps even authorship. Although it is difficult to estimate how frequently people are unfairly denied authorship or some other form of acknowledgment, anecdotal evidence suggests that this practice is not uncommon (Grinnell 1992). The most common victims of this practice include graduate students, post-doctoral researchers, and laboratory technicians (Gurley 1993). This ethical problem probably stems, in part, from the imbalance of power between established researchers and graduate students, technicians, and other people who have less power and authority within the laboratory's hierarchy (PSRCR 1992).

Thus, there appear to be three serious problems when it comes to assigning credit for scientific research: granting authorship that is not deserved, listing too many authors, and failing to recognize important contributions to research. I suggest that an effective way of dealing with this problem would be to create new categories and designations, such as "writer," "data collector," "technician," "statistician," in addition to the forms of recognition that scientists currently use. When different people are responsible for different parts of research, credits and acknowledgments in scientific works should reflect this division of labor. If scientists adopted and used these additional categories, credit allocation could become more clear, fair, and accurate than it is under the current system. These additional designations could also have a beneficial impact on science's reward system and its social institutions by allowing scientists to do a better job of giving credit where and only where credit is due (Resnik, forthcoming). Of course, adopting a new system is not an easy task, and some scientists might wish to cling to the current system's traditional categories, but I believe that the benefits would be worth the hassle of revamping scientific traditions. The motion picture, television, newsprint, and music industries have for many years used clear and accurate methods for allocating credit. Is it too much to ask that science, the paradigm of clarity and accuracy, adopt methods that are more precise than its current ones?

One final issue in credit allocation concerns the order in which authors are listed. This is not a trivial concern, since it is often the case that a person who is listed first will get more recognition than a person who is listed second or third. The name of the first person listed may become associated with the research, especially when there are many co-authors and the article is cited using the first author and the phrase "et al." Scientists have a variety of ways of listing authors and these practices vary from discipline to discipline: in some professions, authors are listed alphabetically; in other disciplines, senior researchers are listed first; in some disciplines junior researchers are listed first; and in some disciplines authors take turns being listed first (LaFollette 1992). I find problems with some of these listing practices: if authors are listed alphabetically, then it is likely that people with last names toward the end of the alphabet will not get the recognition they deserve. If senior researchers are always listed first, then they will tend to accrue even more recognition than they already have. Although some junior researchers may accept second billing on the understanding that they simply must wait their turn, it still distorts and obscures the allocation of scientific credit. Since credit should reflect responsibility, and being listed as a first author is a type of bonus credit, this listing should reflect extra responsibility. Thus, if it is possible to determine which person is most responsible for the research, then that person should be listed first. In general, a listing should reflect an order of responsibility. If it is not possible to determine responsibility, then the idea of taking turns being listed first makes good sense.

One problem that plagues all attempts to allocate credit in science has been labeled by Merton (1973) as the "Matthew Effect."[6] This effect refers to a well-documented tendency in science for noted scientists to get even more notoriety and recognition than they deserve and for unknown scientists to get less recognition than they deserve. Recognition and respect tend to be biased in favor of the already well-known scientists and against the lesser-known, and this biasing increases over time. When a paper is co-authored, it is likely that the well-known scientist will get more recognition than the lesser-known. Well-known scientists are more likely to get prizes, awards, and grants than their equally deserving, lesser-known colleagues, and so on. For example, Anderson French has become famous as the founder of gene therapy even though his contributions to this field are no more impressive than the contributions made by other researchers (Friedman 1997).

The Matthew Effect is bad for science, I believe, because it distorts science's system of allocating credit. It gives more credit to people than they genuinely deserve and it gives less credit to people than they deserve. It is also bad for science because it creates a scientific elite and thereby denies equality of opportunity to other scientists. Since the Matthew Effect has a strong basis in human psychology and sociology, it is unlikely that we can completely overcome it: big stars will always get top billing even when they have only small roles (Merton 1973). However, scientists can (and should) at least attempt to counteract the Matthew Effect by not contributing to it. Scientists should attempt to allocate credit and scientific rewards according to scientific merit, and they should steer away from favoritism, elitism, and cronyism.

Intellectual
Property

The issue of credit allocation is closely related to another important ethical
and political issue in scientific communication, intellectual property and
the ownership of research. Although this book focuses on ethical and
political issues in scientific research, not legal ones, it will be useful to give
a brief overview of the United States' legally sanctioned forms of ownership of intellectual property in order to understand the moral and political
issues relating to intellectual property. Although different countries have
different laws, most Western nations have intellectual property laws similar to the United States' laws.[7] Intellectual property, unlike tangible property, can be shared without diminishing the owner's ability to use it.
Although intellectual property can be shared, many societies have enacted
laws giving the owners of intellectual properties some control over how
their goods are used. The different types of intellectual property recognized by many nations include copyrights, patents, trademarks, and trade
secrets (Foster and Shook 1993).

A copyright is a renewable, legal protection that allows an author to
control the reproduction of an original work. Copyrights do not grant
authors control over the ideas expressed by their original works; they only
give authors control over their particular expressions of those ideas.
Authors who have copyrights over their works have the right to reproduce
their works, prepare derivative works, perform or display works, or author-
ize others to perform the activities. Authors may demand royalties or
other forms of compensation in exchange for permission to copy their
works. However, in the US the courts have developed a doctrine of fair use,
which allows an author's works to be copied without the author's permission, provided that the copying is for educational purposes and it does not
diminish the commercial value of the work. Materials that can be copy-
righted include: literary, dramatic, audio-visual, and choreographic works;
pictorial, graphic, and sculptural artwork; music; motion pictures; and
sound recordings (Foster and Shook 1993).

A patent is a legal permission that gives a patent holder the right to
control the production, use, and commercialization of an invention for a
twenty-year period. Patents cannot be renewed. To obtain a patent, the
inventor must submit an application to the United States' Patent and
Trademark Office (PTO), which describes his or her invention in sufficient
detail that an expert in the field could make it. The PTO will grant a
patent only if the invention is original, useful, and non-obvious. Once an
invention is patented, the patent application becomes public, although the

rights to control the invention remain private. The US courts have ruled that some types of things cannot be patented, such as ideas, scientific principles or theories, or mere results. Inventions designed for the sole purpose of violating the legal rights of others also cannot be patented, nor can inventions that pose a threat to national security (Foster and Shook 1993).

A trade secret is a piece of information useful to a business's activities that is not known to others in the industry or trade. In order to claim ownership of a trade secret, the owners must demonstrate that they have intentionally kept the knowledge a secret and that the secret has business value. Trade secrets do not need to be original or novel, and there are no legal restrictions on how long secrets may be kept. Trade secret laws allow rival companies to discover each other's trade secrets, provided that the discovery occurs through fair and honest means. For example, companies may independently discover the same item of knowledge – trade secrets can be co-discovered. Reverse engineering, i.e. studying an invention to find out how it works, is legal under trade secret law as long as it does not violate copyright or patent laws (Foster and Shook 1993).

A trademark provides ownership of a name, logo, phrase, design, or other symbol that a company might use to distinguish its products from the products of other companies. For example, McDonald's arches and the name "Microsoft" are trademarks (Foster and Shook 1993). Although some scientific knowledge could be protected by trademarks – a biotechnology company could use a transgenic mouse as a trademark – most people with an interest in scientific research will seek other forms of ownership of intellectual property.

Given this sketch of intellectual property laws, we can see that scientists (and other people with an interest in science) could seek to patent inventions; they could copyright original works, such as scientific papers, books, drawings, lectures, and web-pages, or they could protect knowledge through trade secrecy. It should also be clear from this sketch that copyright and patent laws are designed to promote the sharing of information while trade secrecy laws are designed to stop the flow of information. Thus, trade secrecy conflicts with openness in science, while copyrights and patents promote openness by granting ownership in exchange for public disclosure (Dreyfuss 1989). This brief sketch of the laws pertaining to intellectual property gives us an idea of what kinds of ownership are possible under our current system, but this book deals with questions that go beyond intellectual property laws. Many moral and political questions concerning property rights arise in science. The questions that frequently arise in debates about intellectual property include the following: (1) who has a right to claim ownership over a thing?; (2) what kinds of thing can be treated as property? In order to address these questions, we need to discuss some of the moral and political justifications for intellectual property.

The two most influential approaches to intellectual property are the desert approach and the utilitarian approach. According to the desert approach, one can justly acquire property in two different ways, through original acquisition or transfer. If we acquire property through either of these acquisition processes, then we are entitled to the property. The idea of a just transfer of property has proven to be less problematic than the idea of a just original acquisition. A just transfer, one might argue, is a transfer that does not violate moral prohibitions against stealing, dishonesty, exploitation, or unfairness. If I received property as a gift, or through a trade or valid agreement, then the property has been justly transferred. This seems clear enough. But when is original acquisition just?

According to the philosopher John Locke (1980), who developed the entitlement approach, we are entitled to original acquisitions of property if we deserve to own property. Property rights, including intellectual ones, should be granted in order to give people just rewards for their contributions and efforts. If you invent a machine or create a work, you deserve to be able to have some control over that machine or work. One contributes to a thing or puts effort into it by "mixing one's labor" or resources with that thing (Kuflik 1989). In science, labor could include writing papers, designing experiments, collecting data, analyzing data, and other ways that people contribute to scientific research. Resources could include laboratory space, computers, books, equipment, and so on. If we view credit as a form of intellectual property, and we accept the desert approach to intellectual property, it follows that credit allocation practices should reflect contributions and effort.

The desert approach to intellectual property complements my earlier claim that credit and responsibility should go hand-in-hand. The desert approach is usually based on individualistic approaches to morality, such as the natural rights view or Kantianism. Concerning the two questions raised above, the desert approach holds that (1) people can claim ownership over a thing if they have contributed labor or resources to that thing, and (2) a thing can be treated as property, provided that this form of treatment does not violate individual rights.

The utilitarian approach to property holds that all policies relating to property, including those that pertain to transfers and original acquisitions, should maximize socially valued outcomes (Kuflik 1989). Intellectual property can be viewed as a human institution whose main function is the advancement of various social goals. Some of these goals could include happiness, health, justice, the progress of science, quality control of products, a clean environment, or economic prosperity. As one can see from this short list, there can be considerable disagreement about the kinds of outcomes that society should or should not promote, even among those people who accept the utilitarian approach to intellectual property. However, most of the different goals that people might want to promote can be advanced by nurturing the growth of science and technology. Thus, the utilitarian approach to intellectual property holds that intellectual property is justified insofar as it contributes to the progress of science and technology. There are three ways that intellectual property can contribute to this progress. First, it can provide a motivation for researchers who seek monetary rewards for inventions and discoveries. Although many scientists have "pure" motives, i.e. they pursue truth for its own sake, economic interests can play a role in motivating research (Dickson 1984). Second, intellectual property can encourage industrial investment in science and technology by allowing businesses to profit from sponsoring research (Bowie 1994). Third, intellectual property allows for openness and disclosure in science by protecting the interests of individuals and corporations. Without this protection, a climate of secrecy could prevail (Bok 1982).

Concerning the two key questions raised above, the utilitarian approach holds that (1) ownership policies should contribute to the progress of science and technology, and (2) a thing can be treated as property if and only if this policy promotes the progress of science and technology. Thus, the utilitarian approach might hold that some policies and practices relating to intellectual property should not be allowed if they stunt the growth of science and technology.

Having contrasted these two theories, we should note that they agree on a broad range of cases. Neither theory would endorse outright theft, both theories would support property laws and policies, and both theories would forbid the ownership of some classes of things, such as human beings. However, these approaches to intellectual property may offer different perspectives on some hard cases. For the purposes of this book, I will not champion either approach because I think they both have strengths and weaknesses.

However, I would like to note that current patent laws appear to be based on the utilitarian approach, since they reward results, not contributions and efforts (Kuflik 1989). The reason that these laws only award results is that they were designed, in part, to promote private investment in research while allowing for some degree of public disclosure (Bok 1982). Businesses will not invest large quantities of money into research if rival companies can also claim ownership rights to inventions and discoveries. Since nearly half of all research and product development is sponsored by industry, the future of science depends on corporate investment in research (Resnik 1996a). While a period of secrecy usually prevails when a company or inventor is in the process of obtaining a patent or perfecting an invention, our current patent laws encourage companies and inventors to disclose their secrets instead of seeking trade secrecy. Although aggressive pursuit of patents can sometimes hinder scientific and technological progress by stifling cooperation and openness, it is likely that secrecy and competition would prevail over openness and cooperation in science if our society had no laws to protect intellectual property. Our current laws therefore promote progress in science and technology by offering incentives to conduct and sponsor research and by allowing researchers and corporations to profit from their investments in research (Bowie 1994). Since patents generally offer a greater return on investment than copyrights, corporations (and individuals) often pursue patents instead of copyrights.

A final issue to mention concerns the different types of things that might become property. If we think of these issues in utilitarian terms, then we need to ask whether ownership of a kind of thing advances the goals of science or other social goals. If ownership of something promotes these goals, then it may be owned; if ownership of something impedes the realization of these goals, then it may not be owned. Many of the recent debates over intellectual property have been couched in these terms. For example, some people have defended human gene patenting on the grounds that this practice will promote the advancement of science and other social goals (Resnik 1997a). On the other hand, others have worried that human gene patenting could have an adverse impact on scientific research by encouraging companies not to share genetic information while they are trying to develop patents, and by encouraging monopolies instead of free-market competition. Similar arguments have taken place with regard to the patenting or copyrighting of computer programs, organisms, agricultural techniques, drugs, and other new technologies (Merges 1996). In each case, utilitarians examine the costs and benefits of treating some kind of thing as property. From this utilitarian perspective, it makes sense to claim that some things should be viewed as belonging to the common weal if private ownership of those things would significantly impede scientific progress. This is why patent laws do not allow individuals to own theories, principles, or general formulas or methods. If Newton had claimed ownership of his laws of motion, the science of mechanics would have come to a virtual halt.

However, many of the disputes about "what can be owned" go beyond the question of how ownership of something contributes to or impedes scientific progress (or other social goals). Many people oppose the ownership of some things on non-utilitarian grounds. For example, people have argued against patenting life forms on the grounds that living things are sacred or in some way morally sacrosanct and should not be considered property. Others have argued that patenting human DNA or cell lines treats people as property, threatens human dignity, or could lead to the exploitation of indigenous peoples (Resnik 1997a). Thus, intellectual property disputes can raise concerns relating to human rights and dignity, human nature, and social justice. Since these issues transcend the utilitarian perspective, the utilitarian approach to intellectual property cannot settle all the important questions about what may be treated as property (Merges 1996).

To summarize this discussion, I think any adequate discussion and analysis of intellectual property must balance cost/benefit considerations against other important moral concerns, such as human dignity, rights, social justice, and so forth. Obviously, there is much more that needs to be said about intellectual property, but this is as far as I will take the discussion in this book.[8]

Science, the Media, and the Public

Science and the media are not strange bedfellows since they both gather information, value accuracy and objectivity, and have enormous social responsibilities. The media transmits information between science and the general public and between different fields of science. However, since science and the media have different standards, goals, competencies, and funding sources, they can sometimes interact in ways that produce unintended, adverse consequences for the public. Sometimes the public may become misinformed, deceived, or confused as a result of the media's coverage of science. This unfortunate effect can lead to poor policy decisions, ill-informed public opinion, and the inability to make appropriate use of scientific information. In order to prevent these adverse consequences, scientists need to pay special attention to their interactions with the media.

For the purposes of this book, I will distinguish between two kinds of media, professional news journalists and other journalists. The main goal of professional news journalism is to report the news in an objective fashion (Klaidman and Beauchamp 1987). Other journalists, such as columnists, entertainment writers, script writers, and public relations (PR) writers, have other goals that may have little to do with objectivity. Some of these journalists report the news for organizations with explicit political, industrial, philosophical, or religious missions. Although my discussion will focus on professional news journalists, it is worth noting that scientists also interact with many media sources other than the professional news media. There are many different ways that professional journalists gather information about science. These points of contact between science and the professional media include press conferences, news releases, interviews, media attendance at scientific meetings, media summaries of journal articles, books, or electronic publications.

It is not at all unusual for scientists to seek media coverage of their discoveries through press conferences or news releases. In recent years pictures from the Hubbell telescope, the Shoemaker-Levy Comet, cloning research, and the search for life on Mars have been major media events covered by all the major television networks and newspapers. There are several reasons why scientists seek this kind of media spotlight. First, scientists may view a discovery or finding as being so important that they want the public to know about it as soon as possible. Social responsibility often requires that scientists convey important information to the public in a timely fashion. Medical researchers, for example, often have urgent news that can be of vital importance in preventing death and disease or in promoting human health. Second, scientists may wish to impress the public with their results in an effort to increase public support for science in general or for particular research efforts. The first pictures from the Hubbell telescope were not urgent or vital – no one would have died if they had been delayed a few weeks – but they were very useful as a PR tool. Third, some scientists may want to release their results to the press to help establish priority. These scientists fear that they will lose their priority if they report their results through peer review, so they take their results directly to the public. The cold fusion researchers discussed in Chapter 1, for example, may have reported their results at a press conference to help secure priority. As we saw earlier, priority plays a huge role in determining patent rights.

As one might expect, press conferences and news releases raise some very difficult ethical questions for science. The main problem with press conferences or news releases is that sometimes scientists report their results to the media before these results have been confirmed by other scientists. If it turns out that the results are erroneous, then there can be harmful consequences for science and for the public. Science's image suffers when scientific findings reported in haste turn out to be mistaken. It makes scientists look foolish and erodes the public's trust in science. The cold fusion case discussed in Chapter 1 again provides a timely example of this problem. One of the lessons that scientists have learned from cold fusion is that scientists have an obligation to have their work confirmed by their peers before reporting their results to the media. Indeed, some journals will refuse to accept articles that contain results that have already been reported to the media. The main intention of this policy is to encourage scientists not to circumvent the peer review system by obtaining prior publication in the media (Altman 1995).

Most scientific meetings are open to the public, and scientists need to be aware that journalists may attend scientific meetings. Some scientific meetings, such as the AAAS's annual convention, draw hundreds of reporters from all over the world. Professional journalists also sometimes drop in on lesser known scientific meetings. For instance, reporters learned about the cloning of human embryos at a relatively low key meeting of the American Fertility Society. The presence of journalists at scientific meetings can create some ethical conundrums for scientists, however. Sometimes scientists report preliminary results at scientific meetings when they are not prepared to make these results available to a wider audience. Sometimes scientists also discuss work at scientific meetings that is likely to be highly controversial, especially if the work is misunderstood. (Recall the human embryo cloning example from Chapter 1.) One might argue that the press can be banned from some scientific meetings or from some sessions in order to protect preliminary or controversial research. On the other hand, this policy would undermine the public's "right to know" about science and it would restrict journalistic freedom (Klaidman and Beauchamp 1987).

A second issue raised by having journalists at scientific meetings is the question of whether results reported by journalists should not be published in journals. If a reporter writes a story about a piece of scientific research based on what she learns about it at a scientific meeting, does this count as prior publication in the media? This kind of prior publication in the media is not the same as calling a press conference since scientists who present results at meetings are not intending to circumvent the peer review process. Nevertheless, there can be some unfortunate outcomes for science and for society when the press gains access to research that has not been thoroughly peer reviewed.

Interviews with reporters can also create ethical problems and questions for scientists. Most people, including scientists, do not want to be misquoted or quoted out of context (Nelkin 1995). Many scientists refuse to talk to the media after only one episode of irresponsible quotation. But scientists have obligations to science and to society to talk to the press, since media coverage of science can encourage public support of science and it can yield important results for society. For these and other reasons, the phrase "no comment" is seldom an appropriate response to a request for an interview. But saying very little to the press can be almost as bad as saying nothing at all if the few words that are said are quoted out of context or misquoted. The best way to handle this problem is to cooperate with the media and give extensive, in-depth interviews. Interviews give scientists a chance to explain abstract concepts and theories and technical experiments and procedures. Scientists can stress their key ideas, interpret them, and place them in a broader context.

Even if scientists never talk to the media and publish only in technical journals, the professional media may read their books, articles, and other publications. The computer and information revolution makes it easier than ever for non-specialists to gain access to specialized publications, since search engines, indexing systems, faxing services, and other technologies make it easier to find and access scientific information. Though articles that appear in obscure journals are less public than presentations at highly visible meetings, scientists need to realize that their work may be read or studied by non-peers. Awareness of this fact should not stifle scientific creativity or free expression, but it should give scientists some reasons for interpreting and explaining their ideas in some detail, since non-specialist readers may not understand the concepts, methods, or implications of a given piece of research.

Although it is not the aim of this book to blame the media for the ethical problems and dilemmas of the science–media interaction, some of these issues do arise from the media's failure to help the public understand science. These problems are not easy to avoid, since science is by its very nature often difficult to understand, and many laypeople know very little about science and do not care to learn more (Nelkin 1995). Since many important decisions depend on some knowledge of the facts, the public's misunderstanding of science can lead to poor decisions and public policies. A correct understanding of science plays an important role in debates about public health, the environment, product safety, and other important social concerns. When it comes to scientific information, ignorance is usually not bliss. Scientists have an obligation to overcome this ignorance by educating and informing the media and the public about science. Media mistakes can still occur, of course, but scientists still have an obligation to minimize these errors.

One might argue that scientists do not need to worry about how their findings may be misinterpreted or misunderstood because they are not responsible for these problems. The blame for these problems falls on professional journalists and the public, not on scientists. However, this argument is little more than evasion of social responsibility. The principle of social responsibility implies that scientists should attempt to minimize social harms and maximize social benefits when reporting their results to the media and interacting with journalists.

The public's misunderstanding of science may arise in the following ways (Nelkin 1995, Resnik 1997b):

(1) The public may lack information about science.
(2) The public may not understand complex scientific concepts or theories.
(3) The public may not understand the tentative, gradual, piece-meal nature of scientific confirmation and disconfirmation.
(4) The public may not understand statistical arguments and statistical information.
(5) The public may accept junk science.
(6) The public may reject genuine science.
(7) The public may misinterpret scientific findings.
(8) The media may contribute to the misunderstanding of science by misquoting or quoting out of context; oversimplifying key concepts; succumbing to statistical fallacies; using unreliable sources; slanting, sensationalizing, or distorting stories; making errors of fact or reasoning; and failing to cover important stories or follow ongoing stories in depth.

Some prominent examples of the public's misunderstanding of science include the Alar scare, tobacco use, the greenhouse effect, dieting and weight control, carcinogens, and risk assessment. Since examples of the public's and media's misunderstanding of science abound, I will allow the reader to explore these cases for herself.[9]

Education would seem to provide the key to combating the public's and the media's misunderstanding of science. Scientists should strive to inform and educate journalists and the public about scientific theories, methods, discoveries, etc. Since the public needs accurate scientific information in order to make important decisions, scientists should attempt to educate the public about science and to try to prevent research from being misunderstood. Scientists should minimize the misunderstanding of science and promote the understanding and appreciation of science. A well-educated public is likely to make better policy decisions than a scientifically ignorant public.

Although many scientists are not comfortable serving as educators for the public, some scientists have been exemplary public servants. In the 1800s Michael Faraday understood the importance of educating the public about science. He helped promote the teaching of science in the public schools, gave popular lectures to children, and wrote popular books (Meadows 1992). During this century, the late Carl Sagan, Stephen Hawking, Stephen Gould, Jane Goodall, Robert Bakker, and other prominent scientists have helped enhance science's image through popular books, television appearances, and articles. Scientists who can explain scientific concepts and theories to an audience of non-specialists deserve to be commended for their efforts to bridge the gap between science and the public.

Unfortunately, science does not have enough of these great communicators, and science's public image suffers from a lack of public understanding of science.

There are several reasons why the scientific community has a shortage of great communicators. First, to be a good scientist, one needs to devote so much time to research, teaching, and other professional activities, that there is little time left for educating the public. Second, since success in science demands that scientists acquire a great deal of knowledge in a specialized discipline, it may not encourage an interest in other, humanistic disciplines or the development of communication skills. To communicate with the public, scientists need to appreciate the humanities and they need to know how to speak to laypeople (Snow 1964). Third, there are some scientists who actually condemn people like Sagan for a variety of reasons, ranging from pettiness and jealousy to elitism. Many people believe that Sagan was denied admission to the NAS because some members of this body did not approve of his popularization of science (Gould 1997). These attitudes prevail in many academic disciplines, but they can have destructive effects. Academicians who view their work as so deep or important that it should not be watered down for public consumption risk becoming irrelevant, ivory tower snobs. Thus, there are good reasons for encouraging scientists to follow Sagan's example rather than sneer at it.[10]

We should note that educating the public about science can generate a variety of ethical dilemmas, however. Suppose that medical researchers establish a strong statistical connection between drinking one to two glasses of wine per day and a reduced rate of heart disease. How should they go about educating the media and the public about this finding without encouraging people to drink excessively? The principle of education requires scientists to inform the media and the public about these findings; social responsibility requires scientists to prevent harmful effects from the findings (i.e. excessive drinking). This dilemma exemplified by this situation is by no means unique; scientists often must balance their duty to educate and inform against their other social responsibilities.

To help us think about these kinds of dilemmas, it will be useful to draw an analogy between the science–media–public relationship and the doctor–patient relationship. Although the doctor–patient relationship does not include an intermediary, these relationships are very similar in that they involve the gathering and transmission of information, education, and the promotion of specific values or goals. In these relationships, we normally assume that the parties are rational (competent) individuals, but they might not be, and communication with incompetent individuals adds additional complications. If we think of the science–media interaction in this way, then we can discuss several different ways of presenting information to people. These are:

Strong Paternalism: Manipulate information in order to benefit people and prevent harm.

Weak Paternalism: Manipulate information only to prevent harm.

Autonomy: Present all information without distortion so that competent people may make their own decisions.

The main idea behind paternalism is that someone should be allowed to make decisions for someone else because they are better qualified to make those decisions. Since information is often an important part of decision-making, paternalism often involves the manipulation or interpretation of information by one person in order to benefit another person or prevent harm. Most ethicists regard strong paternalism as very controversial and rarely, if ever justified, since rational individuals should be allowed to make their own decisions and act on them (Beauchamp and Childress 1994). Paternalism may be justified in times of war or national emergency, but we should not restrict autonomy simply because we think that we know what's best for people. However, weaker versions of paternalism would seem to be morally sound. For instance, it would seem to be acceptable and perhaps desirable to lie to or misinform a child about his medical condition for the child's own benefit. Children are not competent and we therefore need to control the information they receive in order to make decisions for them. We may also be justified in withholding information from competent individuals in order to prevent harm to them.

How does this apply to science? Scientists, like physicians, may decide to manipulate information in order to promote good consequences and prevent bad ones. For example, a scientist who wants to inform the public about his smoking research might decide not to report the benefits of smoking so that people will not be misled by these results. Scientists may also decide to simplify and/or soften results in order to make them easier for the public to understand and accept. For example, scientists studying the health effects of weight might decide to simplify their research by glossing over certain factors, such as muscle mass, fat location, and percentage body fat when presenting their results to the public. Instead of including all of these different factors, the scientists might decide to instruct people to eat a balanced diet and to maintain their "ideal weight." They might make this recommendation because they believe that it is easier for people to maintain their ideal weight than it is for them to decrease their percentage body fat, increase muscle mass, and so on. They might also believe that it is easier for people to understand a concept like "ideal weight" and a weight chart than it is for them to understand all of the other weight control factors associated with health. Finally, scientists might lie to the public for national security or other reasons. For example, a scientist might lie about the success of a military project in order to prevent enemies from learning that it has not been as successful as advertised. So long as enemies believe that the project is likely to work, it will have an important deterrent effect.

Although it might seem that no kind of paternalism would be justified in science, some forms of paternalism may be justified once we realize that scientists have an ethical responsibility to prevent harmful consequences and promote beneficial ones. So when are paternalistic communications justified? The answer to this question depends on the details of the situation at hand, such as the kind of information to be shared, how it might be withheld or distorted, its possible effects on the public, etc. However, given the importance of education and openness in science, the burden of proof falls on those who would manipulate information for the good of the public; scientists should not act paternalistically toward the media or the public without a strong justification.

CHAPTER 7
Ethical Issues in the Laboratory

This chapter will introduce the reader to a wide variety of ethical problems and issues that can arise within the laboratory environment. As in the previous chapters, I will apply principles of ethical conduct in science to some of these practical problems.

The Ethics of the Mentor–Mentee Relationship

I discussed the importance of mentoring in Chapter 3. Ideally, this relationship should be viewed as a partnership of sorts where mentor and mentee both benefit from working together. Although this relationship usually benefits both parties and the scientific profession, some ethical problems can arise. The first problem is that mentors may exploit mentees. Exploitation can occur in a variety of ways. Sometimes mentors refuse to give mentees proper credit for their contributions. Something like this probably happened when Millikan failed to give Fletcher credit for suggesting that he perform his experiment with oil drops. Sometimes a mentor may try to put excessive blame on his mentees when his research is found to be in error. A graduate student might "take the fall" for erroneous or dishonest research. A mentor may also use his or her position to obtain personal or even sexual favors from mentees. Mentors may require mentees to spend so much time working on the mentor's research that the mentees have little time left for their own research. Many graduate students report abuses relating to work conditions and expectations (PSRCR 1992).

One reason why mentors may exploit their mentees is that this relationship is unbalanced: mentors have more status, knowledge, expertise, training, and power than their mentees. Although one can easily see how mentors can take advantage of their position to suit their own needs or goals, the exploitation of mentees is unethical and should be avoided wherever possible. Exploitation violates science's principle of mutual respect and destroys the trust essential for the mentor-mentee relationship. Without that trust, these important relationships deteriorate, and science suffers (Whitbeck 1995b).

A second problem that can arise is that students may not receive adequate mentoring. Some students may go through graduate school without having a single senior researcher on whom they can depend and from whom they can learn. There are several reasons why students may not receive adequate mentoring. First, as research groups, graduate schools, and laboratories become larger, mentors must supervise more students, and it becomes more difficult for them to give enough attention to each student. The failure to give individual attention to each student can result in ethical problems that result from a lack of communication and supervision. For instance, a mentor might fail to tell her mentees how to write a research paper but still expect them to write one properly, a mentor might not tell her mentees when an experiment should be completed yet still expect them to complete it by a certain time, or a mentor might fail to tell her mentees how to prepare a paper for a presentation at a scientific meeting. Second, many universities do not adequately reward mentors for their important services; mentoring rarely counts for much on tenure and promotion decisions. If a scientist is not adequately rewarded for mentoring, she will be more likely to neglect her mentoring duties in favor of activities that elicit rewards, such as research. Third, female science students may find it difficult to attain mentors. This can occur because there are not enough women in science to serve as mentors for women students who prefer female mentors, or because some male scientists may refuse to accept female mentees because they believe these women will waste the mentor's valuable time by leaving science for personal reasons, i.e. marriage and family.

In order to overcome these problems, universities and other educational institutions should make sure that there are enough scientists who are willing to serve as mentors. To encourage participation in mentoring, it may be necessary to reward scientists for devoting their time to students; mentoring should count for something on a curriculum vitae. Universities also need to conduct workshops on mentoring to help people learn how to mentor and to overcome some myths and biases about mentoring. The mentoring of female students can be improved through the efforts of organizations like the Association of Women in Science, which helps female science students make the most of their educational opportunities. Mentoring of all underrepresented groups can be improved by recruiting and hiring more people from those groups.

Harassment

Although we tend to think of scientists as civil, respectful, and courteous, various forms of harassment can occur in a laboratory setting. Types of harassment that have been reported include insults, verbal or physical intimidation, vandalism, theft, physical assaults, and sexual harassment (PSRCR 1992; Eisenberg 1994). It almost goes without saying that all of these actions are unethical; they violate science's principles of mutual respect and opportunity, they undermine cooperation, trust, openness, and freedom in science. Various forms of harassment are also immoral and often illegal.

In the last two decades, sexual harassment has become a significant ethical concern in science as more women have entered the scientific profession. Sexual harassment can be loosely defined as any type of conduct that uses sex to demean, exploit, or offend people. Beyond this vague definition, there has not been a broad consensus concerning the types of conduct that might be considered sexual harassment. Behaviors that have been viewed as sexual harassment include rape and unwanted sexual advances, requests for dates, *quid pro quo* arrangements, dirty jokes, sexual teasing, and lewd looks (Webb 1995). We lack consensus on this issue, in part, because men and women have different perspectives on sexual harassment. This issue has become a battleground for opposing viewpoints and attitudes on the relations between the sexes.[1] Sexual harassment should be avoided in science because it violates science's principle of mutual respect, it can interfere with scientific education and cooperation, and it can make it difficult for victims of harassment to advance in science. Sexual harassment in employment and education is also legal in the United States and other countries (Aaron, 1993).

In dealing with this issue it is important for scientists to communicate with each other and adhere to the principle of mutual respect. Laboratories should establish definitions of harassment, avenues for reporting harassment, and sexual harassment policies (Swisher 1995b). Since false charges of sexual harassment can still ruin careers and reputations, due process and fairness must be observed in reporting and adjudicating harassment claims, and trivial or unwarranted accusations should be avoided (Guenin and Davis 1996, Leatherman 1997). While scientists should avoid sexual harassment, it is important for scientists to feel comfortable in a laboratory setting. Research and teaching can be significantly hampered when scientists feel too uptight to make conversation or socialize with their colleagues or interact in a normal way. Scientists need to avoid offensive behaviors without inhibiting open and informal expression. Communication, trust, and even some tolerance can go a long way toward achieving this balance (Foegen 1995).

Reporting
Misconduct
in Science

As I noted in Chapter 4, scientists also have an obligation to enforce ethical standards. The obligation to enforce these standards also implies that scientists have a duty to report possible misconduct to the appropriate authorities, such as the lab director, department chair, or a senior researcher. Since accusations of misconduct can threaten careers, scientists should not make trivial or unwarranted accusations and due process should be observed in investigating charges of misconduct. Investigations should not become "witch hunts."

Those who report unethical or illegal conduct in science (or other social institutions) are sometimes called "whistle blowers." Whistle blowing is a hazardous activity, since whistle blowers can face serious repercussions. Evidence suggests that many people who blow the whistle on illegal or unethical activities often do so at great personal expense (Edsall 1995). Whistle blowers in science have been fired, expelled, demoted, blackballed, and so forth. The Baltimore Affair case discussed in the first chapter illustrates this point as well: O'Toole became known as a troublemaker and had trouble finding work after she finished her postdoctorate at Tufts. Many states and the federal government now have laws that protect whistle blowers, and some codes of conduct in the various professions address the need to protect whistle blowers (Edsall 1995). Despite these legal and institutional protections, it is likely that whistle blowing in science will always be hazardous, and it is likely that people who wish to report illegal or unethical conduct in science will have to choose between blowing the whistle and protecting their own personal interests. Whistle blowers should be commended for risking their careers in order to "do the right thing" (Chalk and van Hippel 1979).

In order to protect the rights of the accused and due process, whistle blowers should observe the following guidelines (Clutterbuck 1983):

(1) The whistle blower should have morally good motives; she should blow the whistle in order to report illegal, unethical, or immoral activities, not to advance her own career or thwart a rival.

(2) The whistle blower should have some well-documented evidence before making accusations. The evidence should be more than hearsay or a personal observation.

(3) The whistle blower should make her accusations to the relevant authorities and only go outside the local organization as a last resort.

(4) The whistle blower should carefully deliberate about her actions and avoid a rush to judgment.

Teaching vs. Research

As I mentioned earlier, most scientists who work for universities have institutional obligations to both teach students and to do research. Scientists also have professional obligations to teach and do research, since both of these activities contribute to the attainment of science's goals. The teaching vs. research dilemma can be viewed as a conflict of commitments (see discussion in Chapter 5), since teaching and research are two different commitments that place demands on the scientist's time and energy. In Chapter 4 I argued that all scientists have a duty to educate students, but I acknowledged that this obligation does not bind all scientists at all times. Some scientists may emphasize research over teaching; others may emphasize teaching over research. Some scientists may only teach graduate students; others may teach undergraduates. Some scientists may take sabbaticals to focus on their research; some may opt out of the teaching profession altogether and work for industry or the military. What is important is that the scientific profession, as a whole, promotes education, not that each individual scientist participates in education in the same way or to the same degree. Individual scientists working in university environments will often find it difficult to strike an appropriate balance between teaching and research as they try to resolve this conflict of commitments. Since the future of science depends on having today's scientists participate in science education, scientists should not shun teaching responsibilities, and since research usually complements teaching, universities should allow scientists to devote adequate time to research (Saperstein 1997).

Ethical Issues
in Hiring and
Recruitment

Until this century, there were very few women or minorities in Western science. For many years, women and minorities were banned from science; they were forbidden from studying at universities or from working as professional scientists. Even when women and minorities were allowed to enter science, discrimination, bias, social stigmas, cultural expectations, and stereotypes made it difficult for members of these underrepresented groups to become scientists (Pearson and Bechtel 1989, Committee on Women in Science and Engineering 1991, Tomoskovic-Devey 1993). In the last thirty years, underrepresented groups have made significant strides into science's ranks, but white males still outnumber other groups in Western science. Some sciences have more women and minorities than other sciences, but all sciences still bear the scars of centuries of racial and sexual discrimination.

Since women and minorities are underrepresented in most scientific fields, scientists need to be concerned about their legal and ethical duties to address these inequities and to provide opportunities for underrepresented groups. Many countries have laws that require employers and educators to amend racial and sexual inequities through hiring practices, recruitment, education, and so forth (Sadler 1995). Scientists have an obligation to obey these laws insofar as they pertain to the hiring and recruitment of scientists. (I will not explore current laws relating to employment and educational practices, since this book focuses on ethical issues in science, not legal ones.)

In Chapter 4 I defended a principle of opportunity in science on the grounds that it can promote scientific goals: objectivity is more likely to emerge from the clash of different cultures, personalities, and styles of thought than from the consensus of like minds. Opportunity also has a moral and political basis in egalitarian theories of justice (Rawls 1971). These arguments imply that scientists should take some steps to extend opportunities to underrepresented groups. But how should scientists execute this task? In order to answer this question, we should distinguish between passive and active strategies for promoting opportunities. Passive strategies attempt to remove barriers for underrepresented groups in science; active strategies take steps to draw those groups to science.

One passive strategy that most scientists would accept is to prevent racial, sexual, and other forms of discrimination in science, since discrimination poses a significant barrier to underrepresented groups. For the purposes of this discussion, discrimination is a kind of decision or judgment against a person based on irrelevant characteristics about that person.[2] For example, refusing to hire a woman as an assistant professor of physics because she is a woman would be a form of sexual discrimination. Refusing to hire a woman for the same job because she does not have a Ph.D. would not be a form of sexual discrimination because having a Ph.D. is a relevant characteristic. Another uncontroversial passive strategy would be to take steps to prevent harassment of underrepresented groups, since harassment deters people from pursuing careers in science. Few people would object to the passive policies. Controversies arise, however, when we discuss more active strategies for promoting opportunities in science, such as affirmative action.

Affirmative action can be viewed as any policy that attempts to attract, favor, or recruit underrepresented groups, usually those groups that have suffered past discrimination (De George 1995). Affirmative action can occur in any context where scientists must make decisions pertaining to the allocation of scientific resources or opportunities. These contexts include admission into graduate programs, the awarding of fellowships, scholarships, grants, and prizes, and hiring and promotion. Many writers distinguish between strong and weak affirmative action. Weak affirmative action involves no more than a deliberate effort to recruit and attract underrepresented groups. Scientists might try to identify people from underrepresented groups and mail them brochures, invite them to campus, encourage them to apply to graduate programs, encourage them to apply for jobs, grants, and so forth.

Strong affirmative action implies some form of preferential treatment. Preferential treatment (or reverse discrimination) occurs when someone makes a decision or judgment in favor of a person based on some irrelevant characteristic, such as age or sex (De George 1995). There are stronger and weaker forms of preferential treatment as well. A weaker form of preferential treatment would be to use an irrelevant characteristic to break ties between equally qualified individuals. For example, if two applicants for a scholarship are equally qualified, the scholarship committee might decide to choose a member of an underrepresented group over a white male. A stronger form of preferential treatment would be to allow race, sex, and other normally irrelevant characteristics to override other qualifications. A very strong form of preferential treatment would be to set quotas for hiring and promoting members of underrepresented groups.

Are any forms of affirmative action justified in science? If one accepts my argument for the principle of opportunity in science, then some forms of affirmative action could be justified in order to give opportunities to underrepresented groups. For instance, the active recruitment of underrepresented groups could be justified on the grounds that this policy helps attract women and minorities to science. But what about preferential treatment? Should people be given jobs, scholarships, and other opportunities in science on the basis of race, sex, or other characteristics not related to scientific merit? Although it is not my aim to explore all the pros and cons of affirmative action in this book, I will present a utilitarian argument for some form of preferential treatment in science. Let's start with the assumption that having a diverse community is a legitimate and important goal in science because diversity helps promote objectivity. One might argue that this goal cannot be achieved unless scientists institute some form of preferential treatment; passive strategies will not achieve a satisfactory level of diversity. The reason that passive strategies will not work is that science needs to reach a "critical mass" of underrepresented groups before science will seem like a desirable career to women and minorities (Etzkowitz *et al.* 1994, Jackson 1995). People are attracted to a profession or occupation because they identify with people in that profession or occupation. Science needs people from underrepresented groups to serve as role models for science students. As role models, people from underrepresented groups can aid in the recruitment, education, training, advising, and mentoring of women and minorities in science. Preferential treatment policies can be eliminated once science achieves an acceptable level of diversity, but they need to be implemented for an indefinite period of time in order to achieve an acceptable level of diversity in science.[3]

There are several objections to this argument worth mentioning. Strong forms of preferential treatment could produce more harm than good. If scientists give extra points to people for belonging to underrepresented groups, it is likely that they will select people who are underqualified. The admission of underqualified people into the scientific profession can have some bad consequences for science. First, it can hamper scientific progress because underqualified people are less likely to do good research. Second, when underqualified people are members of underrepresented groups, they may not even be good role models. A role model should be someone that we respect and admire, but we do not usually respect or admire people who we perceive to be underqualified. Thus, stronger versions of preferential treatment are likely to be self-defeating (Puddington 1995). Strong forms of preferential treatment would also not encourage prospective scientists from underrepresented groups to work hard or strive for scientific excellence, since they would be telling these people that it is possible to have a career in science without achieving a high level of excellence or even competence. Strong forms of preferential treatment could also have a negative impact on the careers of people from underrepresented groups who become scientists because they might have to live with the stigma of not being chosen on the basis of merit. These scientists might always wonder whether they advanced in science because they benefited from preferential treatment or because they did good work. Their colleagues might also treat them as "tokens," "the best black," "the best woman," and so on (Carter 1995). Finally, one might argue that using race, sex, or any other characteristic as a basis for any decision relating to hiring or education in science would only perpetuate harmful stereotypes by implying that people from underrepresented groups are intellectually inferior (Carter 1995).

I think these objections present a convincing case against strong forms of preferential treatment in science. They even pose some problems for weaker forms of affirmative action in science, since any use of race, sex, or other criteria not related to merit could contribute to social stigmas and perpetuate racist, sexist, and other stereotypes. A weak form of preferential treatment, i.e. using racial or sexual characteristics to break ties between equally qualified candidates, might avoid some of the objections discussed in the previous paragraph. However, this policy could degenerate into a stronger form of preferential treatment if scientists do not take steps to avoid hiring underqualified people from underrepresented groups.

Nonetheless, this weak form of preferential treatment should not apply to all decisions concerning the distribution of scientific goods. The social, political, and moral problems with preferential treatment imply that affirmative action should be adopted only under exceptional conditions, such as gaining entry into science. All other career-affecting decisions, such as the awarding of prizes, grants, or tenure, should be made on the basis of merit. Once a person from an underrepresented group has become part of a scientific profession, she should be treated no differently from other members of that profession. By limiting the scope of affirmative action policies, scientists can promote diversity without de-emphasizing excellence.

Sharing and Preserving Resources

As I mentioned earlier in this book, a great deal of scientific research involves intra-laboratory, inter-laboratory, inter-disciplinary and international collaboration. Scientists who collaborate (as well as those who do not) frequently face questions about the sharing of scientific resources, such as data, equipment, instruments, research sites, and human resources. Science as a whole would seem to benefit from the sharing of resources since this allows more scientists to have access to the things they need in order to gather and analyze data. The principles of openness and opportunity imply an obligation to share resources. However, since questions relating to the sharing of resources often pit individual, group, professional, and institutional interests against each other, it is often not easy for scientists to work together for science's common good.

As a case study of this problem, consider policies for using the Hubbell telescope. This is a scarce and valuable scientific resource: many astronomers around the world would like to be able to use the telescope to make observations, but not everyone can use it at the same time. Astronomers who would like to use the telescope include people who helped develop the telescope, Nobel Prize winners, senior researchers, junior researchers, graduate students, scientists from industry or the military, scientists from different nationalities, races, sexes, and so on. Who should have access to this telescope?

The allocation of telescope time is an example of a distribution problem under conditions of scarcity. In addressing this problem (and others like it), the following criteria would seem to apply:

(1) Scientific merit. What are the credentials of the different people who wish to use the telescope?

(2) Scientific utility. Which projects will best serve the interests of science?

(3) Opportunity. Which projects will provide important opportunities to scientists?

The first two criteria would seem to be fair, since there is no sense in wasting a scarce resource on someone who cannot make good use of it. Some might question my appeal to opportunity in resource allocations, however. Although I do not favor using race, sex, or other criteria not related to merit to make allocation decisions, considerations of opportunity would support allocating some resources to junior researchers (graduate students, postdoctoral researchers, or untenured faculty) in order to promote their education and professional development. A short-term "waste" of resources on less qualified junior researchers can pay off in the long run. A nominal amount of resources could be set aside for junior researchers; senior researchers could compete for the remaining resources on the basis of merit and utility.

Before closing I should also mention that legally valid property claims can override any of these other considerations. Ergo, if some person, group of people, or social institution owns a scientific resource, then they can (legally) control its use. For example, suppose a rancher in Wyoming wants to allow Wyoming but not Colorado scientists to have access to an archeological site that is on his property. His ownership rights would seem to take precedence over any moral or scientific reasons one might have for allowing Colorado scientists to have access to this site. Since scientists have a *prima facie* duty to follow the law, these legal rights should be respected unless there is some compelling reason to violate them. Universities and other research institutions also control scientific resources, and these organizations may decide to give preference to their constituencies when making allocation decisions.

A great deal of international collaboration and cooperation occurs in science. In Chapter 5, I argued that international collaboration and cooperation should be encouraged and promoted. However, I also noted that sometimes countries will try to stop the flow of scientific information across national boundaries for political reasons. Political considerations may also obstruct the sharing of scientific resources, such as laboratories, computing technology, telescopes, radioactive isotopes, etc. A fuller examination of the politics of international collaboration takes us beyond the scope of this book, however.

In closing this discussion, I will mention that scientists should not misuse or destroy resources. Two types of unethical activities relating to the misuse of resources are the mismanagement of funds and damage to research sites, materials, or equipment. Mismanagement of funds can occur when scientists spend grant money on items not permitted in the grant agreement, when they spend money on frivolous items or waste money, or when scientists file fraudulent reports of their accounting practices. Irresponsible accounting practices are often illegal, and they are unethical because they are dishonest, negligent, or wasteful.

Scientists who damage research sites, materials or equipment during the course of an investigation also waste valuable scientific resources. For instance, a paleontologist might damage a research site by not collecting fossils carefully; a cultural anthropologist might spoil a research site by mistreating and alienating a tribe during her research; a cytologist might severely damage an electron microscope by not operating it according to standard procedures; a computer scientist might destroy a database. Overall, scientists should practice responsible stewardship when it comes to sharing and using scientific resources. (As an aside, some scientists may refuse to share resources because they fear that those who use them will not practice responsible stewardship.)

Research on
Human Subjects

The next two sections of this chapter will give a brief overview of two topics, i.e. the use of human and (non-human) animals in research, that raise very important ethical issues for scientists and for society at large. One could write an entire book about either of these topics, but I will only introduce the reader to some key issues.

Before discussing ethical issues in research on human subjects, it is important to provide the reader with some background information. Prior to this century, medical researchers rarely performed experiments on human beings because they adhered to the Hippocratic oath, which emphasizes non-malificence and beneficence. Since medical experiments can be harmful and not helpful, this tradition shunned human experimentation. During the Scientific Revolution medicine took a more experimental orientation, but attitudes toward human experimentation did not change significantly until the twentieth century, when researchers tested new medicines on human subjects, such as sulfa drugs, and a vaccine for malaria. By the 1940s, many people were taking part in experiments even though there were no generally accepted ethical guidelines for research on human subjects.

This era of virtually unregulated human experimentation ended after the Second World War with the adoption of a set of protocols for human research known as the Nuremburg Code (1949). The Code was established in 1946 during the Nuremburg Trials in order to have some basis for holding Nazi scientists accountable for war crimes.[4] The Code is an internationally recognized declaration that still plays a vital role in governing human experimentation (Capron 1997). The key tenets of the Code are as follows:

(1) *Informed consent:* Human subjects can participate in research only if they give their voluntary, informed consent.
(2) *Social value:* Experiments should be expected to yield fruitful results for society.
(3) *Scientific validity:* Experiments should be scientifically valid and well designed. Experiments should only be conducted by well-qualified scientists.
(4) *Nonmalificence:* No experiments should be conducted that are likely to result in death or disabling injury. Experimenters should take steps to reduce risks and minimize pain.
(5) *Termination:* During the course of the experiment the subject

> may stop participation for any reason; the experimenters must be prepared to stop the experiment if continuation of the experiment is likely to result in injury or death.

There has been an ongoing discussion of the ethics of human experimentation since 1946, and many other rules and regulations have been adopted in the last four decades. Further reflection has resulted in widespread acceptance of the following additional principles (Capron 1997):

(6) *Privacy:* Experimenters should protect the privacy and confidentiality of research subjects.

(7) *Vulnerable populations:* Experimenters should take special precautions to protect subjects for whom informed consent may be compromised, e.g. children or adults who are sick, poor, uneducated, incarcerated, or mentally disabled.

(8) *Fairness:* Selection of subjects to participate in all aspects of an experiment should be fair.

(9) *Monitoring:* Researchers should continually monitor experiments to determine whether the benefits outweigh the risks, whether the experiment is likely to yield significant knowledge, and so on.

Today, nearly all research institutions and many private companies have institutional review boards (IRBs) that review research on human subjects. IRBs serve as ethical and legal gatekeepers for experiments on humans and advise researchers about such issues as obtaining informed consent, protecting privacy, and improving research design. Human subjects are used in the biomedical sciences as well as many social sciences, such as psychology, anthropology, and sociology.

All of the principles discussed above can be justified by moral theories that emphasize the importance of protecting individual rights and dignities. Kantianism offers the most straightforward justification of these guidelines: we can only perform experiments on human beings if we follow rules for protecting the dignity, autonomy, and rights of experimental subjects. Human beings have inherent worth and should not be treated like guinea pigs (Jonas 1969). On the other hand, many of these rules hamper scientific progress because they place limits on our methods for studying human subjects. Many possible experiments cannot be performed because they are regarded as unethical. Indeed, many researchers have broken or stretched these guidelines in order to gain scientific knowledge (Pence 1995). From a utilitarian point of view, society may benefit a great deal from experiments that violate the rights and dignities of a few individuals. Hence, there is tension inherent in all human experimentation that embodies the conflict between producing good results for society and protecting individuals (Lasagna 1971).

Although it is not my intent to explore human experimentation in depth here, I would like to introduce the reader to some issues relating to the doctrine of informed consent. Sometimes it is necessary to perform research on subjects that cannot give valid consent, such as children or unconscious or incompetent adults. Scientists need to do experiments on children because diseases and treatments affect children and adults differently and because it is important to gather information about child development and psychology. When children participate in research, parents or guardians can give proxy consent. However, when people make proxy decisions for individuals they have a duty to act in the best interests of those individuals, and it may not be in anyone's best interests to participate in an experiment (Buchanan and Brock 1989). A parent is free to impose risks on herself, but she should not subject her child to unjustifiable risks. What makes a risk unjustifiable? Many normal childhood activities, such as biking or swimming, impose risks on children. One might argue that a risk is justifiable if it is no more risky than other normal childhood activities or if the benefits of the risk outweigh the harms. For example, the benefits of an experimental leukemia medicine might outweigh the harms to a child, and studying memory in children might be no more risky than other childhood activities.

Difficulties with applying the doctrine of informed consent also arise when adult subjects are used in experiments. Often subjects lack the education or judgment to give completely informed consent. Even well-educated subjects may not understand all the information that is presented, and researchers themselves often lack complete knowledge of an experiment. Since the requirement of completely informed consent is too stringent, a more realistic guideline for researchers would be to obtain adequately informed consent. A person can give adequately informed consent when they have enough information to make a responsible, sound decision. Most people make responsible choices each day in the midst of a great deal of ignorance and uncertainty. We often lack completely informed consent when we decide to take a new job, buy a house, or marry, for example (Veatch 1987). Although this policy sounds reasonable, it is easy to slide from adequate consent to poor consent to no consent at all once we allow deviations from completely informed consent. Two examples illustrate this point.

From 1932 to 1970, physicians at the Tuskegee Institute, a public health clinic in Tuskegee, Alabama, conducted research on African-American men who were suffering from the later stages of syphilis. The research was sponsored by the US Department of Health and involved 399 subjects with latent syphilis, a phase of syphilis that is largely non-infectious. The purpose of the study was to follow the progression and natural history of syphilis, which had not been well documented in 1932. The group of 399 patients was not divided into experimental and control sub-groups; all patients were simply observed without treatment. The study also included a "control" group of 200 men without syphilis who were of similar age to the syphilitic subjects. The purpose of the experiment was to learn about the natural history of syphilis, not to develop treatments for it. Some of the physicians who initially proposed the study said it would last only a year, but it lasted nearly forty years, long after an effective treatment for syphilis, penicillin, became available in the mid-1940s. Subjects who participated in the study were not told that they were receiving no genuine treatment, they were not told about the nature of their disease, nor were they even told that they were participating in an experiment. They were simply offered free medical "care" as well as hot lunches, medical examinations, and free burials. The study was disorganized and lax: the personnel conducting the study changed from year to year, there were no physicians who functioned as central authorities, there were no written protocols, and records were poorly kept. The study continued with little hindrance until 1972, when Peter Buxton, a venereal disease investigator for the US Public Health Service, reported the story to the Associated Press. The story made front page headlines across the US, which prompted a Congressional investigation. In 1973, victims filed a class-action lawsuit against the federal government, which agreed to an out-of-court settlement. The settlement provided compensation for living subjects who still had syphilis and for the families of subjects (Jones 1980).[5]

In 1994 the Department of Energy (DOE), under orders from the Clinton administration, began declassifying documents from the Cold War. The most serious secret to surface is that the US government used its own citizens as guinea pigs in radiation experiments (Schneider 1993, Budiansky et al. 1994, Pence 1995). A wide variety of experiments were conducted on thousands of civilian and non-civilian populations. In many cases people were not told that they were being used in an experiment or they were deceived about the nature of the experiment. The scientific goal of most of these experiments was to discover how radiation affects human beings. The military and political rationale for this research was that its results would be vital in the United States' Cold War efforts. If the US could discover how to mitigate the effects of radiation, then it could find a way to perhaps "win" a nuclear war by increasing the survival rates of American citizens and soldiers or by discovering ways to use radiation to kill or harm enemies. In many of the documents describing this research, scientists and bureaucrats justified the research on the grounds that it is permissible to sacrifice a few people for military strength: the good of the nation is more important than respect for the rights of a few individuals.

Here is a sampling of the experiments:

(1) During the late 1940s at Vanderbilt University, pregnant women were given radioactive iron to study the effects of radiation on fetal development. A follow-up study found that these children had a higher than normal cancer rate.

(2) From 1963 to 1971 at Oregon State Prison, sixty-seven male, mostly African-American prisoners, were paid $200 to have their testicles X-rayed to study the effects of radiation on sperm function. The men were later given vasectomies. They were told about some of the risks but were not told that they could get cancer.

(3) During the late 1950s, twelve terminally ill cancer patients at Columbia University and Montefiore Hospital were given radioactive calcium and strontium to measure the rate at which radioactive substances are absorbed into human tissues.

(4) Joseph Hamilton, a researcher as the University of California at Berkeley, injected plutonium into eighteen unsuspecting cancer patients.

(5) In 1950, federal scientists released a cloud of radioactive iodine in eastern Washington to observe nuclear fallout. The cloud carried hundreds of times more radiation than the cloud released during the Three Mile Island nuclear reactor accident in 1979.

(6) From the 1940s until the 1960s, 1,500 aviators and sailors had encapsulated radium inserted into their nostrils for several minutes. They were not told the purpose of the experiment or why they had been selected, and many of them developed intense headaches after exposure.

The Tuskegee syphilis study and the Cold War radiation experiments are two of the darkest episodes in the history of human experimentation, which involved egregious violations of informed consent as well as many of the principles of research. The bitter irony and hypocrisy of these experiments is that they took place after the research community had established guidelines for the ethical treatment of human subjects. The researchers had to know about the doctrine of informed consent and the Nuremburg Code, but they decided to not give subjects enough information to make informed choices. One might argue that these episodes are nothing more than "deviant or pathological research," and that informed consent is seldom violated or abused in most contemporary human subjects research. While I agree that most human subjects research conducted in the West is ethically sound, I include a discussion of these episodes to let the reader understand that it is easy to violate informed consent in the name of science and slide from partial consent to no consent at all. Hence, researchers must affirm their unwavering commitment to informed consent. Although deviations from this ideal can be justified, we should be wary of experimental designs that offer incomplete or partial consent. However, since partial or merely adequate consent may still occur, human experimentation must involve a great deal of trust, communication, and mutual understanding between researchers and subjects in order to protect human rights and dignity (Veatch 1995).

Deception in human subjects research also creates some questions concerning informed consent since subjects who are deceived about an experiment are not fully informed. The basic argument for deception in research is that it is often necessary in order to obtain valid results, because knowledge of an experiment may affect the subjects' responses (Elms 1994). The placebo effect is a well-documented phenomenon in medicine, which occurs when a subject's belief that she is receiving treatment influences her medical condition. Double-blind experiments attempt to compensate for this effect by giving an experimental group of subjects the treatment under test and a control group a placebo. Neither the subjects nor those researchers who treat the subjects know who gets the placebo treatment and who gets the "real" treatment; subjects are only told that they may receive a placebo. One of the main ethical issues that arises in the use of placebos is whether to stop an experiment and offer the new treatment to subjects receiving placebos once it becomes apparent that the treatment works (Capron 1997). Although subjects in the control group receive standard kinds of palliative care, they do not receive any "real" medicine; they often forgo treatment for the good of medical science. However, although medical ethics would recommend offering treatment to subjects in the control group before an experiment ends, this choice risks invalidating the entire experiment. Thus, clinical trials can raise the ethical dilemma that typifies a great deal of medical research, namely the good of the individual vs. the advancement of science. Some writers argue that physician-researchers can solve this dilemma by only initiating or continuing clinical trials when there exists honest disagreement in the medical community about the merits of different kinds of treatment (Freedman 1992).

Deception is often necessary in the social sciences as well. Although social scientists can employ non-deceptive methodologies, such as field observations, interviews, and role-playing, many social scientists argue that it often necessary to conduct controlled experiments in order to obtain valid and useful results (Elms 1994). In an infamous case of deception in research, Stanley Milgram, a Harvard psychologist, designed an experiment to test obedience to authority (Milgram 1974). The experiment consisted of two subjects, a "teacher" and a "learner." The teacher was told that the purpose of the experiment was to test the effects of punishment on learning. The learner was asked to learn some information and was punished with an electric "shock" each time he gave an incorrect response to a question. The teachers administered the shock by flipping a switch, and the learners would display signs of pain or discomfort when shocks were administered. The severity of the shock increased with each incorrect response until it approached "dangerous" levels. The researcher ordered the teachers to give the shocks and most of them complied with these commands to a certain point. Although the teachers were led to believe that they were administering shocks, they were not. The true nature of the experiment was to see whether the teachers would obey the researchers, the authorities. Although teachers were properly debriefed after the experiments, many of them suffered psychological harm and distress because they realized that they would have hurt someone if the experiment had been real. Many of the teachers did not wish to learn about this aspect of their moral character and conscience. It is clear that this particular experiment would have been ruined if the teachers had not been deceived, since they would have virtually no moral compunctions about carrying out a dramatization and their willingness to obey authority would not have been tested.

Some writers have objected to these experiments on the grounds that there are other, less harmful and deceptive ways to learn about obedience to authority. The value of the knowledge that is potentially gained from these kinds of experiments, some argue, does not justify the violation of standards of informed consent and potential harm to research subjects (Baumrind 1964). Other writers argue that deception can be ethical, provided that it is necessary to obtain valid results, it occurs within the context of informed consent, subjects are debriefed after the experiment, and researchers have non-selfish aims (Elms 1994).

In summary, perhaps informed consent is best viewed as an ideal that we should strive to achieve but not as an absolute rule. If we believe that we should never deviate from this ideal, then we will severely limit research on human beings. Scientific progress will slow down and many practical problems will not be solved. If we believe that we should not slow down research and that we need to solve these practical problems, then we face a difficult choice: when should we settle for less than the ideal? I believe that we can only answer this question by exploring the benefits and risks of human subjects research on a case-by-case basis.

Human subjects research raises many other ethical issues and problems, such as confidentiality, harmful research, frivolous research, research that targets specific racial or ethnic groups, and research on fetuses, embryos, prisoners, soldiers, and unconscious or comatose subjects. I will not explore these other issues here.[6]

Research on
Animal Subjects

Scientists in many different disciplines use animals in basic and applied research for a variety of purposes. Although it is difficult to determine how many animals are used in research each year, the estimates are quite high, ranging from seventeen to seventy million animals per year.[7] Some animal research has benefits for non-human animals, but most animal research is designed to benefit human beings. Research methods vary from field studies to highly controlled experiments. Experiments on animals often involve vivisection or mutilation, and many result in death. For example, Lethal Dose-50 Test is used to determine how high the dosage of a drug needs to be to kill 50 percent of animal subjects. The Draise test was at one time used by the cosmetics industry to determine the toxicity of various substances. In this test, researchers dripped chemicals into the lidless eyes of rabbits in order to test their potential for eye damage. Animals are also used in scientific and medical education. For instance, medical students learn how to do surgical procedures on animals before they attempt to do them on human beings. In these procedures, animals (often dogs) are deliberately injured in some way in order to teach students how to repair wounds, set fractures, and so forth (LaFollette and Shanks 1996).

In the last few decades, animal research has become a highly controversial issue. Animal rights activists have protested animal research by picketing or vandalizing laboratories, destroying years of research in some cases. As a result of these growing concerns about animals, many nations and states have enacted laws pertaining to the use of animals in research and most research institutions have adopted regulations applying to animal research. These various rules prescribe conditions for the humane treatment of animals and specify procedures for reviewing and approving animal research. Most research institutions have committees that enforce these regulations, and any scientist who plans to conduct research on animals must now go through a lengthy and thorough approval process (LaFollette and Shanks 1996).

The basic argument for animal research is that it benefits human beings in many ways (Botting and Morrison 1997). Animal studies play a key role in applied research because animals provide researchers with models for testing drugs and treatments and for studying human diseases. Standard protocols for controlled clinical trials require researchers to conduct extensive animal studies before testing treatments on humans. Animals play a vital role in basic research because humans and animals have many physiological, anatomical, biochemical, genetic, and developmental similarities: our knowledge of the rat brain can aid in our understanding of the human brain. Although there are some alternatives to animal models, they have limited applications. Without using animals in research, human beings would lack safe food, medicine, and cosmetics as well as a great deal of medical and biological knowledge. This human benefits argument is unashamedly utilitarian: we can sacrifice animals in order to maximize good consequences for human beings. It should come as little surprise that most scientists actively involved in animal research accept some version of this argument.

Critics of animal research offer the following objections to this argument (LaFollette and Shanks 1996; Barnard and Kaufman 1997):

(1) The benefits of animal research are exaggerated.
(2) Animals are often not very good models for studying human disease or treatments.
(3) There are useful alternatives to animal research.
(4) There are moral reasons for not using animals in research.

Although the first objection sounds highly implausible, some critics of animal research maintain that there is not a strong correlation between the use of animals in research and discoveries that benefit human beings. They challenge this correlation by citing cases where human studies have contributed more to medical progress than animal studies. Some examples cited include research on hepatitis, typhoid fever, appendicitis, hyperthyroidism, anesthesiology, immunology, and psychology (LaFollette and Shanks 1996). While it is important to remind ourselves of the usefulness of clinical research on human beings, these examples hardly constitute a definitive argument against the contribution of animal research to progress in biology and medicine, since supporters of animal research could cite numerous examples where animal studies have led to scientific and medical progress. The key point here is that animal research has benefited humans and will continue to do so. This assertion would still hold even if it can be shown that proponents of animal research overestimate its utility.

The second objection poses a more serious challenge to animal research. For many years researchers have more or less assumed that results obtained from animal studies can be applied to research on human diseases and treatments because animals are similar to humans in experimentally relevant respects. If a large dose of a substance causes cancer in laboratory mice, scientists infer that it can also cause cancer in human beings, since chemicals that cause cancer in the animal may cause cancer in humans. Animal models are causal analogs of human beings because animals and humans have similar cells, tissues, organs, hormones, metabolic pathways, proteins, genes, and so on. Animals and humans also have a common evolutionary heritage: since humans evolved from animals, humans must be very similar to animals (LaFollette and Shanks 1996).

Many researchers regard the causal analogy between animals and humans as obvious and uncontroversial, but the analogy has come under attack in recent years (Barnard and Kaufman 1997). Many writers have pointed out that animals are not like humans in many important respects and that the same compounds may have very different effects in animals and humans. For example, scientists at one time classified saccharin as a carcinogen because it caused bladder cancer in laboratory rats. Subsequent research showed, however, that saccharin may cause cancer only in rats because rats have high levels of a protein in their urine that causes a build-up of toxic crystals in the bladder. Since humans do not form these crystals, saccharin probably does not pose a serious risk to human health (*Denver Post* 1992).

Those who attack the analogy between animals and humans also point out that many factors frustrate our attempts to apply animal studies to human populations. First, animals in the laboratory are exposed to many unnatural stresses and conditions, such as confinement, handling, and isolation. These factors introduce experimental variables into animal studies that make it difficult to translate these results into human applications. Second, functional similarities among different species may belie significant structural (i.e. physiological, genetic, and biochemical) differences. For example, mammals and birds both use lungs for exchanging gases with the environment, but the structures of the lungs in mammals and birds are very different. Third, if we view organisms as complex, hierarchically organized, dynamic systems, there may be "emergent" properties possessed by a more complex species that are not possessed by its parts or other, less complex species (LaFollette and Shanks 1996). For example, many medical and psychological problems that occur in humans, such as bulimia and alcoholism, do not occur in less complex species. Other problems can be induced in non-human species, such as anorexia, but these problems are very different in non-human species. A rat does not become anorexic because it wants to fulfill social expectations.

I think the second objection to animal research is a valid point that requires further study. Although the objection does not constitute a solid argument against animal experimentation, it raises some important questions about experimental designs and research methods. Given these doubts about analogies between animals and humans, researchers cannot assume that animals always provide good causal models for human diseases and treatments. Though many animal studies may be relevant to human beings, researchers must provide methodological rationales for using animals in experiments (LaFollette and Shanks 1996).

The third objection raises an important point that needs to be addressed, but it also does not constitute a solid argument against animal research. Although the research community has made tremendous advances in cell and tissue cultures and computer simulations in recent years, these alternatives have some significant drawbacks. A piece of an organism is not the same thing as a whole organism, and a computer simulation will never reproduce the complexities of the "real thing." Although scientists can gain some important information from cell and tissue cultures or computer simulations, it is often necessary to understand how a whole, real organism responds to a compound or treatment (Botting and Morrison 1997).

The final objection has occupied center stage in most debates about the use of animals in research. I cannot hope to explore this objection in depth here, but I will discuss some reasons why people oppose animal research on moral grounds. As I noted in my discussion of research on human beings, a moral concern for protecting individual rights and dignity requires us to follow ethical guidelines for human experimentation. Most people accept the idea that human beings have some inherent moral worth that should not be violated in the name of a social good. I think most people also accept the notion that some animals also have some moral worth: we should not torture, abuse, or cause unnecessary harm to animals. Defenders of animal experimentation recognize these commonsense ideas but maintain that animals have significantly less worth than human beings. Though it is wrong to torture a mouse to satisfy sadistic pleasures, it is not wrong to use a mouse in an experiment that is likely to benefit human beings. Better that a thousand rats suffer than one human child dies of leukemia. Animals can be used to promote human ends.

Those who oppose animal experimentation challenge this viewpoint by asserting that animals have much more moral value than their opponents assume. According to Singer (1975) if we should not perform an experiment on a human, then we should not perform the same experiment on an animal. Those who think otherwise embrace an unjustifiable form of discrimination known as speciesism, the view that our species is morally superior to other species and that members of our species deserve to be treated differently. Singer equates speciesism with racism because he believes that both doctrines allow for differential treatment of individuals based on morally irrelevant characteristics. According to Singer, humans and many animals both share a key moral characteristic, the capacity to feel pain. If it is wrong to inflict pain on human beings in experiments, then it is also wrong to inflict pain on animals in experiments.

A more radical position challenges all animal experimentation, not just experimentation that causes pain. According to Regan (1983) animals have moral rights based on their interests. Animals have interests in not being killed, harmed, or placed in captivity, for example. Since animals have rights, they can only be in experiments if they can give consent or if we can give consent for them; they should not be conscripted and sacrificed on the altar of science. Since animals do not choose to be in research and we cannot make choices on their behalf, virtually all animal experimentation should be stopped.

To explore any of these arguments in adequate depth would require more space than I have here, but let me suggest that many of these issues boil down to questions about similarities and differences between humans and animals (Varner 1994). If an organism is very similar to humans in morally relevant respects, then it deserves the treatment accorded to humans. Speciesism is not like racism because organisms from different species, unlike organisms from different human races, can be different in morally relevant respects. To avoid the "speciesism" objection, one of these morally significant features should not be "membership in *Homo sapiens*." The features we need to examine should transcend any particular species even though they may be manifested by our species (LaFollette and Shanks 1996). Though I cannot defend this list here, some morally relevant features might include:[8]

(1) The capacity to feel pain.
(2) Consciousness.
(3) The ability to grasp concepts or form beliefs.
(4) Abstract concepts, self-concepts.
(5) Reasoning.
(6) Language use.
(7) The ability to experience moral emotions, such as sympathy, love, and guilt.
(8) The ability to understand and follow moral rules.

These are traits that are shared by most members of our species and they are traits that can confer moral value on organisms. It is an open question whether any particular organism, species, or machine has these characteristics.

Do animals have some of these traits? Are they like human beings in morally relevant respects? For many years scientists, under the spell of behaviorism, would not address these questions. According to behaviorism, questions about animal mentality and cognition are unscientific because (1) we cannot observe the inner workings of an animal's mind, and (2) inferences about animal cognition or mentality commit the anthropomorphic fallacy, i.e. the mistake of projecting human traits onto non-human phenomena. However, in the last two decades scientists have challenged these assumptions and a new approach to the study of animals has emerged known as cognitive ethology (Griffin 1992). Cognitive ethologists attempt to study consciousness, intelligence, reasoning, emotions, norms, memory, concepts, and beliefs in animals. They typically base their inferences about animal cognition and emotion on neurobiological, behavioral, and evolutionary similarities between humans and animals. This new field is quite young and behaviorism still has a great deal of influence over ethologists, but we have at least started down the path toward answering these important questions about animals.

Although we lack a complete scientific theory of animal cognition and emotion at this point in time, we can tentatively conclude that many different species feel pain, that some species are conscious and experience various emotions, and that some species may even have the ability to reason, use a language, experience moral emotions, grasp concepts, or follow moral rules. If this view is correct, then many animal species may exhibit morally relevant characteristics, and we may have strong obligations not to use some species in experiments. However, this view does imply that all species deserve equal treatment, since differential treatment can be justified when species have morally significant differences. Treatment should be based on cognitive and emotive abilities: species with more of these abilities deserve better treatment.[9] Since chimpanzees have more of these abilities than mice, they deserve better treatment than mice, and many of the experiments that we conduct on mice we should not conduct on chimpanzees. The general ethical premise in this approach is that moral similarities and differences are based on cognitive and emotive similarities and differences; science enters the debate in determining the cognitive and emotive abilities of various animal species.[10]

The view I put forth here suggests a scaling of moral status based on cognitive and emotive features. Only organisms at the high end of the scale, such as human beings, have moral rights and duties. To have moral rights and duties, a being must belong to a species whose members are capable of understanding and following moral rules and experiencing moral emotions. Organisms toward the lower end of the scale lack moral rights and duties but they may still have some moral status. Beings that have moral duties may have an obligation to protect or promote the welfare of a species that lacks rights or duties. For example, human beings have a duty to protect the welfare of elephants, though elephants have no moral rights.

Before closing this discussion of animal experimentation, I should mention one other important consideration in deciding whether to use an animal in an experiment, i.e. whether it belongs to an endangered species. If we accept the idea that we have a moral duty to protect endangered species, then this duty can provide us with additional reason to refrain from experimenting on some animals (Rodd 1990). For example, the black-footed ferret is an endangered species whose cognitive and emotive abilities may not be much greater than a prairie dog's. If a researcher can use either black-footed ferrets or prairie dogs in an experiment, he should use the prairie dogs, since the prairie dog is not endangered. We have very strong reasons for not experimenting on gorillas, since they have significant cognitive and emotive abilities and they are endangered.

To summarize this section, though none of the four objections by themselves constitute a sound argument against animal experimentation, in conjunction they provide us with reasons for constantly examining and scrutinizing animal research. Though we may conduct animal experiments in order to benefit human beings, we need to develop alternatives to animal research, obtain a better understanding of the relevance of animal models, learn more about the cognitive and emotive characteristics of animals, and be willing to change the status quo as we learn more about animals and develop new methodologies.

CHAPTER 8
The Scientist in Society

This chapter will introduce the reader to a variety of ethical issues and dilemmas that arise as a result of science's interaction with society at large. Like the previous three chapters, this chapter will discuss ethical questions in light of the standards of conduct defended in Chapter 4.

Social Responsibility

In Chapter 4, I argued that scientists have a responsibility to serve society. The general idea behind social responsibility is that the people who produce knowledge should be responsible for its consequences. Since I have already defended social responsibility in Chapter 4, I will not repeat those arguments here. Although some scientists avoid interacting with the public, many of today's scientists are paragons of social responsibility. These scientists devote a great deal of time to educating the public about science, raising the public's interest in science, and informing the public about the consequences of research. In Chapter 6 I mentioned that some scientists have served the public by popularizing science. Others have used their knowledge and expertise to advocate for science and technology policies. For instance, after the United States dropped two atomic bombs on Japan during the Second World War, many prominent physicists, such as Albert Einstein and Robert Oppenheimer, led a movement to use atomic energy for peaceful purposes (Cantelon *et al.* 1991). During the 1960s, many scientists, led by Rachel Carson and Barry Commoner, raised the public's awareness about a variety of environmental concerns, such as pollution, overpopulation, pesticides, hazardous waste disposal, species extinction, and so on (Carson 1961, Commoner 1963). Today, many scientists are also environmental activists (Pool 1990). There are now many organizations dedicated to educating the public about health care, nutrition, household hazards, and environmental risks. For instance, the Center for Science in the Public Interest informs the public about nutrition and health and has lobbied for legislation to regulate food labeling and advertising (Williams 1995). There are also scientific organizations, such as the Committee for the Scientific Investigation of the Claims of the Paranormal and the Skeptics Society, that critically examine pseudo-science, junk science, paranormal phenomena, and superstition.[1] Many scientists have devoted their careers to exposing and debunking junk science (Gardner 1981, Milloy 1995).

It should be clear to readers that the scientists and scientific organizations mentioned above have done a great deal of good for society. The public needs to be educated about important scientific developments and the consequences of research, and it needs to be protected from junk science and misinformation. However, some ethical questions and problems can arise when scientists attempt to serve the public by advocating for specific policies or positions. When a scientist engages in a public debate, she occupies two roles, the role of a professional scientist, and the role of a concerned citizen. These roles may create conflicting obligations: professional scientists should strive for objectivity, honesty, and openness, but citizens are free to express subjective opinions, to speculate, and to manipulate information in order to advance their social and political agendas. When a scientist acts as a professional, her voice carries expert authority; when a scientist acts as a citizen, her voice carries no special authority. Scientists need to respect these different roles in order to contribute knowledge and expertise to public debates without violating the public's trust, but they may not always know how to fulfill these different responsibilities and commitments (Ben-David 1971, von Hippel 1991).

To see how conundrums can arise, consider the following example. A great majority of scientists are convinced that the greenhouse effect can lead to global warming unless people take some steps to regulate hydrocarbon emissions (Houghton *et al.* 1992). However, scientists disagree about many key issues related to global warming, such as the validity of certain studies or models, how severe the warming will be, when it will occur, how it will affect the oceans and weather patterns, etc. (Karl et al 1997). A small minority of scientists also reject the entire notion of global warming (Stevens 1996). Global warming is thus very similar to other established scientific theories, such as evolution, because it has been and will continue to be the subject of considerable debate in the scientific community even though most scientists accept its basic principles. Global warming, like evolution, has tremendous social, political, and economic implications. If global warming occurs, sea levels may rise, weather patterns may change, croplands may dry up, moderate climates may become tropical, and so on. Many environmentalists recommend that nations around the world take some steps to reduce hydrocarbon emissions in order to mitigate or prevent global warming. However, business and industry representatives oppose these regulations, since they will have detrimental, short-term economic impacts. Opponents of environmental regulations also argue that global warming is only a scientific theory with very little evidence in its favor. They see the current controversies over global warming as evidence that the theory does not have any solid backing. Why risk causing an economic disaster in order to avoid an outcome that has very little scientific proof?

This volatile mix of science and politics poses an ethical dilemma for scientists who study global climate change: should they act as professionals and provide the public with an objective assessment of the facts or should they act as concerned citizens and advocate a particular policy? Should scientists present the public with an objective account of global warming, one that includes all information and current opinions, or should they offer biased accounts in order to prevent politicians and the public from making a bad decision in the face of some uncertainties about global warming?

There are at least two reasons why scientists should remain as objective as possible when they are expected to offer professional expertise. First, when scientists are asked to give professional opinions, the public expects that they will give an unbiased, objective assessment of the facts. In newspaper interviews, Congressional hearings, and in the courtroom, scientists supply the facts and technical expertise that serve as a foundation for the resolution of disputes (Huber 1991, Hardwig 1994, Bimber 1996). Scientists who abandon this role betray the public's trust and can undermine the public's support for science. Although the public wants scientists to be socially responsible, people may react negatively to scientists who advance their own political agendas while answering requests for professional expertise. Second, if scientists routinely sacrifice their commitment to objectivity to support social or political goals, science may become completely politicized. Scientists must safeguard their commitment to objectivity in order to avoid sliding down a slope toward bias and ideology. Although moral, social, and political values can have an impact on science, scientists should continually strive to be honest, open, and objective when they conduct research or are asked to give expert opinions. However, scientists are free to take off this objective straitjacket when they act as concerned citizens, since they have as much of a right to advocate for political or social policies as anyone else. When scientists are not asked to serve as experts, they are free to slant or bias the facts, offer subjective opinions, and engage in varieties of persuasion and rhetoric.

Thus, to solve the problems created by the mix of science and politics, scientists need to understand their different roles in society (Golden 1993). Scientists should strive to act objectively in situations where their professional opinions are sought, but they may step out of this role at other times. Scientists should also strive to make it clear to the public when they are speaking as citizens and when they are speaking as scientists, so the public will know when scientists are providing professional expertise and when they are touting political or social values. Thus, a climatologist is free to act as citizen and advocate when writing an editorial for a magazine, when organizing a protest, when discussing issues with other citizens, and so on; but she should strive for objectivity when giving expert testimony before Congress, when answering questions for the media, and so on. It is not always easy for scientists to juggle these different roles, and some scientists may have such strong personal interests in some public issues that they cannot separate the roles of citizen and scientist successfully. A scientist whose personal interests interfere with her ability to offer professional expertise could be viewed as having a conflict of interest if asked to give a professional opinion. The proper response to a conflict of interest is to try to remove one's self from the situation that creates the conflict. (See the discussion in Chapter 5.)

Although scientists should strive for objectivity in professional contexts, professional ethics may allow scientists to sacrifice honesty and openness for social or political goals in some rare cases. Many of the social sciences, such as anthropology, have social or political goals. For example, according to the American Anthropological Association's code of ethics, one of the main goals of anthropology is to promote the interests of peoples and cultures studied by anthropologists. When conflicts arise, these interests take precedence over other considerations, such as objectivity and openness (American Anthropological Association 1990, Daly and Mills 1993). However, given the importance of objectivity in science, the burden of proof falls on scientists who would distort or suppress facts in order to promote social or political ends.

Finally, it should be noted that two types of uncertainty make it difficult to practice socially responsible science. The first kind of uncertainty is epistemological: it is often impossible to foresee the consequences of research. Very often the significant consequences of research are unanticipated technological applications. Einstein, Plank, and Bohr could not have anticipated that their research on quantum theory in the early 1900s would eventually lead to the development of the atom bomb. Particle physics was regarded as a field of research far removed from practical concerns, and most scientists at this time would have regarded chemistry as a more likely source of the world's next great weapon (Cline 1965). Other examples abound: when computers were first developed most people thought they would only be useful in missile guidance or number crunching for science; few people realized that the steam engine would play a key role in the industrial revolution or that the discovery of DNA would lead to genetic engineering (Volti 1995).

The second kind of uncertainty is moral or political: even when the consequences of research can be anticipated, people may disagree about their social value. For example, it is fairly obvious that the development of RU-486, a drug that can cause an abortion early in pregnancy, will make it easier for women to obtain abortions (Dixon 1994). Different sides of the abortion dispute disagree about the social value of RU-486 research: pro-choice groups embrace its social consequences, but anti-abortion groups abhor them. Other examples of scientific and technological developments that have generated moral and political disputes include nuclear power, genetic engineering of plants and animals, and the internet and world-wide web.

How should scientists respond to these uncertainties? Given that a scientist's professional duty is to provide the public with facts and expert opinions, one might argue that scientists should not discuss consequences of research with the public when any such discussion would be no more than speculation. One might also argue that scientists should not discuss morally and politically controversial research in order to remain objective and impartial. I find neither of these arguments convincing. Scientists are usually more qualified than other people to speculate about the consequences of research, since they have more knowledge and expertise. Expert opinions about the implications of scientific and technological developments may often be wrong, but it is better to have a well-informed opinion than no opinion at all. Furthermore, objectivity does not require scientists to avoid discussing controversial research; it only demands that scientists do not take sides when they are offering professional opinions. A scientist who seeks to offer an objective opinion about the consequences of research should discuss all of the different possible consequences, both good and bad (Rollin 1995).

Expert Testimony
in Court

As mentioned earlier, scientists should be honest, open, and objective when serving as expert witnesses in court. While expert opinions can have an impact on legislative debates, many legal cases hinge on the testimony of expert witnesses. The stakes in these cases can be very high: murder or rape convictions and billion dollar lawsuits can be decided on the basis of expert testimony. Since experts play such an important role in our legal system, one of the most important stages in a trial is when the judge decides when an expert opinion may be admitted as evidence. In the US, both sides in a court case may seek to obtain the testimony of experts, and experts are usually recognized based on their professional credentials. Juries must assess these different expert opinions as they weigh evidence presented in court. Though experts offer evidence, juries decide matters of guilt, innocence, and liability (Huber 1991).

The use of experts in the courtroom raises some important legal and ethical issues, but I will only discuss the ethical ones here. First, can experts bias their testimony? Can they slant the facts or suppress evidence? Although experts might be tempted to use their testimony in order to sway a jury in favor of a particular judgment, the arguments I made for honesty and openness apply to expert testimony. Scientists who are asked to give expert testimony are serving in a professional role that demands objectivity, and those who ignore this responsibility betray the public's trust. The obligation to remain objective would hold even if the expert is convinced of the guilt or innocence of a defendant or the liability of a litigant. Scientists should state facts and give expert opinions when appearing on the witness stand; it is not their prerogative to bias a jury in favor of guilt, innocence, or liability (Capron 1993).

Second, can an expert witness have a conflict of interest? If so, how should they respond to this situation? Expert witnesses can have a conflict of interest when they have strong personal or financial interests relating to the outcome of a court case. A conflict could arise when the expert's interests clash with her professional obligation to provide objective testimony before the court. For example, a physician who gives expert testimony against a breast implant company would have a conflict of interest if his wife could be awarded a significant sum of money if the company is found liable of manufacturing a dangerous product. People who have conflicts of interest should not serve as expert witnesses, since these conflicts compromise their judgment.

Third, does a fee taint a witness's ability to provide objective testimony? Witnesses are paid for their testimony in order to provide them with compensation for time taken away from work, travel costs, and so on. If a scientist can be paid an honorarium to give a lecture or workshop, it seems reasonable to pay a scientist some money to testify in court. So long as an expert's fee is not linked to the outcome in the case, the fee does not taint her testimony or create a conflict of interest. It would be unethical for an attorney to offer an expert a bonus for a favorable outcome in a case, but it is not unethical to pay an expert witness a fee for providing testimony per se.

However, the ethics of paying expert witnesses fees for services is more questionable when we realize that some people earn so much money serving as expert witnesses that they have made careers out of providing expert testimony (Huber 1991). If these experts obtain employment, in part, because their testimony results in favorable outcomes, then I would say that they have a conflict of interest, since they know that the testimony they offer in the courtroom can lead to future employment opportunities and other forms of financial remuneration. For example, there are some experts today who make a living testifying about DNA fingerprinting evidence. These techniques can be used to compare the DNA of a defendant with DNA found at a crime scene. Experts who testify on behalf of these techniques estimate that they have a one in ten million chance of falsely implicating an innocent person; experts who testify against these techniques argue that evidence can be contaminated or degraded and that there is not a sound statistical basis for estimating the probability that an innocent person will be falsely implicated (Hubbard and Wald 1993). One might argue that these experts have a conflict of interest since they know that their testimony for or against DNA fingerprinting can lead to future employment. On the other hand, one might argue that these experts should still be allowed to testify since their testimonies can cancel each other out. (Lawyers put it this way, "for every Ph.D. there is an equal and opposite Ph.D.")

The last issue I would like to discuss concerns the criteria for deciding who can give expert testimony. I will introduce this issue with a case study. George Franklin was convicted in 1990 of raping and killing an 8-year-old girl in 1970. The key evidence in the case came from his daughter Eileen's recollections of witnessing the crime. The unusual aspect of this case is that her memories had emerged as a result of a new and controversial psychological technique known as memory retrieval. Psychologists who developed memory retrieval techniques testified in this trial as expert witnesses; other psychologists offered testimony that challenged memory retrieval. Franklin was the first person convicted on the basis of memory retrieval in the US, but since then memory retrieval testimony has helped to secure other convictions in murder, rape, and child molestation cases. Many psychologists believe that the process of memorial retrieval is highly fallible. Psychologists no longer view memory as a storage space in which items can be placed, lost, found or retrieved in the way one might store data on a computer disk. People are constantly reshaping their memories of the world based on their current outlooks and experiences. If memory works this way, then it may be impossible to recall any event in exact detail – memory is not photographic. There may be no way to distinguish between genuine retrieved memories, fanciful stories, dreams, and memories that have been induced by memory retrieval techniques, which often involve hypnosis. The False Memory Syndrome Foundation was founded in 1992 to assist people claiming to be falsely accused on the basis of retrieved memories (Ofshe and Waters 1994, Loftus 1995).

Should memory retrieval evidence be allowed in court? What are the standards for admitting expert testimony? These are questions that affect all citizens, not just judges, since legal proceedings impact individuals and society. There are two basic approaches for admitting testimony from scientific experts, the strict approach and the loose approach. According to the strict approach, only well-qualified scientists should be able to testify in court. Judges should evaluate scientists based on testimony from peers, publications in established journals, professional appointments, public service, and other criteria that can be used to certify scientific qualifications. Although the legal system allows expert witnesses on both sides of a case, juries can be misled by junk science and may fail to understand or appreciate good science. Juries that are swayed by junk science can make poor decisions, such as false convictions or findings of liability. In order to avoid the legal errors caused by junk science, judges should maintain strict standards for admitting expert witnesses. Some writers have even suggested that the scientific community should designate certified experts (Huber 1991).

According to the loose approach, judges should be fairly liberal when it comes to admitting expert testimony, because a strict approach can prevent novel and controversial evidence from entering the courtroom. In Chapter 6 we noted that scientists often resist novel or controversial research. Moreover, they may also regard scientists who do this type of research as weird or incompetent. Thus, scientists who do novel or controversial research may lack publications in established journals or recognition from peers. It is important to allow novel or controversial evidence into the courtroom because lawyers should have access to important developments in science before they become well-established. For example, DNA fingerprinting techniques were once regarded as controversial or unreliable, but they are now routinely used. Those who defend the loose approach admit that it may allow some junk science to enter the courtroom, but the effects of junk science on jury deliberations can be mitigated by good science (for every Ph.D. there is an equal and opposite Ph.D.). It is better to let in too much evidence than to exclude some important evidence.

I see advantages and disadvantages to both of these approaches, but I should mention a consideration that supports a strict approach over a loose one, i.e. the public's ignorance about science. Although lawyers and scientists can help to educate judges and juries when science enters the courtroom, this kind of remedial education has limitations. If the public already lacks a great deal of scientific knowledge, then a crash course on various scientific techniques may not do much good. (Many lawyers and judges report that jurors roll their eyes and glaze over when scientific experts testify in court.) A loose approach to expert testimony makes sense when the public understands science; a strict approach makes more sense when the public has little grasp of science. These observations once again highlight the importance of educating the public about science.

Industrial Science

I would like to switch gears a bit by discussing ethical dilemmas that arise when scientists leave the academic environment and conduct research for industry or the military. Although there are many differences between the military and private industry, they raise similar ethical issues because they both have goals and policies that are often at odds with scientific goals and standards of conduct. In private industry, profit maximization is the primary goal and pursuit of this end frequently conflicts with openness, honesty, freedom, and other principles of research ethics. The military's main objective is to protect national security, and this goal also can conflict with many scientific standards, including openness, freedom, honesty, and respect for human and animal subjects. When these conflicts arise, people conducting research in non-academic settings must choose between science's standards of conduct and other standards.

Industry's employment of scientists (and engineers) has increased steadily over the last hundred years.[2] During the Renaissance, scientists worked for universities or sponsored their own research. Industry had very little contact with science until after the scientific revolution, when people began to realize science's practical potency (Jacob 1997). Perhaps the first significant interface between science and industry occurred in the late 1700s when James Watt, a scientist-inventor, collaborated with John Roebuck and Matthew Boulton, two English industrialists, in producing steam engines. In the 1860s, the German dyestuffs manufacturers pioneered the use of scientists in industry by setting up their own company laboratories. Collaborations between science and industry soon became more formal, and the modern industrial laboratory was born. Today, most of the world's major corporations employ scientists and have industrial laboratories, and many businesses sponsor research that occurs in university laboratories. Businesses and universities have also established mutually beneficial partnerships on many campuses (Bowie 1994).

Research in industrial laboratories usually occurs through highly structured bureaucracies, which control the selection of research problems, the appropriation of materials, tools, and employees, and other aspects of research. Scientists who work in these laboratories are usually not allowed to set the research agenda, and they often sign contracts giving away their intellectual property rights in exchange for employment, royalties, and other types of compensation (Ziman 1984). Although industrial research often produces knowledge, the advancement of this goal is not sought for its own sake. If an area of investigation may yield a significant profit for a company, then the company will explore it; if not, then the company may ignore it, even if the area of investigation could produce socially valuable consequences. However, some companies sponsor pure research in certain areas because they believe that it will have some direct, practical payoffs, and this is often the case. For instance, companies that sponsor research on solid-state physics have used their knowledge to design smaller, more efficient transistors.

Before ruminating on the ethical concerns raised by the science–business connection, it is worth noting that industrial research yields a great deal of social benefits. First, industry employs scientists to develop products and technologies that benefit society, such as the automobile, microwave ovens, personal computers, and instant coffee. Second, private industry provides employment for millions of scientists and other people involved in research. These jobs tend to be the high-wage, high-skilled jobs that play a vital role in building a community's or country's economic base. Third, private industry funds scientific research. Due to budgetary restrictions, the government sponsorship of research has declined in recent years but private industry has continued to sponsor research (Resnik 1996a). Although the research sponsored by private industry is often highly applied, it can have theoretical spinoffs. For instance, in 1965 two researchers at Bell Laboratories, Arno Penzias and Robert Wilson, discovered the uniform, background radiation that has become a crucial piece of evidence for the big-bang theory in cosmology. The researchers came upon this important finding when they were conducting research on microwave antennas and found that some background noise could not be eliminated. Fourth, academic institutions often benefit from working with private industry. When companies operate in university settings, they help universities to obtain private funding for equipment, work sites, and human resources (Bowie 1994).

Industrial research has created many ethical issues and dilemmas. Although I cannot examine all of these questions here, I would like to introduce the reader to one key issue in industrial research, secrecy.

As we noted in Chapter 6, companies can control intellectual property through patents, copyrights, trademarks, and trade secrets. Secrecy usually plays an important role in the development and control of intellectual property in industry. If a company is seeking to patent an invention, it may require secrecy in order to protect research before a patent application has been accepted. Although patents encourage the disclosure of information, a period of secrecy usually prevails until a company obtains a patent. In order to maintain a competitive advantage, most companies also keep trade secrets as well. For example, the formula for Coca-Cola is not patented; it is a trade secret. Although scientists who work for industry often publish their results, companies censor and suppress research results in order to promote their interests. By maintaining secrecy, companies maximize their own profits but they also hamper the advancement of knowledge. Perhaps a certain amount of secrecy is a small price to pay for the many benefits of industrial research. Since industrial research benefits both science and society, banning secrecy in industrial research would be like killing the goose that laid the golden egg: this move might yield some good results in the short run, but in the long run it would do more harm than good. Furthermore, though the advancement of science might be improved if all industrial secrets were made public, science is doing quite well without complete openness. I think these arguments provide a good justification for secrecy in industrial science and they allow most companies to practice secrecy without facing external pressures to reveal information.

However, there are some notable exceptions to this policy, since secrecy may conflict with scientific ethics or with moral and political values. Sometimes a company can do a great deal of harm by keeping secrets. The research on nicotine addiction sponsored by tobacco companies illustrates this point. Testifying before a Congressional hearing on tobacco companies, Victor DeNobel and Paul Mele discussed research they conducted for Philip Morris in the early 1980s on nicotine addiction. DeNobel and Mele testified that they discovered a substance which increases nicotine's addictive effects when added to cigarettes. They also testified that their colleagues had discovered an artificial version of nicotine whose toxic effects on the heart are less than the effects of natural nicotine. The purpose of their research was to develop a nicotine substitute to make cigarettes less harmful; it was part of a research program to learn everything possible about nicotine and its effects on the body. Their work was kept so secret that they were not allowed to discuss it with fellow employees and animals used in the research were brought in the laboratory under covers. DeNoble and Mele reported their findings in a paper submitted to a scientific journal, *Psychopharmocology*, which accepted the paper for publication. Philip Morris learned about the paper and forced DeNoble and Mele to withdraw it. Soon Philip Morris shut down their laboratory and DeNoble and Mele left the company. DeNoble and Mele were allowed to discuss this research only after Congressman Henry Waxman arranged for the two researchers to be released from a lifelong agreement they made with Philip Morris not to discuss their research without the company's permission (Hilts 1994a). Although it was widely known during the early 1980s that nicotine is addictive, its addictive properties were still not well understood. If DeNoble and Mele's work had been available to psychologists, pharmacologists, and other researchers, perhaps they could have developed better techniques for combating nicotine addiction. If the FDA and the Surgeon General had known about this research, then perhaps these agencies could have issued more informative warnings about the dangers of tobacco use and they might have altered some of their educational and regulatory policies. If DeNoble and Mele's research had been made public in the 1980s, it is likely that fewer people would have been addicted to nicotine or more people would have recovered from nicotine addiction. The harms caused by nicotine are well known: it directly causes harm to people by increasing the risk of heart disease and it indirectly causes harm to people by compelling them to use tobacco products, which have been linked to lung, mouth, and throat cancer as well as emphysema. Thus, by keeping trade secrets concerning nicotine's addictive properties, Philip Morris probably caused a great deal of harm to people. (Of course, tobacco products sold by Philip Morris are harmful anyway, but this fact does not lessen the added harm of keeping nicotine research secret.)[3]

Careless research can also pose significant harms to the public. Consider the tragic case of the space shuttle Challenger, which exploded after launch on 28 January 1986 (Westrum 1991). Six astronauts and a school teacher died in the explosion. An investigation of the accident showed that a seal on its booster rocket, the O-ring, had leaked due to cold temperatures and that this leak allowed rocket fuel to ignite in the booster. Many people involved with the mission had known that it was too cold for a safe launch, and many authorities at NASA and at Morton Thiokol, the company that made the boosters, had known that the O-rings were not safe at low temperatures, yet they had continued to allow shuttle launches despite this known hazard. It would be too expensive to make new O-rings that could withstand colder temperatures, even though these rings would be safer. Since authorities did not anticipate launching the shuttle in excessively cold weather, the O-ring problem posed an acceptable risk. The day before the tragic launch Roger Boisjoly estimated that the O-rings would leak at a temperature of 50 degrees Fahrenheit and he called a teleconference with Morton Thiokol and NASA officials to discuss the situation. Morton Thiokol initially recommended against going ahead with the launch but NASA officials asked the company to reconsider. NASA was under tremendous pressure to go ahead with the launch and Morton Thiokol changed its decision. Subsequent investigations revealed that not only were the O-rings defective, but the shuttle also had problems preventing ice formation and an inadequate communication system. For a second example, consider the tragic case of misread Pap smears. In 1995 BioChem Corporation and two of its employees were charged with homicide for misreading the Pap smears of two women who died of cervical cancer. Doctors testified that if their smears have been read correctly, the women would have had a 95 percent chance of survival (Kolata 1995). Witnesses also claimed that the Pap smears were probably misread because BioChem was requiring its employees to read up to 31,000 slides per year; the American Society for Cytology recommends that technicians read no more than 12,000 slides per year.

In the both of these cases it is likely that two business values, speed and cost-effectiveness, helped cause errors in research. Administrators at NASA wanted to go ahead with their launch schedule and did not want to pay the extra money for O-rings that could function in cold temperatures. Executives at BioChem overworked their employees in order to maximize their profits by saving money on human resources. The adage, "haste makes waste," applies to all areas of research, not just research that takes place within the academic environment.

Dishonest research may also cause harms to the public. Although it is difficult to estimate the frequency of dishonest research in industry, it is likely that industrial scientists, like their colleagues in academia, also fabricate, falsify, or misrepresent data. Indeed, one might expect that the rate of fraudulent research would be higher in industry, since the economic incentives for fraud are often greater in industrial research than they are in academic research. If deception is more profitable than honesty, then why be honest? For example, in 1994 four former employees of Empire Laboratories accused the company of falsifying results in order to make concrete appear stronger than it really was. The company was testing concrete to be used on runways at Denver International Airport. Empire's lawyers conceded that some test results were altered, but the employees argued that this practice was widespread (Kilzer *et al.* 1994). In 1993 the Public Citizens' Health Research group accused Eli Lilly Corporation of covering up a problem with an experimental hepatitis drug that killed five patients in an NIH trial. The group charged that the company knew that the drug could cause liver toxicity but failed to disclose the information to the FDA. The group charged that the lives of three of the five patients who died would have been saved if Eli Lilly had disclosed this information, since the FDA would have stopped the trial. Eli Lilly officials denied these accusations (*Denver Post* 1993).[4]

What should a scientist do when he or she believes that keeping research a secret is likely to harm the public? This question brings up the issue of whistle blowing, which we discussed in another context in Chapter 5. It also brings to light a conflict between a scientist's professional obligations and her obligations to private corporations. The scientist's professional obligations require her to blow the whistle on unethical or illegal research; her obligations to private corporations require her to maintain secrecy. Since industrial researchers also often sign contracts agreeing to maintain secrecy, scientists who blow the whistle on industrial research may also violate the law (Schlossberger 1995).

If we think of this dilemma as a conflict between science and industry, then it may be intractable. However, we can appeal to moral standards to help us resolve these issues. As members of society, scientists also have obligations to do no harm, to benefit other people, and to maximize social utility. We can appeal to these moral obligations to provide a rationale for blowing the whistle in some cases (Baram 1983, Clutterbuck 1983). However, since complete openness would undermine industrial research, and industrial research benefits science and society, employees must have a compelling reason for blowing the whistle on industrial research. Secrecy should remain the norm in industrial research, and whistle blowers should follow the guidelines outlined in Chapter 5, i.e. they should acquire documentation, proceed through appropriate channels, etc. Scientists who blow the whistle on industrial research can be viewed as heroes because whistle blowers often face significant repercussions, such as loss of employment, blackballing, lawsuits, and in some cases death.[5]

What about exposing secret research in order to do good for society (as opposed to preventing harm)? One might argue that a great deal of research is and ought to be kept secret even though the public might benefit from having it made public. The long-run benefits of secrecy, i.e. increased industrial investment in research and the development of useful products, are more important than the short-term gains that result from disclosing information. Scientists who would break their agreements with companies in order to benefit the public must have a clear and convincing case for taking such action. Consider the following case.

In 1995 Boots Company convinced Betty Dong to withdraw a paper that had been accepted for publication in the *Journal of the American Medical Association*. The paper showed that several forms of levothyroxine work as well at treating hypothyroidism as Synthroid, a drug manufactured by a company owned by Boots. The paper also stated that the US could save $356 million a year if the eight million patients with under-active thyroids used these alternative forms instead of Synthroid. Boots had funded Dong's research in the hope that she would obtain evidence that Synthroid is superior to alternative drugs. Boots spent several years attempting to discredit Dong's research and allegedly threatened to sue Dong if she published her paper, since Dong and her colleagues signed a contract promising not to publish results without written consent from the company. Officials from Boots deny these allegations, and they claim that they tried to stop publication of the paper in order to prevent flawed research from putting millions of patients at risk (Wadman 1996). The company eventually relented and allowed Dong to publish her paper, which appeared in the *New England Journal of Medicine* (Altman 1997). Although the paper was eventually published, the episode raises a number of ethical questions. Would it be ethical for Dong to violate her agreements with Boots and publish her results before the company allowed her to do so? What amount of public benefit justifies disclosing secret industrial research? Does the validity of Dong's research (or lack thereof) make any difference in this case? Was Boots' agreement with its researchers unethical? I think that Dong would be justified in breaking her agreements with Boots in this case, but questions like these do not have easy answers. We need to think more about the long-run benefits and costs of secrecy to science, society, and industry.

The science–industry relationship raises many other ethical issues that I do not have space to discuss here. Some of these are: government funding for industrial research, the ownership of industry-sponsored research conducted in public facilities, secret industrial research conducted at university and college campuses and the threat to the climate of openness, conflicts of interest (discussed in Chapter 5), the redirection of human and technical resources from pure toward applied research, organizational biases in industrial research, and the conflict between private research and other university responsibilities, such as education, advising, and public service. These and other issues merit further public discussion so that society can benefit from the relationship between science and industry.[6]

Military Science

The connection between science and the military dates to ancient Greece and Rome, where many scientists also designed weapons. During the Renaissance, governments employed scientists in designing and building cannons, guns, bombs, fortresses, ships, and other necessities of war. By the Enlightenment, scientists advised military officers on the use of weapons, tactics, and strategies. Prior to the twentieth century, scientists played an important role in the military, but the relationship between science and the military was still largely informal and small-scale. But all that has changed since the Second World War, when scientists, engineers, and technologists played a key role in developing weapons, tactics, and strategies. Scientists were employed in large, top-secret activities, such as the Manhattan Project, and the government began spending a great deal of money supporting military research. The atom bomb is an especially appropriate and frightening symbol of this emerging interdependence between science, technology, and the military. Today, it is estimated that 500,000 scientists and engineers work for the military and that one fourth of the world's research and development (R & D) budget is devoted to military research (Dickson 1984). In the United States, the federal government spends twice as much on military R & D as it does on all other R & D budgets.

Scientists who work for the military may work in government laboratories, such as Los Alamos National Laboratory in New Mexico, or in university settings. They include researchers from many different disciplines ranging from the hard sciences, such as physics and chemistry, to the softer ones, such as psychology and computer science. Although one might think that military research is highly applied, the military also sponsors a great deal of pure research; research need not have a direct payoff for the development of weapons technologies in order to be important for national security. Military research has greatly increased our general knowledge of many subjects, including physics, chemistry, biology, aeronautics, meteorology, medicine, psychology, and computer science, and military technologies can have important non-military applications. For instance, satellite- and missile-tracking technologies developed by the military have been employed in directing commercial air traffic. Surveillance technologies used to spy on enemies can be used by police to monitor criminal activities.

Most military research occurs under the auspices of highly structured bureaucracies, such as the Department of Defense (DOD). These bureaucracies control all aspects of military research from the selection of research problems and the allocation of funds to the appropriation of materials, tools, and employees. Although individual researchers do the work that yields military gains, they usually do not own the property rights to their research. The military decides when and how the research is to be used.

Although some military research is open to public scrutiny, most military science is kept under a cloak of secrecy. "Loose lips sink ships," is a motto that fits most military research, and the military has developed very elaborate and effective means of keeping secrets (Howes 1993). Most military research is available only on a "need to know" basis: a person in the military will be allowed to know only enough information in order to perform their duties. The justification for this procedure is that the less a person knows, the less damage they can do if they are captured by the enemy or commit acts of treason. Military personnel and civilians who work for the military are bound by oaths and contracts not to reveal classified information. Disclosure of such information can result in severe punishments ranging from jail sentences to capital punishment. For instance, Julius and Ethel Rosenberg were executed after being convicted of revealing important military secrets to the Soviet Union. Many people working closely with their colleagues on confidential research do not even know what their colleagues are doing. Indeed, many of the people who worked on the Manhattan Project did not know exactly what they were doing for the military. Even Vice-President Truman was not allowed to know the details of this project until he became President. Research can be declassified when it is determined that it is no longer in the interests of national security to maintain secrecy. For instance, in 1994 the Clinton administration began declassifying top-secret research on the effects of radiation on human subjects (Weiner 1994a).

Military research raises many different ethical and political and issues. Before discussing these concerns, we should rehearse the main argument for the moral legitimacy of military research. The argument begins with a defense of the military's role in society: a military force, one might argue, is necessary to protect a sovereign state's security and interests. Military force is required because it is often not possible for a sovereign state to protect itself or its citizens through political means, such as diplomacy. In an ideal world it might not be necessary for sovereign nations to have standing armies, but this world is far from perfect. Since knowledge enhances military power and influence, a sovereign nation may conduct military research to enhance its military power. Thus, military research can be justified when a sovereign nation needs to conduct research in order to protect and promote its national security and interests (Fotion and Elfstrom 1986). Military research is a legitimate and necessary part of our imperfect and violent world. I think this is a convincing argument for military research. We should note, however, that the argument does not apply to "outlaw" nations; a nation is justified in having a military force only if it recognizes the sovereignty of other nations and abides by international agreements pertaining to warfare and the control of terrorism. Having presented an argument for military research, I will now consider some ethical questions that this kind of research generates.

For many scientists, the main ethical dilemma is whether they should work for the military under any conditions. Scientists may refuse to work for the military on the grounds that they do not want to conduct confidential research, that they are not interested in military research, or that they do not wish to contribute to violence and warfare (Kemp 1994). On the other hand, scientists have at times regarded military research as a civic duty. In the 1930s, German physicist Fritza Strassman discovered the process of nuclear fission by bombarding uranium atoms with neutrons. The US did not obtain knowledge of how to split atoms until 1939, when scientists fled Nazi Germany with their knowledge of fission. In 1939, a group of influential refugee physicists persuaded Einstein, who by then was a world famous scientist, to write a letter to President Roosevelt warning him that the Nazis would soon develop a nuclear weapon and that the US should accelerate its fission research. This letter helped convince Roosevelt to launch the Manhattan Project, which employed Enrico Fermi, Robert Oppenheimer, Hans Bethe, and other renowned physicists. These scientists worked on the Project out of a sense of social responsibility, since they feared that Nazi Germany would ruin civilization if the Allies lost the Second World War (Morrison 1995).

Those scientists who decide to work for the military face ethical dilemmas relating to secrecy. Before discussing some of the ethical problems associated with military secrecy, we should remind ourselves of the obvious point that secrecy is necessary in order to accomplish military objectives. It is difficult to defend a country or win a war when adversaries can learn about your weapons, tactics, strategies, technological capabilities, and troop movements. Thus, if military research can be justified in order to protect national sovereignty, then secrecy can also be justified as a necessary means for conducting military research and carrying out military operations. However, military research, like business research, violates traditional, scientific standards relating to openness. Since military ethics and the law require scientists to not disclose classified information, the burden of proof falls on those who would break confidentiality. If we follow my earlier analysis of secrecy in industrial research, then scientists may break confidentiality in order to prevent harm to the public. Although sometimes great harms occur when military secrets are exposed, sometimes more harms result from secrecy than from openness.

For example, sometimes military secrecy may be used to cover-up research that abuses human subjects. Consider the military's secret research on the effects of radioactivity on human beings that I discussed in the last chapter. If this secret research had been made public, it probably would have been stopped or would never have occurred. The experiments were so morally corrupt that they could only be conducted under a cloak of military secrecy. Although some damage to US national security might have resulted from disclosing this confidential research, it is likely that secrecy resulted in much greater harms to the public. Thus, scientists who knew about this research would be justified in making it public.

Secrecy may also be used to cover-up fraudulent or invalid research. One of the most embarrassing moments for the Pentagon occurred in

August 1994, when it was revealed that researchers on the Strategic Defense Initiative (SDI) had rigged some crucial tests and faked data in an attempt to deceive Congress, the public, and the Soviet Union. SDI was a thirty billion dollar program to develop anti-missile technologies. The Reagan administration launched this defense effort and touted it as a way of providing the US with a protective shield against a nuclear attack from the Soviet Union or some other foreign power (Broad 1992). Some of the SDI devices included lasers and anti-missile missiles. One of the key tests of the program was to determine whether it was possible to make a missile that could destroy another missile in flight. The first few attempts to intercept missiles in flight were dismal failures. As a result of these failures, researchers faced the prospect of losing funding and the Reagan administration faced the possibility of losing support for the program. In order to keep the program going and produce results, SDI researchers faked an interception test: they put a beacon on a targeted missile and a receiver on the intercepting missile. The test worked beautifully: Congress was convinced that SDI could work and the program continued (Weiner 1994b). One might argue that researchers who worked on SDI would be justified in blowing the whistle on fraudulent research in order to allow Congress and the public to have accurate information about this program's feasibility.

We could discuss many other cases of questionable military research, but my basic point still holds: scientists who work for the military are sometimes justified in disclosing confidential information for the good of the public. However, I should also mention that it is often very difficult to know the consequences of disclosing military secrets. For example, scientists who worked on the Manhattan Project discussed whether they should share military secrets with the Soviet Union after the Second World War in order to promote nuclear parity. Some scientists argued that the cause of global peace and stability would be best served by keeping information about nuclear weapons secret; others argued that openness would promote peace and stability (Bethe *et al.* 1995). Since the disclosure of military secrets can have disastrous, international consequences, scientists who contemplate disclosing secrets should err on the side of caution: scientists should reveal military secrets only when they have clear and convincing reasons for believing that the consequences of secrecy will be much worse than the consequences of openness.

One final issue relating to military secrecy concerns the military's control over research that is not sponsored by the military. Consider the example of cryptography, the science of making and breaking codes. In any given military operation, information and commands are encoded in various way in order to prevent enemies (or other people) from disrupting the operation. Research on cryptography became especially important during the Second World War, and it is likely that it will have even more military significance as we enter the digital battlefield of the twenty-first century (Stix 1995). For many years, mathematicians and computer scientists have been interested in cryptography and in problems that have a direct bearing on cryptographic research. However, the US military has taken steps to suppress, restrict, or classify research on cryptography on the grounds that such research, if made public, could threaten national security. For example, in 1978 George Davida applied for a patent on a device to decipher and encode computer information. He soon received a notice warning him that his patent application contained information which could be detrimental to national security if disclosed to the public. The notice also told him that he would face a $10,000 fine and two years in prison if he published his invention or disclosed any details relating to it. Several months after this incident, the Information Group of the Institute of Electrical and Electronic Engineers was preparing for an international conference which would include discussions of cryptography. The group received a letter from a member of the National Security Agency (NSA) warning it that a discussion of cryptography at the meeting could violate international treaties on the export of arms. The NSA sought to disassociate itself from its employee's actions, saying he was not acting on its behalf, yet many people involved with the conference believed that he was acting for the NSA (Dickson 1984).

As one might expect, these and other episodes in the history of cryptographic research have caused an uproar in the academic community. Many people maintain that research conducted outside of the military setting should be not be classified. On the other hand, one cannot deny that the military may have a legitimate interest in controlling non-military research when it threatens national security. If a private company develops a new and powerful weapon, for example, the military has a legitimate interest in seeing that this weapon does not fall into the wrong hands. Questions like those raised by cryptographic research are likely to arise in the future as scientists and engineers produce discoveries and inventions with military implications. They are best settled by agreements that respect scientific freedom and openness yet do not compromise national security. For example, the NSF and NSA have an agreement concerning cryptographic research. The NSF has agreed to let the NSA review all of its applications on cryptographic research. The NSA can then decide to sponsor some of this research, which then becomes classified. The NSF also sponsors its own cryptographic research, which remains unclassified (Dickson 1984).

Although I have offered a general defense of military secrecy in this chapter, I also believe that secrecy is a dangerous type of governmental authority. When any governmental organization has the power to suppress and control information, it also has the power to control political processes and to shape society. The net political effect of governmental confidentiality is to create an elite group of people who have tremendous power and a culture of secrecy. The concentration of power in the hands of a few can easily lead to governmental tyranny and the erosion of democratic rule if left unchecked. This raises an interesting paradox for modern democracies: in order for a democratic society to survive in a violent world, it must permit and even promote social practices that could undermine democratic rule. A society may risk tyranny in attempting to preserve democracy. In order to prevent tyranny, it is therefore necessary to have social institutions, such as the media and various interest groups, that seek to declassify governmental information for the good of the people. Wherever governmental secrecy exists, social institutions and individuals must safeguard the public's right to know.

Military research raises many ethical questions that I cannot discuss here. Some of them are: the use of propaganda and disinformation, the use of human and animal subjects in military research, pacifism, military research as a civic duty, the conflict between the military and academia, and the military-industrial complex.[7]

The Public Funding of Research

Questions about the public funding of research take scientists out of the laboratory and into the middle of the political arena. Although the main focus of this book is ethics, not politics, it is important for scientists to understand the politics of research so they can be prepared to engage in public debates and defend their work. Scientists need to be able to describe their research to the public and explain its value and significance. Scientists do not have a blank check from the government to conduct research, and they need to be able to justify their work and understand the views of those who object to funding scientific research. Even though public funding is largely a political issue, scientists also sometimes face ethical dilemmas relating to public funding.

The three questions I would like to address in this section are:

(1)   Should the government fund scientific research?
(2)   Should the government fund pure or applied research?
(3)   Should funding decisions be based on political considerations?

Concerning the first question, there are three basic arguments for the government's support of research:

(a)   Research produces important technological applications for medicine, engineering, industry, and the military.
(b)   Research produces a wealth of knowledge that can be used by current and future generations.
(c)   Research contributes to education and intellectual development.

Although arguments (b) and (c) are important reasons for governmental support of research, they have little persuasive force in contemporary political debates. While most people value knowledge, education, and intellectual development, few people would allow the US government to spend over fifty billion dollars a year in research unless they expected to obtain some practical results from this investment (Goodman *et al.* 1995). In this era of tight budgets, science that does not produce practical results is regarded as academic pork. Case in point, the beleaguered and now defunct Super Conducting Super Collider, which would have cost at least twenty billion dollars to build (Roberts 1993, Horgan 1994). This project would have produced tremendous advances in particle physics, but its proponents were not able to convince politicians and the public that it was more important than other items in the federal budget.

The idea that science funding should be tied to practical results dates back to the nineteenth century, when governments began to see research as a wise economic investment (Mukerji 1989). During the twentieth century, governments realized that science and technology investments enhance military strength. Many of the important military technologies of this century, such as radar, the A-bomb, and the computer, resulted from scientific research. Since the Second World War, the US has had a strong commitment to funding scientific research and funding levels climbed steadily from 1946 to 1984 (Horgan 1993). During this era, research investments could be justified on the grounds that they were necessary to counter the Soviet threat. Policy makers appealed to this argument to justify military and non-military research on the grounds that all research investments can have important consequences for military and economic power. While the military argument for funding scientific research still has a great deal of persuasive force in the US and many other countries, the end of the Cold War has weakened its role in US (and Russian) politics. Today, the primary rationale for funding scientific research has shifted back to economic rather than military concerns. The Reagan, Bush, and Clinton administrations have all argued that science should be given high priority in the federal budget because it plays a key role in economic development and prosperity. The US should fund research not to stop the Soviet threat but to keep its high standard of living and to out-compete global economic powers such as Japan, China, and Germany (Cohen and Noll 1994). However, some writers continue to stress the national security argument for science funding (Gergen 1997).

Turning to the second question of this section, this pragmatic justification for the funding of research implies that governments should spend more money on applied research than on pure research, since applied research is more likely to yield practical results (Brown 1993, Slakey 1994). If economic prosperity and military strength are the names of the game, then disciplines like chemical engineering, medicine, computer science, and molecular genetics may end up big winners, while disciplines like astrophysics, evolutionary biology, and anthropology may end up big losers. Political realities may direct funds to research with direct economic and/or military significance.

However, there are several reasons why governments should not abandon their commitment to pure research. First, as many writers have argued, pure research often has practical applications. For example, the study of heat led to the development of the steam engine, nuclear physics led to atomic power, DNA research produced biotechnology, and the study of mathematical logic laid the foundation for computers. It is usually impossible to forecast the practical applications of pure research, and these applications may occur many decades after the research is completed, but the history of science indicates that pure research yields practical results (Mukerji 1989). Second, in order to conduct applied research, scientists need to have a large amount of general, scientific knowledge at their disposal (Weisskopf 1994). In order to conduct research on manufacturing integrated circuits, one needs to have a great deal of general knowledge about electricity, solid state physics, and so on. Since pure research aims at providing this type of knowledge, it plays a vital role in applied research. Pure research is part of a nation's informational infrastructure.

Third, the history of science also indicates that all research (not just pure research) flourishes in a social setting with a high degree of intellectual freedom. A country that directs research to specific practical goals and does not provide funding for pure research is likely to hamper the research climate by limiting intellectual freedom. German science during the Nazi era provides a good example of the error of trying to direct all research to practical goals. Before the 1930s, most of the best scientists in the world lived in Germany. But when the Nazis came to power, they put many restrictions on intellectual freedom and tried direct scientific research toward specific, practical goals. Many scientists emigrated from Germany, and German science declined (Merton 1973). I would argue that American science is so highly successful, in part, because freedom is important in the United States, and the US government has traditionally provided funds for pure research.

Finally, the military will always find reasons to fund research directly linked to national security and industries will also find reasons to fund profitable research. But these institutions may have few incentives to fund pure research. Although businesses sometimes sponsor pure research, most industrial research is highly applied. The military sponsors some pure research, and probably always will, but most military research is also applied. Moreover, since military and industrial research is often secret, pure research conducted within these institutions may not enter the public domain. Thus, if we agree that pure research should be conducted, then it needs to be sponsored by governments so that it can be available to the public. To borrow a term from economic theory, pure research should be regarded as a public good. (A public good is a good that cannot be consumed privately; the act of purchasing or making the good allows it to be available to others.) Pure research should be viewed as a public good that is as important as safe roads and bridges, a police force, sewage treatment, or education.

Turning to the third question of this section, it is certainly the case that politics enters into many research funding decisions today. Politicians often decide to direct research funds towards specific areas in order to satisfy particular constituencies or interests. For example, during the mid-1980s AIDS research was low on the US government's list of funding priorities. Today, the US government spends over a billion dollars on AIDS research, which is more money than it spends to study any other disease. There are several reasons behind this dramatic change: AIDS had only been recently discovered in the 1980s, but took on pandemic proportions during the 1990s, and AIDS activists lobbied for more research. Although there are some "scientific" reasons why AIDS research has risen to the top of the US government's list of medical research priorities, one should not underestimate the role that politics has played and will continue to play in AIDS research funding (Grmek 1990, Bayer 1997).

Politicians also succumb to constituencies and interests when deciding to cut or deny funding to specific areas of research.[8] For example, consider President Reagan's executive order to not allow NIH funds to be spent on fetal tissue research. Many scientists believe that fetal tissue transplants may offer some hope for patients who suffer from Parkinson's disease, since fetal tissue transplants have a low rejection rate and they can differentiate into adult tissues. Fetal tissue can become nerve tissue in a human adult's brain and can secrete dopamine, an important neurotransmitter that is deficient in Parkinson's patients.[9] The Clinton administration restored federal funding for fetal tissue research when it came to power (Kolata 1994). (As of the writing of this book, President Clinton had placed a moratorium on federal funding for research on human cloning, however.)

Since research has important social implications and costs a great deal of money, politics will always (and should always) play an important role in funding decisions. In a democratic society, citizens should be able to decide how the government allocates its budget; funding decisions should not be left entirely in the hands of bureaucrats or experts (Dickson 1984). Although the public should always have some say in decisions pertaining to the funding of research, there are at least two reasons why scientists, not politicians, should make most funding decisions. First, since the public does not want to waste its resources on unsound research, scientific merit should play an important role in the decision to fund any research proposal. Although the public can decide the social worth of research, most people are not qualified to determine the scientific merit of particular research proposals. Hence, the government needs to draw on the expertise of qualified scientists when making funding decisions. Second, it is highly inefficient for the public to review every research proposal, since the government receives hundreds of thousands of proposals each year. It would be more efficient to delegate most of these decisions to people who are qualified to make them. These two arguments support the idea that scientists should evaluate individual research proposals, although the public should oversee the evaluation process. This is pretty much the way science funding works in the United States. The public sets funding priorities, but funding agencies use a process of peer review to make individual funding decisions (Martino 1992). Scientists make the micro-management decisions relating to scientific merit, while the public sets science funding policy. This process mitigates the role of politics in science funding without eliminating it.

Other Social, Political, and Moral Issues

There are many more social, political, and moral issues that arise from the relation between science and society that I do not have time to discuss here. Some of the more important ones are:

(1) Restrictions on research: should research ever be banned for moral, political, or social reasons? (The human cloning example discussed in Chapter 1 raises this issue.)[10]

(2) Racism and sexism in science: is science sexist or racist? (My earlier discussions of research bias, human subjects research, sexual harassment, mentoring, and affirmative action touch on this issue.)[11]

(3) The relation between science and religion: should evolution be taught alongside creationism? Does science undermine religion, support religion, or neither undermine nor support religion? (We have had very little discussion of this topic so far, but it deserves to be included in discussions of science and ethics.)[12]

(4) The relation between science and human values: is science value-free? Is there a scientific basis for morality? What's the relation between science and morality, ethics, and human culture? (This is a big topic beyond the scope of this book but still worth discussing.)[13]

(5) Science and education: how should science be taught? Should public school curricula emphasize science, mathematics and technology education over other subjects, such as literature, languages, history, and art? (This topic is also beyond the scope of this book but still worth discussing.)

POSTSCRIPT
Toward a More Ethical Science

In this book I have explored some of the concepts, principles, and issues relating to ethics in science. In order to give a fair treatment of this subject, I have attempted to address more than one point of view on most topics. Although I expect that most readers will benefit from this balanced approach, some may also find it frustrating, since I have offered very little in the way of specific recommendations. This approach may leave readers with the impression that I do not have very many strong opinions on these issues, but I do. I have kept these opinions at bay in order to shed light on the subject. It should be clear by now that I have very strong opinions about the importance of ethics in science. I think that it is important for both science and society that scientists follow appropriate standards of conduct, that scientists learn how to recognize important ethical concerns in science and to reason about them, and that scientists see science as part of a larger social context with important consequences for humankind. Both science and society suffer when researchers adopt the attitude that they can ignore ethical standards and concerns in order to carry on the search for knowledge. Having said this much in favor of ethics in science, I think it is appropriate at this point to discuss some strategies for promoting ethical conduct in science.

Education is the most important tool in insuring the integrity of science (Hollander *et al.* 1995). Unless scientists are taught certain standards of conduct, it is not likely that they will learn them. Just as scientists need to be taught how to analyze data, make observations and measurements, in order to insure the epistemological soundness of research, scientists also need to be taught certain standards of conduct in order to insure the ethical soundness of science (PSRCR 1992). I think there is no doubt that scientists need to teach their students ethics in research, but there are some interesting questions about how to carry out this task. We have moved beyond the philosophical question, "can ethics be taught?," to the more practical question, "how can ethics be taught?"

Since ethics has to do with human action, the goal of ethics education should be to shape or affect human conduct. Ethics is of little use as an abstract system of ideas; it must be lived in order to have any redeeming value. Changing or shaping human conduct is no easy task, since many of our actions generally result from habits that must be acquired or enforced over a period of years. Just as one does not become a musical virtuoso overnight, one does not become an ethical scientist in a short period of time. Thus, the motto of teaching ethical conduct must be "practice, practice, practice!"

This being said, there are two ways that scientists can teach ethics. First, scientists should promote informal ethics instruction by serving as role models and mentors and by engaging students in informal discussions about ethics. The best way that scientists can teach their students how to be ethical scientists is by setting a good example (Feynman 1985, Gunsalus 1997). It is likely that most ethical knowledge in science is acquired informally, almost by osmosis.

Although informal instruction is probably the most important way of teaching ethics, it often does not go far enough, and it is also useful to rely on formal instruction in ethics. Formal instruction may involve teaching ethics in a classroom setting, reading about ethics, writing about it, discussing cases and problems, and so on. Just as there is a definite need to have formal instruction in research methods in various disciplines, there is also a need for formal instruction in research ethics. Formal instruction in ethics can help prepare students for ethical problems and issues that they will be likely to face when they enter the "real" world, it can sensitize students to important ethical issues and problems, it can help students learn to think about ethical issues and to resolve ethical dilemmas, and it can help provide further motivation for ethical conduct by allowing students to understand the justifications for standards of conduct in science (Rest and Narvaez 1994).

As far as informal instruction is concerned, it should begin as soon as students are taught science. From the very moment that students perform their first experiments, they should have good examples to follow and they should at least have a sense of appropriate conduct in science. As their science education becomes more sophisticated and refined, they will develop a keener sense of what amounts to ethical science. At all stages of education, students will need good examples to follow. Since science education usually begins in elementary school, educators who teach at the elementary, junior high school, and high school levels all have a responsibility to set good examples for doing methodologically and ethically sound science. Educators in colleges and universities have the same responsibility.

As far as formal instruction is concerned, I see no reason to begin it before college. Most students will not have the critical thinking and writing skills necessary for formal instruction in ethics until they enter college, and many students will simply not need or desire such instruction. Formal instruction in research ethics seems most appropriate for students when they have decided or are in the process of deciding to pursue careers in science. At this point they will be prepared to respond to such instruction and they will also be more willing to receive it. Thus, it would be appropriate for students to take courses in research ethics when they are advanced undergraduates majoring in science and/or when they are beginning their graduate education in science.

Despite the best efforts of scientists to teach research ethics, some people will violate ethical standards and there will therefore arise a need to enforce them. If standards are to be enforced, they need to be made public in the appropriate communication forum, which may vary from discipline to discipline. Some example of places where ethical standards can be publicized include the codes of conduct published in scientific journals, publications by various research organizations, such as the NSF and NIH, ethical codes adopted by various professional societies, and the rules and regulations of organizations that sponsor research, such as universities and government laboratories.

Standards that are made public should also be clearly defined, since people cannot be expected to adhere to vaguely or poorly stated rules and regulations. Of course, ethical standards in science are by their very nature highly vague, ambiguous, and often controversial, but this does not mean that we should not attempt to express them as clearly as possible or that they should not be enforced.

Cases of possible misconduct should be handled at a local level by people working within the relevant disciplines, wherever possible. When further investigation and adjudication is required, cases may work their way up science's regulatory hierarchy, but external investigations of science should be the exception rather than the rule. Scientists working within various disciplines should be allowed to police themselves; people should be brought in from outside the discipline or outside science only as a last resort. Although science should be held accountable to the general public, people from outside of a particular scientific discipline usually lack the knowledge or the expertise to pass judgment on scientific conduct within that discipline. In order to promote justice and protect individual rights, any investigation of alleged misconduct must also protect the rights of the accused and the accusers. Anyone who is accused of misconduct should receive a fair and impartial hearing, and scientific whistle blowers should not suffer repercussions. Since cases of scientific misconduct now frequently make big headlines in the media, it is especially important to protect due process in science, since trials by the media can amount to witch hunts.

Sanctions for misconduct should vary in their degree of severity. There are two reasons why there should be sanctions which vary in severity. By having punishments which vary in severity we can give violators the punishments they deserve: the more severe the crime, the more severe the punishment. Concerning the nature of such sanctions, that issue is best decided by scientists. Some possible sanctions include: warnings or strong expressions of disapproval, publication of errata or retractions in journals, censorship, exclusion from scientific societies, a ban on publication or presentation at scientific meetings, denial of research funds, dismissal from a university position, fines, or even ostracism.

Science needs various governing bodies to promote ethics education and enforcement. Science already has some important governing bodies, such as professional societies, ethics committees for funding organizations, and university committees on the conduct of research. Despite these important beginnings, science still needs to develop a well-organized system for administering scientific justice. This system would help scientists coordinate ethics education and enforcement. To this end, I would make the following recommendations:

(1) Every research organization should have a committee for research ethics. The function of these committees would be to investigate cases of possible misconduct within the organization, to administer sanctions, where appropriate, and to promote ethical standards through education and publicity.

(2) Every leader of a research team in any scientific organization should be aware of the appropriate channels for reporting possible misconduct in science. Leaders of research teams are responsible for insuring that scientists under their direction are familiar with various ethical standards and that they follow them.

(3) All broader scientific research institutions, including professional societies and funding organizations, should have research ethics committees. The function of such committees would be similar to the function of the committees at lower levels, except their jurisdiction would be broader in scope, i.e. national or possibly international, and they would serve as a medium for resolving disputes that cannot be resolved or handled at lower levels.

(4) There should be international committees on research ethics, sponsored by scientific societies or by governments. Because much research these days involves scientists from different

nationalities and scientific research has global consequences, we need to address concerns about research ethics at an international level. International committees on research ethics could help establish international standards of conduct while recognizing some important variations among different nations. They would also help to investigate or resolve possible cases of misconduct or ethical disputes that are international in character (Krystyna 1996). The race to isolate the AIDS virus and the ensuing priority dispute between French and American scientists and the problems of protecting intellectual property rights at an international level provide us with perfect examples of why we need international committees on research ethics (see Hilts 1991a).

These recommendations, if put in place, should go a long way to promoting ethical science. However, one might wonder whether we need even stronger, more formal rules and regulations. If we take seriously my earlier claim that science is a profession, then perhaps science should follow the model we find in well-established professions, such as medicine or law. In these professions various states and nations have governing bodies that issue licenses to practice the profession. These governing bodies play an important role in upholding professional standards through education and enforcement and they have the power to take away these licenses if people violate professional standards. In order to uphold standards of conduct in science, one might argue, scientists could establish agencies that issue licenses to practice science that have the power to punish scientists who violate professional standards.

I think most scientists would resist the idea of establishing formal agencies with the power to issue or take away licenses to practice research. There are some good reasons for not following a model one finds in other more established professions (Woodward and Goodstein 1996). First, a highly professionalized science would place too many constraints on scientific freedom and would undermine scientific creativity. Second, a highly professionalized science would discourage or in some cases halt contributions by scientific amateurs, who often make significant impacts on science. An amateur might be a self-employed, perhaps intellectually isolated, experimenter or theorizer, such as the young Einstein. An amateur might be someone who is well-qualified in one discipline, but who has crossed disciplinary boundaries to try to work on a problem in another discipline, such as Francis Crick. People who cross disciplines bring up another problem with the more professional model, namely that it would not be able to accommodate inter-disciplinary research very well. If a person is licensed as a chemist can they publish a paper on electrical engineering? For now, it seems best to view science as a profession though one that is (and should be) less professional and more flexible than other professions.

Finally, in Chapter 1 I mentioned that the contemporary research environment probably contributes to unethical conduct in science (Woodward and Goodstein 1996). Though I have no quick fixes for the research environment, I have a few suggestions:

(1) Make hiring and promotion decisions based on the quality of research, not the quantity of publications.

(2) Reward scientists for mentoring; make mentoring a key part of science education.

(3) Stress accountability in authorship practices; develop new categories for acknowledging contributions to scientific works that accurately reflect different responsibilities.

(4) Set policies that promote due process in the investigation of misconduct.

(5) Set policies that promote fair opportunities in science for underrepresented groups and junior researchers.

APPENDIX
Case Studies

This appendix contains some hypothetical cases for analysis and discussion. Most of these cases are based on real situations, however. I have included some questions at the end of each case, but readers may wish to raise and ask additional questions. Since I have provided relatively brief descriptions of these cases, readers may wish to discuss the additional information that would be helpful in reaching a decision or options that I have not mentioned.

1. Omitting data

Jane Doe is a graduate student helping Dick Jonas analyze data on a spiral galaxy in order to determine its velocity, luminosity, and rate of spin. The data were produced by an infra-red telescope at a nearby mountain. Jonas intends to publish the results in an astronomical journal and list her as a co-author. In order to have an example of how to analyze the data, she reads a paper Jonas published several years ago that uses the same statistical techniques. She begins a search for the old data used to write this paper and to her surprise she finds that the records do not agree with the results the professor reported in the paper. It appears as if Jonas omitted about 10 percent of the recorded data. Jane talks to Jonas about this discrepancy and he explains that he omitted some of the data because he felt the telescope was not working correctly when it produced these poor results. She presses him further on this issue and he tells her to trust his judgment. Should Jonas have included all of the data in his paper? If so, how should he have discussed problems with the data? Should Jane pursue this matter any further?

2. Benign data fabrication?

Victor Johnson and Susan Klein are graduate students analyzing soil samples for Roberto Martinez, who is conducting a study on soil acidity for the state of Idaho. The study began six months ago and is supposed to be completed this week. Martinez plans to list Johnson and Klein as co-authors when he submits the research to a journal. Each day Johnson and Klein have collected and analyzed soil samples from different parts of the state. They are almost near the end of their study when they realize that they forgot to record the data for six soil samples taken three weeks ago. They remember the approximate locations of the samples, but not the exact locations. Johnson suggests that they should go ahead and record some exact locations for these samples since this act will not have a significant affect on the outcome of the study and they do not have time to go back to the sites and collect samples again. Klein is not sure that they should make up these results. Should Klein abide by Johnson's suggestion? Should she talk to Martinez about this issue?

3. Traffic statistics

Obuto Kimura and Nathan Riley are studying the effects of seat-belt laws on traffic fatalities in Utah. They have collected the following data on traffic fatalities:

Year	Fatalities
1991	290
1992	270
1993	250
1994	245
1995	230
1996	215

Utah's seat belt-law went into effect on 1 January 1994. During the three years before the law went into effect, Utah averaged 270 traffic fatalities per year; after the law went into effect this number dropped to 230 fatalities per year. They submit their findings to the Utah Department of Transportation and prepare a press release. In discussing the data, Kimura and Riley will conclude that the new seat-belt laws caused a 15 percent reduction in traffic fatalities. Have they misrepresented the data?

4. Publishing a correction

Collin, Wood, and Butamo have written a paper on the effects of UV radiation on plant mutations. After reading the paper, Butamo notices that it contains a minor mathematical error. Butamo mentions this error to Wood, who wrote the section of the paper that contains the error. Wood tells Butamo that the error will not affect the paper's findings and that they should ignore it. Should they submit a correction to the journal? What should Butamo do if his colleagues do not want to submit a correction?

5. Funding and fraud

The DOD has undertaken a project to develop a space-based anti-missile system. The plan will place several satellites in orbit around the earth armed with powerful lasers to destroy ballistic missiles. Gloria Grant and Hugh Long have been working for this program since its inception and currently have a two million dollar grant from the DOD that expires in a few months. In order to renew the grant they need to present the DOD with some results. Although Grant and Long will have no trouble convincing the DOD to renew their funding, during the course of their research they come to a disturbing conclusion: the space-based defense system won't work. Grant and Long discuss their conclusion with some other researchers who are working on the project, and these other researchers agree with their assessment. However, none of the researchers want to share this information with the DOD, since accepting this conclusion would jeopardize their funding. In order to continue obtaining funding, these other researchers express enthusiasm for the program to the DOD, Congress, and the media. Grant and Long also would like not to jeopardize the program, since the DOD money funds their research, but at the same time they feel an obligation not to deceive the public. Should they continue to express enthusiasm for the program or should they reveal their reservations? Is an expression of enthusiasm tantamount to fraud? Do any of these researchers have a conflict of interest?

6. Research on soluble fiber

Ian McGruder is conducting research on the effects of soluble fiber on cholesterol levels, which is being sponsored by Oatcorp. In clinical trials, he obtains results that indicate that a diet high in soluble fiber can lower blood cholesterol levels by 40 percent. After completing his experiments, he buys 400 additional shares of Oatcorp and submits a paper to the *Journal of the American Medical Association*. (He already owned 100 shares of the company before he completed the study.) In the paper, McGruder discloses his source of funding and his ownership of the company's stock. Does McGruder have a conflict of interest? Should the journal publish his paper if it stands up to peer review? Has McGruder done anything wrong?

7. Reviewing a book manuscript

Jill Westerhoff has been sent a book manuscript to review for Wadman Publishing. The manuscript is an introduction to developmental psychology, and she is currently working on a textbook on the same topic. If this rival textbook is published and is well received, then her own textbook may not receive adequate recognition. Does she have a conflict of interest? If she does, what should she do?

8. Sharing information

Sarah Huxely and Curtis Weston are developing a new, more efficient process for desalinating water, which they hope to patent. At a conference they discover that Bream and Lorenzo are conducting similar experiments and are also close to perfecting a new desalination process. After the conference, Bream and Lorenzo send Huxely and Weston an email message asking them for some more information about their experimental designs and preliminary results. Should Huxely and Weston refuse this request?

9. Beaten to the punch

Twelve months ago, John Edwards and his colleagues submitted a paper on newly developed super-conductive materials to a journal and they have not heard the journal's decision. They decide to call up the editors and they are told that the paper has been held up by a reviewer who has not had time to read it yet. They are pretty sure that the reviewer is one of several colleagues who are working on the same topic. To their dismay, they learn that one of these colleagues has "beaten them to the punch" since he will be presenting a paper on the very same topic at an international conference. They suspect foul play: either their ideas have been stolen or a reviewer has delayed publication of their paper in order to win a race for priority. But they cannot prove these suspicions. What should they do?

10. Too good to be true

Ibu Aramuto is reading a paper on the effects of a new fertilizer on the growth of corn. The research was funded by Growfast and was conducted by several scientists working at Iowa State University. Aramuto doubts the validity of the research even though it has been published in an established journal because the new fertilizer is purportedly twice as effective as any previously developed fertilizer and the results appear "too neat": there is nearly a linear relationship between the amount of the fertilizer given to corn and growth. He suspects that the data may have been erroneous or fraudulent because they are "too good to be true." He decides to repeat the experiments described in the paper but cannot reproduce its results. He contacts the authors about their paper and they are vague and evasive. Are his suspicions well founded? What should he do?

11. Owning data

Li Park is a postdoctoral student in microbiology at University T. During her stay at T, she has been working on the development of an enzyme that inhibits the growth of blood vessels. She hopes that the enzyme could be useful in treating cancer by preventing the flow of blood to tumors. She has just received an appointment to conduct the same research in a private laboratory, BioErg. The private laboratory requests that Park take all of the data with her to BioErg. However, her supervisor, Gregor Grunbaum, insists that the data must stay in his lab. Grunbaum would like to use the data in his own research, and he is concerned that if BioErg acquires the data it will not be available to other scientists. Who should be allowed to control this data? If BioErg develops any products from this data, should it provide royalties to University T?

12. Nazi data

Raymond Martin is studying the effects of heat exhaustion on human beings. His research is funded by the NIH and has been approved by his university's IRB. He has been using volunteers who have been fully informed of the dangers of this research. He has been carefully monitoring their responses and has been very cautious. He believes that his research can have valuable consequences for society, since it may lead to better ways to treat heat stroke and heat prostration. But Martin recognizes that there are limits to his research: he cannot, for ethical and legal reasons, cause significant harm to his subjects or bring them to the point of death.

A colleague informs Martin that the Nazis did experiments on heat prostration that went much further than his experiments will go. Martin would like to gain access to this data, to assess its reliability, and possibly to use it in his own work. He realizes that this research was obtained under heinous conditions and that it is tainted by the Nazi legacy, but he believes that it could still be quite useful. He applies for a supplemental grant from the NIH to study the Nazi data. Should Martin be allowed to gain access to this data? Should the NIH fund his attempt to evaluate the Nazi data? If he does obtain the Nazi data and it turns out to be valid, should he be allowed to publish it in a paper on heat exhaustion?

13. Allocation of telescope time

The Department of Astronomy at the University of Montana has a brand new radio telescope. It has received many requests to use this instrument and it can only grant about half of them. Of the sixty requests, twenty of them are from younger researchers, i.e. graduate students and postdoctoral researchers. None of the proposals from the younger researchers seem as impressive as most of the proposals from the older researchers. Some people have suggested that the department give the younger people a break and accept some of these proposals anyway. Others have replied that this would simply be a waste of valuable telescope time. What should the department do?

14. Private fossil collecting

Buck Anderson owns a fossil collecting company, Fossil Hunters, that collects fossils and sells them to museums and private patrons. Anderson used to be a professor of paleontology at the University of Colorado before leaving academia to manage his business. He is one of the world's foremost authorities on finding, collecting, and preserving fossils. Last year he sold a Tyrannosaurus Rex skull to a Japanese collector for two million dollars. The skull was found on privately-owned land in Wyoming. Anderson has recently arranged a deal with the Governor of Wyoming and a legislative review panel for fossil prospecting on State lands. The State will allow his company to collect fossils on State lands. In return, Fossil Hunters will pay the State a special 30 percent tax on all fossils sold that are collected on State property. Half of these funds will go into Wyoming's General Education Fund and half will help support the University of Wyoming. The State's Finance Office estimates that Wyoming could collect up to five million dollars a year under this arrangement. Many people in the legislature view this deal as a good way to increase Wyoming's tax base, which has steadily declined due to decreasing revenues from oil industry levies. However, many faculty members and students at the university object to this deal on the grounds that the fossils are a valuable resource for science which should not be sold to private collectors. The fossils should remain public property and should be available for research and education. Critics of this agreement are also concerned that Fossil Hunters will damage research sites and other fossils that they do not sell. Anderson replies that his excavators are very careful and methodical, and that science will lose more fossils to weathering than to private collecting. Is this arrangement between the Wyoming and Fossil Hunters unethical?

15. Plagiarism?

Stanley Goldwire is writing a paper on civil war photography for a class on the history of technology. As he is doing his research, he finds a paper in an obscure journal that says everything he wants to say and more. He decides to use and cite the paper extensively in his own paper; almost every paragraph contains a reference to this paper. Though he does not copy any sentences from this paper, many of the sentences in his paper are very similar to sentences in the other paper; he makes only minor changes to reflect his own wording. Is this plagiarism? Is it unethical?

16. Unethical teamwork?

Shirley Steadman and Agnes Horowitz are good friends and share the same apartment. They collaborate on many assignments. They are both writing a paper on teaching evolution in schools for their introductory biology class. They do most of their research together and their papers have virtually identical outlines and bibliographies. Although the wording in their papers is different, their ideas are very similar. They do not cite each other or mention their collaboration when they turn in their papers. Have Steadman and Horowitz committed plagiarism? Have they acted unethically? How should their professor respond to this situation if he notices that the papers are very similar?

17. Honorary authorship

Richard Ramsey opens a new issue of the journal *Cell* and discovers that he is listed as a co-author on one of the papers and he cannot recall having contributed anything to the research. The first author is a former doctoral student. He emails the first author who tells him that he stuck Ramsey's name on the paper because he benefited from Ramsey's insights, and he thought having Ramsey's name on the paper would give it more prestige and make it more likely to be read. Ramsey is flattered but upset. What should he do?

18. Credit where credit's due

Two years ago, Stanley Smith agreed to supervise Herbert McDowell's master's thesis on cockroach mating, and he is currently supervising McDowell's Ph.D. thesis. While reading Smith's latest paper, McDowell notices that many of the speculations in the discussion section of the paper are ideas that he had suggested to Smith during some of their many informal discussions. Smith did not give any form of acknowledgment to McDowell in the paper. Does McDowell deserve to be listed as an author? Does he deserve a mention in the acknowledgments section? Did Smith exploit McDowell?

19. Credit for lab technicians?

John Jonart and Sara Stumpf are biotechnicians employed by the University U. They have signed an agreement to transfer their patent rights to the university, and they have also agreed (informally) not to ask for authorship on published papers. Normally, they do not offer much conceptual or theoretical insight, but after ten years of experience they now have a great deal of working knowledge of experimental procedures. As it turns out, they have offered some valuable advice and suggestions for the testing of a new drug to treat epilepsy. They now wish to be listed as co-authors and receive copyright and patent rights, based on their valuable contributions. But the university and its researchers refuse their request. Should they be given at least some credit or intellectual property rights? Are their prior agreements fair?

20. The first author

Arendorf, Dun-Ow, Hanscum, Hernstein, Mirabella, Robertson, Ramos, and Williams are meteorologists at eight different universities in the western United States. They have each made a major contribution to a study on the relation between thunderstorm size and tornado activity. The study has been accepted in a prestigious scientific journal and will probably be cited many times in the literature. Since many people will cite their study as "first author et al," the first author of the study will receive significantly more recognition than the other authors. Three of the authors, Ramos, Williams and Hanscum, have indicated that they do not care whether they are listed first, but the other writers all have a desire to be the first author. Mirabella and Robertson did most of the writing for the paper; Arendorf and Dun-Ow did most of the grant writing; and Hernstein organized the whole project. All authors collected and analyzed data. Who should be listed first? How should the authors make this decision?

21. Press conference

Anthony Lopez and Adrian White have just completed some experiments demonstrating that a commonly used food additive causes severe birth defects in laboratory rats. They plan to submit the paper to a journal before making a public announcement about the food additive, but they feel compelled to hold a press conference first in order to inform the public and prevent any further birth defects from the food additive. What should they do?

22. Softening results

A. J. Hoyt and Cathy Compton have shown that the notion of ideal weight is a myth: most of the so-called ideal weights set by insurance companies and health organizations are not very helpful in finding out a person's most optimal weight. They have recently published a new set of recommendations based on body type, muscular strength, and percentage body fat in the *Journal of Nutrition*, and they plan to hold a press conference soon. Hoyt would like to announce their recommendations in full detail, but Compton does not think that the public could understand or accept the complete truth, because their recommendations are complicated and physically demanding. Compton recommends that they greatly simplify and soften their recommendations in the press conference in order to more effectively motivate compliance with their recommendations. Those who want the whole truth and nothing but the truth can always consult their journal article. Should Hoyt and Compton simplify and soften their results for public consumption?

23. Press distortion

Kia Kurfunkle is the lead author of a study showing a statistical connection between moderate alcohol consumption and reduced heart disease. A reporter for the *Daily Reporter* interviews her about her research and she carefully explains the study and its significance. The next morning a story appears in the paper with the headline, "Alcohol consumption reduces heart disease." She continues to read the story and finds that it does not stress the importance of moderate consumption nor does it discuss the fact that the results do not apply to alcoholics. The story will be distributed to hundreds of papers over the associated press. What should she do?

24. Publishing embarassing results

Stephen Polgar has been studying patterns of family violence in Appalachian Communities for five years. He has focused on people living near the community of Blue Elk, North Carolina, and has conducted his research through interviews, an examination of police and school reports, and field observations. Throughout his research, he has consulted with community leaders and various authorities in the area. He has also obtained informed consent from his subjects. He has now completed his work and is ready to publish his results. After reading a draft of his paper, some of the leaders object to publishing the results on grounds that they are not very flattering: Polgar's research indicates high levels of child abuse, spousal abuse, and other types of domestic violence, and it shows that domestic violence is associated with alcohol abuse and crime. Polgar promises to protect confidentiality by changing the names of subjects, towns, streets, rivers, but the leaders say that people will still be able to tell that their community is the subject of the study. Polgar knows that the law allows him to publish his results, but he is worried about making the people in the community upset. He and his colleagues have been studying the people of Blue Elk for years, and they do not want to destroy the research site by alienating this community. Should Polgar publish the results as they stand? Should he publish them but try to "candy coat" them in such a way that they don't sound so bad? Should he not publish his results?

25. Ownership of herbal medicine

Bruce Heyman has been conducting research in the Amazon jungle on the use of herbal medicines by indigenous tribes. He has been living with a tribe for several years and has become good friends with the tribe's medicine man, who has shown Heyman where some of the plants grow and how to prepare them. Heyman's research is being sponsored by Johnson Laboratories, which hopes to develop some marketable products from herbal medicines. In the last few months, the medicine man has used a herbal remedy to reverse tumor growth in the breasts of women in the tribe. Heyman concludes that the remedy could play an important role in curing breast cancer and so he asks the medicine man for a sample of the herbal preparation. He analyzes the chemical ingredients in the remedy and sends his results back to Johnson Laboratories. Johnson Laboratories reports that their chemists were able to synthesize some of the compounds in the herbal remedy and they want to begin controlled studies of this medicine. However, they need more samples of the cure before they can begin these studies. Heyman tells the medicine man about Johnson Laboratories' interest in the herbal remedy and he asks for more samples. He also informs him that Johnson Laboratories will generously compensate the medicine man and the tribe for their help. The medicine man decides that he does not want his herbal knowledge to be used in this fashion. He believes that the knowledge is sacred and should stay within the tribe and should only be used by medicine men or their assistants. Dr. Heyman knows that he can probably force the medicine man to yield his herbal knowledge by asking the local authorities for their help and promising them that Johnson Laboratories will compensate them for obtaining the medicine man's cooperation. What should he do? Who owns this herbal knowledge?

26. Education, research, and money

Robert Carlson is a professor of entomology at the University of Georgia. He is currently conducting research on fire ants which is funded by Myrmex. Although this research takes up much of his time, the university has allowed him to have fewer educational responsibilities than other faculty members. Nevertheless, he still teaches one graduate seminar each semester, advises and supervises graduate students, and serves on various committees. Myrmex asks Carlson to devote his time almost exclusively to developing a new fire ant poison, and Carlson asks his department chairperson, Lisa Knopf, to petition the administration for a redirection of his teaching responsibilities. Knopf is hesitant to grant this request for several reasons. First, it will not be easy for the Department of Entomology to take over Carlson's teaching responsibilities. Second, some other faculty members have already expressed their dissatisfaction with Carlson, claiming that his research accomplishments make him a "prima donna" who receives special treatment. Third, she believes that allowing Carlson to do nothing but research could set a bad precedent in that other professors might seek a similar reclassification, which could further disrupt departmental unity and create a kind of academic hierarchy. On the other hand, Carlson is an internationally recognized researcher and an excellent mentor/teacher. Knopf knows that he could easily get a job at another university or in private industry if she refuses his request. What should she do?

27. Affirmative action

High Plains University has told its Department of Physics that they must hire a woman this year. The department has no women on its faculty. After advertising their position and encouraging some well-qualified women to apply, the department is ready to make its hiring decision. It has received 115 applications, only three of which are from women. After interviewing two women and two men, the department determines that while the two women are competent, they are clearly less qualified than the men they interviewed. Should the department try to hire one of the two women or try to hire the most qualified person they can get?

28. An affair in the lab

Marianne Yoder has been having an affair with one of her chemistry graduate students, Sam Green, for three months. The affair was secret at first, but now all of the graduate students in her laboratory know about it and they are beginning to resent her involvement with Sam Green. Several students talk to Salvador Seleno, the department chairman, about this situation. They say they do not feel comfortable working with Green and Yoder when the two are together, and they believe that Yoder is showing favoritism toward Green. Yoder is one the best professors in the University, and Green is a promising student. Is this affair unethical? What should Seleno do about this situation?

29. Grant management

Anne Wilson has obtained a $50,000 grant from the NSF to study the effects of magnetism on conductivity. In her proposal, she said that she would conduct experiments on two metals, copper and aluminum. While conducting these experiments, Wilson decided to do some exploratory research on the effects of magnetism on several other metals. She funded these experiments by using money that was designated for travel and salaries for graduate assistants. Did Wilson do anything wrong? Should she have consulted with the NSF about her exploratory research?

30. Personalities and tenure decisions

The senior professors at the Department of Physics at Hastings University are deciding whether they will recommend that Raymond Abenia, a solid-state physicist, should receive tenure. Abenia's case is not an easy one: he is a fine teacher and advisor but his publication record is less than spectacular. He has barely met the minimum number of publications the department requires to be considered for tenure and his letters from outside reviewers are mixed. Four of the department's nine senior members believe that he should receive tenure based on his teaching, advising, and the quality of his research. Four of the senior members are undecided at this point. The person who is best qualified to evaluate Abenia's work, Oliver Ormadoze, has had a "falling out" with Abenia over the supervision of graduate students, one of whom is dating Ormadoze's daughter. Ormadoze believes that Abenia has allowed his students to act unprofessionally in the laboratory: Abenia's students have played rock and roll music in the lab, they have ordered pizza, and they have brought their children into the lab. (Abenia is very popular with the students; Ormadoze is known as a bit of a curmudgeon.) Since Ormadoze and Abenia are the only two solid-state physicists in the department, the four undecided colleagues are likely to put a great deal of weight on Ormadoze's assessment of Abenia's work. If he refuses to offer his opinion of Abenia, the colleagues may take this as a non-endorsement. If the department presents a split tenure decision to the university, it is likely that Abenia will not receive tenure. Ormadoze is having a difficult time deciding how to respond to this tenure case and his personal feelings may be interfering with his ability to make a professional judgment. Should Ormadoze abstain from this decision and/or withdraw from the discussion? Should he try to set aside his feelings and evaluate Ormadoze as a scientist? Would it be unethical for Ormadoze to give his honest assessment of Abenia at the tenure meeting?

31. Unfair treatment of graduate students?

Jessica Parker and Charley Ward are graduate assistants for Harold Arthur. Their duties include grading tests for his introduction to a biochemistry class and assisting him in his own research, which focuses on junk DNA. They are both Ph.D. students and are also working on their own research. One day, Arthur calls Parker and Ward into his office and announces that they need to devote more time to sequencing DNA for his project. Parker and Ward are already working three hours a day sequencing junk DNA, two hours a day leading biochemistry labs, and two hours a day grading and tutoring biochemistry students. They both have to devote a great deal of time to studying for their Ph.D. oral exams, which are in three weeks. They barely have time for their own research. Has Arthur treated his students fairly? How should Parker and Ward respond to Arthur's demand?

32. An irresponsible mentor?

Carol Levingston is writing a master's thesis on the effects of ultraviolet radiation on plant growth. George Nijhoff is her thesis advisor and mentor. Three other professors are on her MS committee. During her oral defense, two members of the committee claim that the thesis is poorly organized and poorly written, and the third member says that it fails to mention several recent and important studies in the section that reviews the literature. The committee votes to deny Levingston an MS in botany and recommends that she rework the thesis so she can complete it at the end of the next semester. The following day Levingston discusses this episode with the chairperson of the Botany Department. She complains that Nijhoff did not supervise her work adequately, that he did not offer any substantial comments on earlier drafts of the thesis, and that he did not tell her about the recent studies that she failed to include. Was Nijhoff an irresponsible mentor? How should chairperson respond to this situation?

33. An AZT Trial

Four physicians from the US are conducting a clinical trial in country Z on the effectiveness of AZT, a drug used to treat HIV and AIDS. Patients are randomly assigned to one of two groups, a group that receives AZT and another that receives a placebo. The clinical trial would be unethical and possibly illegal in the US and other industrialized nations because AZT is a standard treatment for HIV/AIDS in those countries. However, Country Z is very poor, and most HIV/AIDS patients in this nation do not have access to AZT. The physicians maintain that their trial is ethical and humane because it is providing the possibility of treatment to patients who would not receive any treatment at all. Is this trial ethical? Is it possible for a clinical trial to be unethical in one country but ethical in another? Are the researchers exploiting their patients?

34. Continuing a clinical trial

Terry Jones has agreed to enroll patients in a clinical trial which will test an arthritis drug. The trial uses randomized, double-blind techniques that divide the population of patients into a group that receives the drug and a standard arthritis treatment and a group that receives the same treatment and a placebo. As patients enroll in the trial, their treatment will be randomized in that incoming patients will have a 50 percent chance of receiving either the drug under test or a placebo. The trial is supposed to include 400 patients and will last up to four years. After two years of the trial, Jones has found that the drug provides significant relief for arthritis symptoms for 90 percent of his patients. The trial is halfway completed and Jones has agreed to continue his part of the study for another two years. During this time, 50 percent of his patients will receive a placebo when he believes that an effective arthritis drug is now available. Should he stop enrolling patients in this trial and offer all of his patients this new drug?

35. Humane data falsification?

Rudolph Clemens has agreed to participate in a randomized clinical trial to test the effectiveness of an experimental drug in treating prostate cancer. In order to have some control over the variables in the trial, the study's protocols require that patients who are enrolled in the trial meet specific requirements concerning age, date of diagnosis, and previous cancer history. Incoming patients are divided into two groups on a random basis; patients in one group receive the drug; patients in the other group receive standard treatments, which may include prostate removal. (Many patients who have their prostate removed suffer from impotency and other undesirable side effects.) After conducting the study for three years, Clemens has acquired enough data to determine that the new drug offers significant medical benefits to prostate cancer patients. Other physicians enrolling patients in the trial support these preliminary conclusions. At this point, he decides that he should try to help as many patients as possible. In order to do this, he falsifies fifty patient records in order to qualify them for participation in the study so that about half of those patients will qualify for the experimental treatment. (Patients who do not qualify for the study would still be able to choose standard therapies.) Has Clemens acted unethically? Could this study design be modified in some way to allow more patients to benefit from this experimental drug?

36. Research on prisoners

Sam Adams and Wu-lee Wong are conducting cancer research in country X. So far they have only conducted statistical analyses of cancer rates in various populations. They have found that cancer rates are associated with various lifestyles and diets. While conducting their research, they have continually consulted with local authorities. Today, the authorities offer them the opportunity to conduct some experiments on a human population. The experiments are being proposed by some scientists at University Y and would be performed on prisoners serving long sentences. These experiments would offer researchers the opportunity to observe the long-term effects of various diets on cancer and could significantly impact human knowledge of cancer and its prevention. However, Adams and Wong have some strong moral reservations about these experiments, given the country's record on human rights. They believe that the prison system is a highly coercive environment and that their subjects will have no choice but to participate in the experiments. However, their colleagues from this country have no such reservations about doing this research and see it as one way that the prisoners can repay their debt to society. Should Adams and Wong help conduct these experiments?

37. Drug testing in the Navy

The Navy has been training some of its best divers for long-term exposure to cold water temperatures and has been conducting experiments on ways to improve cold water performance. One of these experiments involves the development of a chemical that will function like anti-freeze in human blood, and it will enable the body and its cells to withstand colder temperatures. During animal testing, the chemical has proven to be safe and reasonably effective, but it is still highly experimental. The Navy now plans to test the drug on human subjects and it orders fifty navy divers to participate in experiments with the chemical. Any divers that refuse these orders will be court-marshaled. Are the Navy's actions immoral?

38. A study of aggression in rats

Chris Chisholm and Christie Chase have isolated a hormone in rats that causes aggressive behavior. Rats that are administered this hormone become very aggressive and violent. The hormone is very similar to human testosterone in its structure and function, and they believe that some of their results will have significant implications for human aggression.

When given this hormone, some of the rats become so aggressive that they literally tear each other apart in fits of rage. Many rats die in their experiments and those that live are severely mutilated. Chisholm and Chase have also found that it is difficult to predict the exact dosage of the hormone it takes to produce these fits, since it seems to vary from rat to rat; some rats become very aggressive with low dosages; others can withstand higher dosage without becoming overly aggressive. Some animal rights activists have learned about these experiments and they are staging protests to stop them. Should these experiments be allowed to continue?

39. Super chickens

The Biotech Corporation is developing a procedure for creating a super chicken. Using recombinant DNA techniques, the company will create a chicken that will have extremely high levels of growth hormones. The company estimates that the chicken will grow to four times the size of normal chickens, mature twice as fast, have a higher resistance to disease, and have 50 percent lower body fat. However, preliminary results also indicate that these chickens will suffer some adverse side effects: due to excessively high levels of these hormones, they will be very agitated and "highly strung." They will also have brittle bones and weak muscles and tendons. As a result, they will have abnormally high injury and mortality rates due to physical exertion and normal activities. However, super chicken farming should still be economically lucrative, since injured and dead chickens can still be used in a variety of chicken products. Biotech's patents on their super chicken are being reviewed by the United States' PTO. Should Biotech be allowed to patent this animal?

40. Bear medicine

Since 600 AD, herbalists in Country C have used bear parts to treat a variety of ailments. As a result of continual killing of bears for medicinal purposes, the bear population in C is now becoming endangered and C's government has decided to raise bears in captivity for medicinal purposes. Officials in C view this endeavor as a way of protecting an endangered species and benefiting human beings at the same time. The bears may vanish from the wild, but the population will be preserved in captivity. Is there anything wrong with using bears like this? If you find this use of bears objectionable, would you allow cows or pigs to be raised for medical purposes?

41. A racist conference?

Ellen Iverson is organizing a conference on genetic factors in crime. The conference will draw people from many different fields, including genetics, sociology, criminal justice, political science, anthropology, and philosophy. It will include people who represent different views on the subject, and it will not be one-sided. However, some students and faculty are protesting against this conference on the grounds that it is racist. As a result, the University Q has backed out of its offer to sponsor this conference. Iverson was about to cancel the conference when she received a call from a conservative think-tank offering to fund the entire conference. The conference could take place off university property at a local hotel. However, Iverson is worried that if she accepts this offer, the whole conference will be perceived as racist even if it has no racist implications whatsoever. Should she accept the funding? Should the university have withdrawn its support of the conference?

42. The politics of disease

Several studies on the politics of health care funding indicate that 70 percent of the NIH's funds over the past thirty years have supported research on white, male populations. In order to correct for racial and sexual inequities in the study of disease and increase medical knowledge about human health, NIH has decided to target research on specific populations, such as women and various racial and ethnic groups. In the future, the NIH will set aside up to 30 percent of its funds to sponsor research on diseases that primarily affect these populations. Is this a fair policy? Could it create any ethical problems?

43. Research on perceptual speed

Rebecca Clearheart is a psychologist who has a grant from the NIH to study the effects of aging on perceptual speed. The purpose of her research is to determine whether perceptual speed peaks at a certain age, whether it slows down as people age, and whether people can perform certain activities to enhance perceptual speed. Recently, a senior citizens group has learned about her research. The group has written hundreds of letters protesting her research on the grounds that it could be used to discriminate against the elderly and could contribute to age bias. Should the NIH continue funding this research?

44. Settling ownership claims

The Canadian government and a tribe of Native Americans living on an island off the coast of Canada are engaged in a dispute over land rights. The Native Americans claim the entire island as their natural place of residence. The Canadian government claims that this island is not their natural place of residence and that part of the island belongs to Canada. This case has gone to court, and the Canadian government has asked an anthropologist, Ginger Kearney, to give expert testimony in this case. The anthropologist has studied these people for over twenty years and her research has been funded, in large part, by the Canadian government. In her studies, Kearney has determined that the Native Americans' claims about the island being their natural place of residence are false. If she conveys this information to the court, it is likely that the Native Americans will lose this property dispute. If she refuses to testify in court, it is likely that the government will find another expert witness that will support its position. As an anthropologist, she is committed to serving as an advocate of the people she studies. But in this case her duty to be an advocate conflicts with her legal and ethical obligations to be honest. Should she present the court with an honest, objective appraisal of the tribe's ownership claims? Should she withhold or distort information? Should she refuse to testify? Since her research has been sponsored by the Canadian government, does she have an additional obligation to act on behalf of the Canadian people in this dispute?

45. Environmental activism

The town of Butterfield, NM, is holding a hearing on banning the use of pesticides that control mosquitoes on the grounds that the pesticides are threatening a local toad species, which is on the verge of extinction. Many scientists at a local university, ECO U, have offered their expert testimony and opinions. Each side in this debate has been allowed to call in its own witnesses. Roger Rubble, a professor at ECO University, has taken an active role in the movement to ban this pesticide: he has written newspaper columns, appeared on television, circulated flyers, and gone door-to-door talking to people. Many of Rubble's colleagues and members of the local community are worried that he is overstepping his bounds as a scientist and is now no more than a policy advocate. How can (or should) Rubble participate in this public policy debate?

46. A new pain relief medication

Helen Herskovitz and Stanley Schein have developed a new medication for pain relief while working for Sanguine Laboratories. Preliminary studies indicate that the medication will be dramatically more safe and effective than anything else on the market with none of the side effects associated with non-narcotic pain relievers, such as aspirin, or narcotic ones, such as codeine. It should also be fairly cheap and easy to manufacture once it is fully developed. Herskovitz and Schein brief company officials about this new discovery and the officials decide that the research should be tabled for at least several years. The company also tells Herskovitz and Schein not to publish their results and relinquish the data. The company also manufactures another pain relief medication, neuralgomine, and it needs to recoup the money it has invested in developing and marketing this product before it sells a new one. Herskovitz and Schein are shocked by the company's blatant disregard for the relief of human suffering. They are legally bound to keep their research confidential but they feel a moral obligation to make it public for the good of humanity. Should they publish their research? Should they hold onto their data? What should they do?

47. Co-opted research

Wayne Tillman and several colleagues conduct research on artificial intelligence at MIT and have recently developed a device that can recognize a variety of targets and return gunfire. They have applied for a patent for this device and hope that it will one day be useful in police operations that use special weapons and tactics. However, after applying for this patent, they are visited by officials from the CIA and NSA who inform them that their device poses a threat to national security. The officials ask them to continue their research in a different context: the research would be funded by the DOD and would become highly classified. Lacy Jones, one of Dr. Tillman's colleagues, tells the group that the CIA and NSA would probably lose a legal battle over the control of this research and that the research team need not work for the military in order to continue its work. Even so, many members of the team feel threatened by the CIA and NSA and they would rather simply work for the military than fight its attempt to control their research. What should Tillman and his colleagues do?

48. Environmental consulting

Jerry Jones and Tracy Trek are working for an environmental consulting company, BioData, that is providing information for an oil company, Bedrock Oil (BO). Jones and Trek have been studying a site for BO's proposed oil well. The site is on BO property, five miles outside of the town of River Rock (population 12,500), Wyoming. During some exploratory drilling, Jones and Tek discover a previously uncharted underground tributary close to the drilling site. They suspect that the stream may lead to an aquifer outside of River Rock, the town's sole source of water and they are concerned that an oil well might contaminate the tributary and the town's aquifer. Jones and Trek report this finding to their supervisor, Ken Smith, the Vice President of BioData. Smith tells them to go ahead and prepare their report for BO without mentioning the underground tributary. Jones and Trek protest that the report should include all the information, but Smith tells them that BioData will probably lose BO's contract if it reports all of the information. IF BO does not like its report from BioData, it may stop using BioData as an environmental consultant and hire companies that will give more favorable reports. Smith believes the tributary may not even lead into the aquifer, and that if it does that town's water supply can be adequately protected by shielding the drilling site. Moreover, he also is concerned that environmental activists and health advocates might raise a tremendous protest if information about the tributary becomes public. The protest would create political pressures that would probably prevent BO from drilling at its proposed site. Should Jones and Trek follow Smith's instructions? Should they inform the public about the tributary?

49. A drug company's white lies

Superfoods is a food company that is developing a fat substitute, Fatfree. In order to obtain FDA approval for Fatfree, Superfoods must submit test data to the FDA, which also will test Fatfree. Julie Schwartz has been hired by Superfoods to oversee its testing procedures. In her examination of one of the lab records on Fatfree, she discovers a side-effect that was not reported to the FDA. Seven out of 1,000 subjects experienced dizziness after ingesting Fatfree. She asks her supervisor why this data was not reported to the FDA and he explains that the side-effect is not significant enough or frequent enough to cause concern. He explains that if this side-effect turns out to be more significant or frequent, then the FDA will be able to discover it as well. Telling the FDA about the side-effect, on the other hand, might slow down the approval process. Is it wrong for Superfoods not to tell the FDA about this side-effect? What should Julie do?

50. Sex determination

Two geneticists, Elizabeth Xanatos and Michael Fullwinder have developed two drugs that regulate the sex of offspring. One drug kills sperm that carry an X chromosome; another drug kills sperm that carry a Y chromosome. (In mammals, males carry an X and a Y chromosome; females carry two X chromosomes.) In animal studies on several different mammalian species, the drug has been 95 percent effective at determining the sex of offspring. Xanatos and Fullwinder have applied for patents on these drugs for agricultural uses. They are also planning to begin clinical trials on human subjects. Should these drugs be developed for human use? Should research on human applications of these drugs be banned?

Notes

Chapter 1

1 Unethical behavior or misconduct occurs when a community has a clear consensus about standards but member(s) of the community fail to live up to those standards. An ethical issue is a situation where a community lacks a clear consensus about standards.
2 Instead of citing all of the references for this case, I will provide readers with a list of sources. These include the original paper that allegedly contained fraudulent data (Weaver *et al.* 1986), *New York Times* stories (Hilts 1991b, 1992, 1994b, 1996), and other sources (Sarasohn 1993, Weiss 1996).

Chapter 2

1 For further discussion of meta-ethics see Pojman (1995).
2 For more on moral theories see Pojman (1995).
3 For further discussion of moral pluralism see Hooker (1996).
4 For more on these priority issues see Wueste (1994).
5 For further discussion of ethical relativism, see Gibbard (1986) and Pojman (1990).

Chapter 3

1 I use the term "scientific knowledge" to distinguish the kind of knowledge sought by scientists from other kinds of knowledge. I recognize that there are other kinds of knowledge besides scientific knowledge, such as legal knowledge, moral knowledge, commonsense knowledge, and so on. See Pollock (1986).
2 A growing number of writers who do social, cultural, and historical studies of science

would disagree with my claim that science is the quest for objective knowledge. According to these writers, knowledge is relative to a particular worldview, a particular set of assumptions, or some particular social and political interests. This general idea goes by many different names, such as "relativism," "postmodernism," and "social constructivism." I will not attempt to refute this position in this book, but I will provide the reader with references. For a defense of the social constructivist approach, see Barnes (1974), Latour and Woolgar (1979), and Bloor (1991). For a critique of this view Laudan (1990), Kitcher (1993), and Gross and Levitt (1994).

3 For further discussion of scientific method, see Grinnell (1992).

4 Relativist might reply, of course, that we can still make sense of ethical standards in science if we view them as part of what defines science's socio-historical context. In some social contexts, such as golf, people are expected to be honest. Just as lying about a score is inappropriate in golf, it is also inappropriate in science. In both cases deception is unethical because it violates certain rules not because it undermines any quest for objectivity.

Chapter 4

1 For more on different types of dishonesty, see Bok (1978).

2 See Broad and Wade (1993) for documented cases of fraud in science.

3 See Sergestrale (1990) for further discussion of Millikan's oil drop experiments.

4 Huff (1954) provides a classic and entertaining account of how people misuse statistics.

5 The Panel on Scientific Responsibility and the Conduct of Research provides an implicit ranking of scientific obligations by distinguishing between "Misconduct in science," "Questionable research practices," and "Other misconduct" (PSRCR, 1992). I question the validity of these distinctions for precisely the same reasons why I am hesitant to rank the various principles of scientific conduct.

6 To explore this argument in depth would take us too far afield. As example of how diversity can promote objectivity, Longino (1990) shows how sexist biases have affected research on primatology and endocrinology. She argues that a better understanding of these sciences occurred after women contributed their insights to these fields.

7 For other accounts of standards of conduct in science, see Glass (1965), Reagan (1971), AAAS (1980), PSRCR (1992), Shrader-Frechette (1994), Schlossberger (1993).

8 For some examples of professional codes of ethics in science, see American Anthropological Association (1990), American Psychological Association (1990), American Physical Society (1991), American Chemical Society (1994), American Medical Association (1994), Association of Computer Machinery (1996), Institute of Electrical and Electronics Engineers (1996).

Chapter 5

1 Violations of science's principle of honesty can be considered "fraud" in some cases. Although "fraud" can be equated with "dishonesty" or "deception," it has legalistic connotations that I would prefer to avoid in discussions of the ethics of science.

2 For further discussion of the use and misuse of statistics in science, see Ellenberg (1983), American Statistical Association (1989).
3 The observer effect occurs when the desire to observe something allows one to "observe" something that is not really there (National Academy of Sciences 1994).
4 It is possible to use the notion of bias to distinguish between different feminist critiques of science. According to radical feminists, science is completely biased; it is male invention designed to suppress women (Harding 1986). According to more moderate feminist views, various parts of science, such as certain theories or concepts, have been or might be biased (Longino 1990). Although I reject radical feminism, I find great value in feminist critiques that seek to expose particular sexist biases in scientific theories, concepts, or methods.
5 The question of research bias can also be useful in understanding other ideological critiques that seek to expose the social and political values that underlie Western science. While I admit that political, social, and other biases can affect research, I subscribe to the view that scientists can and should strive for objectivity. The mere fact that some research is or has been biased does not mean that all research is biased or that scientists cannot eliminate biases from research. For further discussion see Gross and Levitt (1994).
6 Sharon Traweek (1993) has an interesting story that illustrates the value of "junk" data. According to Traweek, a group of female physicists in Japan made use of data that their male counterparts had decided to throw away. The male physicists regarded the data as useless "noise" that could be tossed. The female scientists saved the data from the rubbish bin and used it to obtain some significant results.

Chapter 6

1 For more on writing scientific papers, see Hawkins and Sargi (1985).
2 See Hull (1988) for a fascinating and detailed account of biases and personal vendettas in biology. For some empirical research on bias in peer review, see Chubin and Hackett (1990), Fletcher and Fletcher (1997).
3 Self-plagiarism entails dishonesty but not intellectual theft. A person who self-plagiarizes fails to give credit to their own work. The most extreme example of self-plagiarism would be a case of publishing the exact same paper more than once without proper acknowledgments, attributions, or permissions (LaFollette 1992). While it is sometimes appropriate to publish the same paper in different journals in order to reach different audiences, authors should disclose a work's record of previous publication.
4 For more on some of these reports, see PSRCR (1992). See Kohn (1986), and Broad and Wade (1993), for infamous episodes of plagiarism in science.
5 Readers interested in examining a recent, highly publicized priority dispute are encouraged to examine the debate between Robert Gallo and Luc Montagnier concerning the discovery of HIV (Hilts 1991a). This dispute became an international incident and led to high-level negotiations between the United States and France.
6 The "Matthew Effect" gets its name from a passage in the Bible's book of Matthew 25:29, which states that "For those that have more shall be given, and for those that have not more shall be taken away."
7 Nothing in this chapter should be construed as legal advice. I suggest that readers consult with an attorney on legal questions concerning intellectual property rights.

8 For further discussion, see Nelkin (1984) and Weil and Snapper (eds) (1989).
9 For more examples, see Nelkin (1995), Wilkins and Patterson (1991), Cary (1995).
10 Carl Sagan even has his own neologism, "saganize," which means to deride someone for popularizing technical works.

Chapter 7

1 In more than 90 percent of cases of harassment, men are accused of harassing women (Aaron 1993). Other forms of harassment are possible, of course.
2 There is a morally neutral sense of the word "discriminate" as well. To "discriminate," according to this sense, means to "make a decision or judgment." Of course, this is not the sense of the word most people have in mind when they discuss racial or sexual discrimination (De George 1995).
3 There are other moral and political arguments for and against affirmative action, of course. My discussion in this chapter only addresses arguments for and against affirmative action that focuses on science's goals and concerns. For further discussion of affirmative action, see Sadler (1995). For further discussion of some concrete strategies for increasing the participation of women in science, see Committee on Women in Science and Engineering (1991).
4 During the Second World War physicians in Nazi Germany performed many different experiments on humans. The subjects, who were conscripted from concentration camps, included homosexuals, Russian officers, convicted criminals, Polish dissidents, and Gypsies. The Nazi physicians did not obtain informed consent from their subjects. Many of the experiments involved a great deal of pain and injury and often resulted in death. Although some of the experiments achieved scientifically valid results, many of the experiments lacked sound experimental procedures and/or were done simply to satisfy prurient or sadistic interests. The most infamous of all Nazi "scientists" was Josef Mengele, the so-called "Angel of Death," who was stationed at the Auschwitz concentration camp. Mengele conducted many experiments with identical twins in order to determine the relative contributions of genetics and the environment in the development of various traits. His goal was to be able to produce "perfect" human beings, i.e. people with blonde hair, blue eyes, healthy bodies and no genetic diseases, by controlling the environment. In one experiment, he injected dye into the eyes of six children in an attempt to make them blue. He then cut out their eyes and hung them on his wall, along with other organs that had been removed from human bodies while the subjects were still alive. Mengele forced twins to have sex to see if they would produce twins; he interchanged blood between twins; he grafted two non-identical twins together to create a "Siamese" twin; he put seven dwarfs on display for visiting German physicians; and he killed twenty-five subjects in electric shock experiments. For further discussion, see Pence (1995).
5 People commenting on this infamous case have pointed out that it violated many ethical standards; the research has been criticized as careless, racist, and deceptive (Crigger 1992).
6 For further discussion of many of these issues, see President's Commission (1983), Veatch (1987), Beauchamp (1997), Capron (1997).
7 Humans are animals too of course. I use the term "animal" here to refer to non-human animals.
8 For further discussion, see LaFollette and Shanks (1996).

9 This view implies that a species that is superior to humans would deserve better treatment.

10 One of the ironies of animal experimentation is that similarity arguments can go both ways: an animal might be similar enough to a human being to serve as a good causal model but different enough to have little moral value.

Chapter 8

1 Although most people recognize that there is an important distinction between valid science and junk science or pseudo-science, it is not easy to define these terms. For more on the distinction between science and other activities, see Gardner (1981), Kitcher (1983), Ziman (1984).

2 Since more engineers than scientists are employed by industry, it is likely that engineers face the types of ethical dilemmas discussed here more often than scientists. For more on engineering ethics, see Schaub et al. (1983), Schlossberger (1993).

3 The development of the Ford Pinto is another striking example of harmful research. See Cullen et al. (1984), De George (1995).

4 For further discussion of fraud and carelessness in industrial research, see PSRCR (1992), Broad and Wade (1993), Bowie (1994).

5 Many people believe that Karen Ann Silkwood was murdered for blowing the whistle on unsafe practices at a nuclear power plant.

6 For further discussion of these issues, see Cape (1984), Bela (1987), Lomasky (1987), Bowie (1994), Zolla-Parker (1994), Spier (1995).

7 For further discussion, see Zuckerman (1966), Nelkin (1972), Sapolsky (1977), Fotion and Elfstrom (1986), Howe and Martin (1991), MacArthur (1992), Kemp (1994), Lackey (1994).

8 For a fascinating account of how politics can enter into research funding decisions, consider the ill-fated Office of Technology Assessment (OTA). See Bimber (1996).

9 Scientists who were conducting research on fetal tissue once this restriction went into effect faced some difficult ethical choices. If they had continued to conduct research while receiving NIH funds, they would have violated the law and acted dishonestly. But if they had discontinued their research, many Parkinson's patients would fail to benefit from a new and possibly effective treatment. Since restrictions on the use of federal funds do not apply to private industry, Parkinson's researchers also had the option of seeking private funding for their work On the other hand, corporations fund research if they believe that they will get a good return on their investment, and fetal tissue research is not currently a sound investment.

10 For more on restrictions on research, see Feyerabend (1975), Cohen (1979), Cole (1983), Nelkin (1994), Wasserman (1995).

11 For a range of perspectives on sexism in science, see Keller (1985), Harding (1986), Goldberg (1991), Longino (1994), Koertge (1995). For more on racism in science, see UNESCO (1983), Pearson and Bechtel (1989), Johnson (1993), Tomoskovic-Devey (1993), Beardsley (1995), Fraser (1995).

12 For a variety of perspectives on the relation between science and religion, see Kitcher (1983), Davies (1990), Barbour (1990), Dennett (1995).

13 For more on the relation between science and human values, see Rudner (1953), Bronowski (1956), Hempel (1960), Snow (1964), McMullin (1982), Jacob (1988), Longino (1990), Putnam (1990), Scriven (1994).

Bibliography

Aaron, T. (1993) *Sexual Harassment in the Workplace*, Jefferson, NC: McFarland and Co.

Alexander, R. (1987) *The Biology of Moral Systems*, New York: de Gruyter.

Altman, L. (1995) "Promises of miracles: news releases go where journals fear to tread," *New York Times*, 10 January: C3.

—— (1997) "Drug firm relenting, allows unflattering study to appear," *New York Times*, 16 April: A1, A16.

American Anthropological Association (1990) "Statements on ethics and professional responsibility."

American Association for the Advancement of Science (AAAS) (1980) *Principles of Scientific Freedom and Responsibility*, revised draft, Washington: AAAS.

—— (1991) *Misconduct in Science, Executive Summary of Conference*, Washington: AAAS.

American Chemical Society (1994) "The chemist's code of conduct."

American Medical Association (AMA) (1994), "Code of medical ethics."

American Physical Society (1991) "Guidelines for professional conduct."

American Psychological Association (1990) "Ethical principles of psychologists."

American Statistical Association (1989) "Ethical guidelines for statistical practice."

Aristotle (1984) *Nichomachean Ethics*, in J. Barnes (ed.) *Complete Works of Aristotle*, Princeton, NJ: Princeton University Press.

Armstrong, J. (1997) "Peer review for journals: evidence of quality control, fairness, and innovation," *Science and Engineering Ethics* 3, 1: 63–84.

Association of Computer Machinery (1996) "Code of ethics."

Babbage, C. (1970) *Reflections on the Decline of Science in England*, New York: Augustus Kelley.

Bacon, F. (1985) *The Essays*, ed. J. Pitcher, New York: Penguin.

Bailar, J. (1986) "Science, statistics, and deception," *Annals of Internal Medicine* 104 (February): 259–60.

Baram, M. (1983) "Trade secrets: what price loyalty?," in V. Barry (1983).

Barber, B. (1961) "Resistance by scientists to scientific discovery," *Science* 134: 596–602.

Barbour, I. (1990) *Religion in the Age of Science*, San Francisco: Harper and Row.

Barnard, N. and Kaufman, S. (1997) "Animal research is wasteful and misleading," *Scientific American* 276, 2: 80–82.

Barnes, B. (1974) *Scientific Knowledge and Sociological Theory*, London: Routledge and Kegan Paul.

Barry, V. (ed.) (1983) *Moral Issues in Business*, 2nd edn, Belmont, CA: Wadsworth.

Baumrind, D. (1964) "Some thoughts on the ethics of research: after reading Milgram's 'behavioral study of obedience'," *American Psychologist* 19: 421–23.

Bayer, R. (1997) "AIDS and ethics," in R. Veatch (1997).

Bayles. M. (1988) *Professional Ethics*, 2nd edn, Belmont, CA: Wadsworth.

Beardsley, T. (1995) "Crime and punishment: meeting on genes and behavior gets only slightly violent," *Scientific American* 273, 6: 19, 22.

Beauchamp, T. (1997) "Informed consent," in R. Veatch (1997).

Beauchamp, T. and Childress, J. (1994) *Principles of Biomedical Ethics*, 2nd edn, New York: Oxford University Press.

Bela, D. (1987) "Organizations and systematic distortion of information," *Journal of Professional Issues in Engineering* 113: 360–70.

Benedict, R. (1946) *Patterns of Culture*, New York: Pelican Books.

Ben-David, J. (1971) *The Scientist's Role in Society*, Englewood Cliffs, NJ: Prentice-Hall.

Bethe, H., Gottfried, K., and Sagdeev, R. (1995) "Did Bohr share nuclear secrets?," *Scientific American* 272, 5: 85–90.

Bimber, B. (1996) *The Politics of Expertise in Congress*, Albany, NY: State University of New York Press.

Bird, S. and Housman, D. (1995) "Trust and the collection, selection, analysis, and interpretation of data: a scientist's view," *Science and Engineering Ethics* 1: 371–82.

Bird, S. and Spier, R. (1995) "Welcome to science and engineering ethics," *Science and Engineering Ethics* 1, 1: 2–4.

Bloor, D. (1991) *Knowledge and Social Imagery*, 2nd edn, Chicago: University of Chicago Press.

Bok, S. (1978) *Lying*, New York: Pantheon Books.

—— (1982) *Secrets*, New York: Vintage Books.

Botting, J. and Morrison, A. (1997) "Animal research is vital to medicine," *Scientific American* 276, 2: 83–85.

Bowie, N. (1994) *University-Business Partnerships: An Assessment*, Lanham, MD: Rowman and Littlefield.

Broad, W. (1981) "The publishing game: getting more for less," *Science* 211: 1137–39.

—— (1992) *Teller's War*, New York: Simon and Schuster.

Broad, W. and Wade, N. (1993) *Betrayers of the Truth*, new edn, New York: Simon and Schuster.

Bronowski, J. (1956) *Science and Human Values*, New York: Harper and Row.

Brown, G. (1993) "Technology's dark side," *New York Times* magazine, 30 June: B1.

Browning, T. (1995) "Reaching for the low hanging fruit: the pressure for results in scientific research – a graduate student's perspective," *Science and Engineering Ethics* 1: 417–26.

Budiansky, S., Goode, E., and Gest, T. (1994) "The Cold War experiments," *US News and World Report* 116, 3: 32–38.

Buchanan, A. and Brock, D. (1989) *Deciding for Others*, New York: Cambridge University Press.

Cantelon, P., Hewlett, R., and Williams, R. (eds) (1991) *The American Atom*, 2nd edn, Philadelphia: University of Pennsylvania Press.

Cape, R. (1984) "Academic and corporate values and goals: are they really in conflict?," in D. Runser (ed.), *Industrial-Academic Interfacing*, Washington: American Chemical Society.

Caplan, A. (1993) "Much of the uproar over 'cloning' is based on misunderstanding," *Denver Post*, 7 November: D4.

Capron, A. (1993) "Facts, values, and expert testimony," *Hastings Center Report* 23, 5: 26–28.

—— (1997) "Human experimentation," in R. Veatch (1997).

Carson, R. (1961) *Silent Spring*, Boston: Houghton Mifflin.

Carter, S. (1995) "Affirmative action harms black professionals," in A. Sadler (1995).

Cary, P. (1995) "The asbestos panic attack," *US News and World Report*, 20 February: 61–63.

Chalk, R. and van Hippel, F. (1979) "Due process for dissenting whistle blowers," *Technological Reviews* 8: 48.

Chubin, D. and Hackett, E. (1990) *Peerless Science*, Albany, NY: State University of New York Press.

Cline, B. (1965) *Men Who Made Physics*, Chicago: University of Chicago Press.

Clinton, W. (1997) "Prohibition on federal funding for cloning of human beings: memorandum for the heads of executive departments and agencies," The White House, Office of the Press Secretary, 4 March.

Clutterbuck, D. (1983) "Blowing the whistle on corporate conduct," in V. Barry (1983).

Cohen, C. (1979) "When may research be stopped?," in D. Jackson and S. Stich (eds) *The Recombinant DNA Debate*, Englewood Cliffs, NJ: Prentice-Hall.

Cohen, J. (1994) "US-French patent dispute heads for a showdown," *Science* 265: 23–25.

—— (1997) "AIDS trials ethics questioned," *Science* 276: 520–22.

Cohen, L. and Noll, R. (1994) "Privatizing public research," *Scientific American* 271, 3: 72–77.

Cole, L. (1983) *Politics and the Restraint of Science*, Totowa, NJ: Rowman and Littlefield.

Committee on the Conduct of Science. (1994) *On Being a Scientist*, 2nd edn, Washington, DC: National Academy Press.

Committee on Women in Science and Engineering (1991) *Women in Science and Engineering*, Washington: National Academy Press.

Commoner, B. (1963) *Science and Survival*, New York: Viking Press.

Crigger, B. (1992) "Twenty years after: the legacy of the Tuskegee syphilis study," *Hastings Center Report* 22, 6: 29.

Cromer, A. (1993) *Uncommon Sense*, New York: Oxford University Press.

Cullen, F., Maakestad, W., and Cavender, G. (1984) "The Ford Pinto case and beyond: corporate crime, moral boundaries, and the criminal sanction," in E. Hochstedler (ed.) *Corporations as Criminals*, Beverly Hills, CA: Sage Publications.

Daly, R. and Mills, A. (1993) "Ethics and objectivity," *Anthropology Newsletter* 34, 8: 1, 6.

Davies, P. (1990) *The Mind of God*, New York: Simon and Schuster.

Davis, M. (1982) "Conflict of interest," *Business and Professional Ethics Journal* 1, 4: 17–27.

De George, R. (1995) *Business Ethics*, 4th edn, Englewood Cliffs, NJ: Prentice-Hall.

Dennett, D. (1995) *Darwin's Dangerous Idea*, New York: Simon and Schuster.

Denver Post, (1992) "Saccharin may cause cancer only in rats," 9 April: A10.

—— (1993) "Drug maker Lilly accused of cloaking toxic reaction," 10 December: A22.

Dickson, D. (1984) *The New Politics of Science*, Chicago: University of Chicago Press.

Dijksterhuis, E. (1986) *The Mechanization of the World Picture*, trans. C. Dikshorn, Princeton, NJ: Princeton University Press.

Dixon, K. (1994) "Professional responsibility, reproductive choice, and the limits of appropriate intervention," in D. Wueste (1994).

Drenth, J. (1996) "Proliferation of authors on research reports in medicine," *Science and Engineering Ethics* 2: 469–80.

Dreyfuss, R. (1989) "General overview of the intellectual property system," in V. Weil and J. Snapper (1989).

Edsall, J. (1995) "On the hazards of whistle blowers and on some problems of young biomedical scientists of our time," *Science and Engineering Ethics* 1: 329–40.

Eisenberg, A. (1994) "The Art of Scientific Insult," *Scientific American* 270, 6: 116.

Ellenberg, J. (1983) "Ethical guidelines for statistical practice: an historical perspective," *The American Statistician* 37 (February): 1–4.

Elmer-Dewitt, P. (1993) "Cloning: where do we draw the line?," *Time Magazine*, 8 November: 64–70.

Elms, A. (1994) "Keeping deception honest: justifying conditions for social scientific research strategems," in E. Erwin, S. Gendin, and L. Kleiman (1994).

Erwin, E., Gendin, S., and Kleiman, L. (eds) (1994) *Ethical Issues in Scientific Research*, Hamden, CT: Garland Publishing Co.

Etzkowitz, H. *et al.* (1994) "The paradox of critical mass for women in science," *Science* 266: 51–54.

Feyerabend, P. (1975) *Against Method*, London: Verso.

Feynman, R. (1985) *Surely You're Joking, Mr. Feynman*, New York: W.W. Norton.

Fletcher, R. and Fletcher, S. (1997) "Evidence for the effectiveness of peer review," *Science and Engineering Ethics* 3: 35–50.

Fleischmann, M. and Pons, S. (1989) "Electrochemically induced nuclear fusion of Deuterium," *Journal of Electroanalytic Chemistry* 261: 301.

Foegen, J. (1995) "Broad definitions of sexual harassment may be counterproductive for business," in K. Swisher (1995a).

Foster, F. and Shook, R. (1993) *Patents, Copyrights, and Trademarks*, 2nd edn, New York: John Wiley and Sons.

Fotion, N. and Elfstrom, G. (1986) *Military Ethics*, Boston: Routledge and Kegan Paul.

Fox, R. and DeMarco, J. (1990) *Moral Reasoning*, Chicago: Holt, Rinehart, and Winston.

Frankena, W. (1973) *Ethics*, 2nd edn, Englewood Cliffs, NJ: Prentice-Hall.

Franklin, A. (1981) "Millikan's published and unpublished data on oil drops," *Historical Studies in the Physical Sciences* 11: 185–201.

Fraser, S. (ed.) (1995) *The Bell Curve Wars*, New York: Basic Books.

Freedman, B. (1992) "A response to a purported difficulty with randomized clinical trials involving cancer patients," *Journal of Clinical Ethics* 3, 3: 231–34.

Friedman, T. (1997) "Overcoming the obstacles to gene therapy," *Scientific American* 276, 6: 96–101.

Fuchs, S. (1992) *The Professional Quest for the Truth*, Albany, NY: State University of New York Press.

Gardner, M. (1981) *Science – Good, Bad, and Bogus*, Buffalo, NY: Prometheus Books.

Garte, S. (1995) "Guidelines for training in the ethical conduct of research," *Science and Engineering Ethics* 1: 59–70.

Gaston, J. (1973) *Originality and Competition in Science*, Chicago: University of Chicago Press.

Gergen, D. (1997) "The 7 percent solution: funding basic scientific research is vital to America's future," *US News and World Report*, 19 May: 79.

Gibbard, A. (1986) *Wise Choices, Apt Feelings*, Cambridge, MA: Harvard University Press.

Gilligan, C. (1982) *In A Different Voice*, Cambridge, MA: Harvard University Press.

Glass, B. (1965) "The ethical basis of science," *Science* 150: 1254–61.

Goldberg, S. (1991) "Feminism against science," *National Review*, 18 November: 30–48.

Golden, W. (ed.) (1993) *Science and Technology Advice to the President, Congress, and Judiciary*, 2nd edn, Washington, DC: AAAS.

Goldman, A. (1986) *Epistemology and Cognition*, Cambridge, MA: Harvard University Press.

—— (1992) *Liaisons*, Cambridge, MA: MIT Press.

Goldman, A.H. (1989) "Ethical issues in proprietary restrictions on research results," in V. Weil and J. Snapper (1989).

Goldstein, T. (1980) *The Dawn of Modern Science*, Boston: Houghton Mifflin.

Goodman, T., Brownlee, S., and Watson, T. (1995) "Should the labs get hit? The pros and cons of federal science aid," *US News and World Report*, 6 November: 83–85.

Gould, S. (1981) *The Mismeasure of Man*, New York: W.W. Norton.

—— (1997) "Bright star among billions," *Science* 275: 599.

Griffin, D. (1992) *Animal Minds*, Chicago: University of Chicago Press.

Grinnell, F. (1992) *The Scientific Attitude*, 2nd edn, New York: Guilford Publications.

Grmek, M. (1990) *The History of AIDS*, trans R. Maulitz and J. Duffin, Princeton, NJ: Princeton University Press.

Gross, P. and Levitt, N. (1994) *Higher Superstition*, Baltimore, MD: Johns Hopkins University Press.

Guenin, L. and Davis, B. (1996) "Scientific reasoning and due process," *Science and Engineering Ethics* 2: 47–54.

Gunsalus, C. (1997) "Ethics: sending out the message," *Science* 276: 335.

Gurley, J. (1993) "Postdoctoral researchers: a panel," in Sigma Xi (1993).

Harding, S. (1986) *The Science Question in Feminism*, Ithaca, NY: Cornell University Press.

Hardwig, J. (1994) "Towards an ethics of expertise," in D. Wueste (1994).

Hart, H. (1961) *The Concept of Law*, Oxford: Clarendon Press.

Hawkins, C. and Sargi, S. (eds) (1985) *Research: How to Plan, Speak, and Write About It*, New York: Springer-Verlag.

Hedges, S. (1997) "Time bomb in the crime lab," *US News and World Report*, 24 March: 22–24.

Hempel, C. (1960) "Science and human values," in R. Spillar (ed.) *Social Control in a Free Society*, Philadelphia: University of Pennsylvania Press.

Hilts, P. (1991a) "US and French researchers finally agree in long feud on AIDS virus," *New York Times*, 7 May: A1, C3.

—— (1991b) "Nobelist apologizes for defending a paper found to have faked data," *New York Times*, 4 August: A1, A7.

—— (1992) "A question of ethics," *New York Times*, 2 August: 4A: 26–28.

—— (1994a) "Tobacco firm withheld results of 1983 research," *Denver Post*, 1 April: A14.

—— (1994b) "MIT scientist gets hefty penalty," *Denver Post*, 27 November: A22.

—— (1996) "Noted finding of science fraud is overturned by a federal panel," *New York Times*, 22 June: A1, A20.

—— (1997) "Researcher profited after study by investing in cold treatment," *New York Times*, 1 February: A6.

Hixson, J. (1976) *The Patchwork Mouse*, Garden City, NJ: Doubleday.

Hollander, R., Johnson, D., Beckwith, J., and Fader, B. (1995) "Why teach ethics in science and engineering?," *Science and Engineering Ethics* 1: 83–87.

Holloway, M. (1993) "A lab of her own," *Scientific American* 269, 5: 94–103.

Holton, G. (1978) "Subelectrons, presuppositions, and the Millikan-Ehrenhaft dispute," *Historical Studies in the Physical Sciences* 9: 166–224.

Hooker, B. (1996) "Ross-style pluralism versus rule-consequentialism," *Mind* 105: 531–552.

Horgan, J. (1993) "Wanted: a defense R & D policy," *Scientific American* 269, 6: 47–48.

—— (1994) "Particle metaphysics," *Scientific American* 270, 2: 96–106.

Houghton, J. *et al.* (eds) (1992) *Climate Change 1992: The Supplementary Report to the IPCC Scientific Assessment*, Cambridge: Cambridge University Press.

Howe, E. and Martin, E. (1991) "Treating the troops," *Hastings Center Report* 21, 2: 21–24.

Howes, R. (1993) "Physics and the classified community," in M. Thomsen (1993).

Hubbard, R. and Wald, E. (1993) *Exploding the Gene Myth*, New York: Beacon Press.

Huber, P. (1991) *Galileo's Revenge*, New York: Basic Books.

Huff, D. (1954) *How to Lie with Statistics*, New York: W.W. Norton.

Huizenga, J. (1992) *Cold Fusion*, Rochester, NY: University of Rochester Press.

Hull, D. (1988) *Science as a Process*, Chicago: University of Chicago Press.

Huth, E. (1986) "Irresponsible authorship and wasteful publication," *Annals of Internal Medicine* 104: 257–59.

International Committee of Medical Journal Editors (1991) "Guidelines for authorship," *New England Journal of Medicine* 324: 424–28.

Institute of Electrical and Electronic Engineers (1996) "Code of ethics."

Jacob, M. (1988) *The Cultural Meaning of the Scientific Revolution*, Philadelphia: Temple University Press.

—— (1997) *Scientific Culture and the Making of the Industrial West*, New York: Oxford University Press.

Jackson, J. (1995) "People of color need affirmative action," in A. Sadler (1995).

Jardin, N. (1986) *The Fortunes of Inquiry*, Oxford: Clarendon Press.

Jennings, B., Callahan, D., and Wolf, S. (1987) "The professions: public interest and common good," *Hastings Center Report* 17, 1: 3–10.

Johnson, H. (1993) "The life of a black scientist," *Scientific American* 268, 1: 160.

Jonas, H. (1969) "Philosophical reflections on experimenting with human subjects," *Daedalus* 98: 219–47.

Jones, J. (1980) *Bad Blood*, New York: Free Press.

Joravsky, D. (1970) *The Lysenko Affair*, Cambridge, MA: Harvard University Press.

Kant, I. (1981) *Grounding for the Metaphysics of Morals*, trans. J. Ellington, Indianapolis, IN: Hackett.

Kantorovich, A. (1993) *Scientific Discovery*, Albany, NY: State University of New York Press.

Karl, T., Nicholls, N., and Gregory, J. (1997) "The coming climate," *Scientific American* 276, 5: 78–83.

Kearney, W., Vawter, D., and Gervais, K. (1991) "Fetal tissue research and the misread compromise," *Hastings Center Report* 21, 5: 7–13.

Keller, E. (1985) *Reflections on Gender and Science*, New Haven, CT: Yale University Press.

Kemp, K. (1994) "Conducting scientific research for the military as a civic duty," in E. Erwin, S. Gendin, and L. Kleiman (1994).

Kennedy, D. (1985) *On Academic Authorship*, Stanford, CA: Stanford University.

Kiang, N. (1995) "How are scientific corrections made?," *Science and Engineering Ethics* 1: 347–56.

Kilzer, L., Kowalski, R., and Wilmsen, S. (1994) "Concrete tests faked at airport," *Denver Post*, 13 November: A1, A14.

Kitcher, P. (1983) *Abusing Science*, Cambridge, MA: MIT Press.

—— (1993) *The Advancement of Science*, New York: Oxford University Press.

Klaidman, S. and Beauchamp, T. (1987) *The Virtuous Journalist*, New York: Oxford University Press.

Koertge, N. (1995) "How feminism is now alienating women from science," *Skeptical Inquirer* 19, 2: 42–43.

Kohn, R. (1986) *False Prophets*, New York: Basil Blackwell.

Kolata, G. (1993), "Scientists clone human embryos, and create an ethical challenge," *New York Times*, 24 October: A1, A22.

—— (1994) "Parkinson patients set for first rigorous test of fetal implants," *New York Times*, 8 February: C3.

—— (1995) "Lab charged with homicide over misread pap smear," *Denver Post*, 13 April: A1, A19.

—— (1997) "With cloning of a sheep, the ethical ground shifts," *New York Times*, 24 February: A1, B8.

Krystyna, G. (1996) "The computer revolution and the problem of global ethics," *Science and Engineering Ethics* 2: 177–90.

Kuflik, A. (1989) "Moral foundations of intellectual property rights," in V. Weil and J. Snapper (1989).

Kuhn, T. (1970) *The Structure of Scientific Revolutions*, 2nd edn, Chicago: University of Chicago Press.

—— (1977) *The Essential Tension*, Chicago: University of Chicago Press.

Kyburg, H. (1984) *Theory and Measurement*, Cambridge: Cambridge University Press.

Lackey, D. (1994) "Military funds, moral demands: personal responsibilities of the individual scientist," E. Erwin, S. Gendin, and L. Kleiman (1994).

LaFollette, H. and Shanks, N. (1996) *Brute Science*, New York: Routledge.

LaFollette, M. (1992) *Stealing into Print*, Berkeley: University of California Press.

Lakoff, S. (1980) "Ethical responsibility and the scientific vocation," in S. Lakoff (ed.) *Science and Ethical Responsibility*, Reading, MA: Addison-Wesley.

Lasagna, L. (1971) "Some ethical problems in clinical investigation," in E. Mendelsohn, J. Swazey, and I. Traviss (eds) *Human Aspects of Biomedical Innovation*, Cambridge, MA: Harvard University Press.

Latour, B. and Woolgar, S. (1979) *Laboratory Life*, Beverly Hills, CA: Sage Publications.

Laudan, L. (1990) *Science and Relativism*, Chicago: University of Chicago Press.

Leatherman, C. (1997) "Ohio State withdraws its job offer to Yale professor accused of harassing student," *Chronicle of Higher Education*, 10 January: A10.

Lederer, E. (1997) "Britain to cut off funding to sheep cloning project," *Denver Post*, 2 March: A6.

Locke, J. (1980) *Second Treatise of Government*, ed. C. Macpherson, Indianapolis, IN: Hackett.

Loftus, E. (1995) "Remembering dangerously," *Skeptical Inquirer* 19, 2: 20–29.

Lomasky, L. (1987) "Public money, private gain, profit for all," *Hastings Center Report 17*, 3: 5–7.

Longino, H. (1990) *Science as Social Knowledge*, Princeton, NJ: Princeton University Press.

Longino, H. (1994) "Gender and racial biases in scientific research," in K. Shrader-Frechette.

MacArthur, J. (1992) *Second Front*, New York: Hill and Wang.

Macrina, F (ed.) (1995) *Scientific Integrity*, Washington, DC: American Society for Microbiology Press.

Markie, P. (1994) *A Professor's Duties*, Lanham, MD: University Press of America.

Marshall, E. (1997) "Publishing sensitive data: who calls the shots?," *Science* 276: 523–25.

Martino, J. (1992) *Science Funding*, New Brunswick, NJ: Transaction Publishers.

McMullin, E. (1982) "Values in science," in P. Asquith and T. Nickles (eds) *PSA 1982*, vol. 2, East Lansing, MI: Philosophy of Science Association.

Meadows, J. (1992) *The Great Scientists*, New York: Oxford University Press.

Merges, R. (1996) "Property rights theory and the commons: the case of scientific research," in E. Paul, F. Miller, and J. Paul (eds), *Scientific Innovation, Philosophy, and Public Policy*, New York: Cambridge University Press.

Merton, R. (1973) *The Sociology of Science*, ed. N. Storer, Chicago: University of Chicago Press.

Milgram, S. (1974) *Obedience to Authority*, New York: Harper and Row.

Mill, J. (1979) *Utilitarianism*, ed. G. Sher, Indianapolis, IN: Hackett.

Milloy, S. (1995) *Science Without Sense*, Washington, DC: CATO Institute.

Morgenson, G. (1991) "May I have the pleasure," *National Review*, 18 November: 36–41.

Morrison, P. (1995) "Recollections of a nuclear war," *Scientific American* 273, 2: 42–46.

Mukerji, C. (1989) *A Fragile Power*, Princeton, NJ: Princeton University Press.

Munthe, C. and Welin, S. (1996) "The morality of scientific openness," *Science and Engineering Ethics* 2: 411–28.

Naess, A. (1989) *Ecology, Community, and Lifestyle*, trans. D. Rothenberg, New York: Cambridge University Press.

National Academy of Sciences (1994) *On Being a Scientist*, Washington, DC: National Academy Press.

Nelkin, D. (1972) *The University and Military Research*, Ithaca, NY: Cornell University Press.

—— (1984) *Science as Intellectual Property*, New York: Macmillan.

—— (1994) "Forbidden research: limits to inquiry in the social sciences," in E. Erwin, S. Gendin, and L. Kleiman (1994).

—— (1995) *Selling Science*, revised edn, New York: W.H. Freeman.

Newton-Smith, W. (1981) *The Rationality of Science*, London: Routledge and Kegan Paul.

Nozick, R. (1974) *Anarchy, State, and Utopia*, New York: Basic Books.

Nuremburg Code (1949) In *Trials of War Criminals before Nuremburg Military Tribunals*, Washington, DC: US Government Printing Office.

Ofshe, R. and E. Waters (1994) *Making Monsters*, New York: Charles Scribner's Sons.

Panel on Scientific Responsibility and the Conduct of Research (PSRCR) (1992) *Responsible Science*, vol. 1, Washington, DC: National Academy Press.

Pearson, W. and Bechtel, H. (1989) *Blacks, Science, and American Education*, New Brunswick, NJ: Rutgers University Press.

Pence, G. (1995) *Classic Cases in Medical Ethics*, 2nd edn, New York: McGraw-Hill.

Petersdorf, R. (1986) "The pathogenesis of fraud in medical science," *Annals of Internal Medicine* 104: 252–54.

Pojman, L. (1990) "A critique of moral relativism," in L. Pojman (ed.) *Philosophy*, 2nd edn, Belmont, CA: Wadsworth.

—— (1995) *Ethics*, Belmont, CA: Wadsworth.

Pollock, J. (1986) *Contemporary Theories of Knowledge*, Totowa, NJ: Rowman and Littlefield.

Pool, R. (1990) "Struggling to do science for society," *Science* 248: 672–73.

Popper, K. (1959) *The Logic of Scientific Discovery*, London: Routledge.

Porter, T. (1986) *The Rise of Statistical Thinking*, Princeton, NJ: Princeton University Press.

President's Commission for the Study of Ethical Problems in Medicine and Biomedical and Behavioral Research (1983) *Implementing Human Research Regulations*, Washington, DC: President's Commission.

Puddington, A. (1995) "Affirmative action should be eliminated," in A. Sadler (1995).

Putnam, H. (1990) *Realism with a Human Face*, Cambridge, MA: Harvard University Press.

Rawls, J. (1971) *A Theory of Justice*, Cambridge, MA: Harvard University Press.

Reagan, C. (1971) *Ethics for researchers*, 2nd edn, Springfield, MA: Charles Thomas.

Regan, T. (1983) *The Case for Animal Rights*, Berkeley: University of California Press.

Reiser, S. (1993) "The ethics movement in the biological sciences: a new voyage of discovery," in R. Bulger, E. Heitman, and S. Reiser (eds) *The Ethical Dimensions of the Biological Sciences*, New York: Cambridge University Press.

Resnik, D. (1991) "How-possibly explanations in biology," *Acta Biotheoretica* 39: 141–49.

—— (1996a) "The corporate responsibility for basic research," *Business and Society Review* 96: 57–60.

—— (1996b) "Social epistemology and the ethics of research," *Studies in the History and Philosophy of Science* 27: 565–86.

—— (1997a) "The morality of human gene patents," *Kennedy Institute of Ethics Journal* 7, 1: 31–49.

—— (1997b) "Ethical problems and dilemmas in the interaction between science and the media," in M. Thomsen (ed.) *Ethical Issues in Physics*, East Lansing, MI: Eastern Michigan University.

—— (forthcoming) "A proposal for a new system of credit allocation in science," *Science and Engineering Ethics*.

Rest, J. (1986) *Moral Development*, New York: Praeger.

Rest, J. and Narvaez, D. (eds) (1994) *Moral Development in the Professions*, Hillsdale, NJ: Lawrence Erlbaum.

Roberts, C. (1993) "Collider loss stuns CU researchers," *Denver Post*, 14 November: A20.

Rodd, R. (1990) *Biology, Ethics, and Animals*, Oxford: Clarendon Press.

Rollin, B. (1995) *The Frankenstein Syndrome*, Cambridge: Cambridge University Press.

Rose, M. and Fisher, K. (1995) "Policies and perspectives on authorship," *Science and Engineering Ethics* 1: 361–371.

Rosen, J. (1996) "Swallow hard: what *Social Text* should have done," *Tikkun*, September/October: 59–61.

Rosenberg, A. (1995) *Philosophy of Social Science*, 2nd edn, Boulder, CO: Westview Press.

Ross, W. (1930) *The Right and the Good*, Oxford: Clarendon Press.

Rudner, R. (1953) "The scientist qua scientist makes value judgments," *Philosophy of Science* 20: 1–6.

Saperstein, A. (1997) "Research vs. teaching: an ethical dilemma for the academic physicist," in M. Thomsen (ed.) *Ethical Issues in Physics*, Ypsilanti, MI: Eastern Michigan University.

Sadler, A. (ed.) (1995) *Affirmative Action*, San Diego: Greenhaven Press.

Sapolsky, H. (1977) "Science, technology, and military policy," in I. Spiegel-Rosing and D. de Solla Price (1977).

Sarasohn, J. (1993) *Science on Trial*, New York: St. Martin's Press.

Schaub, J., Pavlovic, K., and Morris, M. (eds) (1983) *Engineering Professionalism and Ethics*, New York: John Wiley and Sons.

Schneider, K. (1993) "Secret nuclear research on people comes to light," *New York Times*, 17 December: A1, B11.

Schlossberger, E. (1993) *The Ethical Engineer*, Philadelphia: Temple University Press.

—— (1995) "Technology and civil disobedience: why engineers have a special duty to obey the law," *Science and Engineering Ethics* 1: 169–172.

Scriven, M. (1994) "The exact role of value judgments in science," in E. Erwin, S. Gendin, and L. Kleiman (1994).

Segerstrale, U. (1990) "The murky borderland between scientific intuition and fraud," *International Journal of Applied Ethics* 5: 11–20.

Shadish, W. and Fuller, S. (eds) (1993) *The Social Psychology of Science*, New York: Guilford Publications.

Shrader-Frechette, K. (1994) *Ethics of Scientific Research*, Boston: Rowman and Littlefield.

Sigma Xi (1986) *Honor in Science*, Research Triangle Park, NC: Sigma Xi.

—— (1993) *Ethics, Values, and the Promise of Science*, Research Triangle Park, NC: Sigma Xi.

Singer, P. (1975) *Animal Liberation*, New York: Random House.

Slakey, P. (1993) "Public science," in M. Thomsen (1993).

—— (1994) "Science Policy in a Tug-of-War," *New Scientist* 142: 47.

Snow, C. (1964) *The Two Cultures and the Scientific Revolution*, Cambridge: Cambridge University Press.

Sokal, A. (1996a) "Transgressing the boundaries: toward a transformative hermeneutics of quantum gravity," *Social Text* 46/47: 217–52.

—— (1996b) "A physicist experiments with cultural studies," *Lingua Franca* (May/June): 62–64.

—— (1996c) "Transgressing the boundaries: and afterward," *Philosophy and Literature* 20, 2: 338–46.

Solomon, M. (1994) "Social empiricism," *Nous* 28, 3: 355–73.

Spiegel-Rosing, I. and de Solla Price, D. (eds) (1977) *Science, Technology, and Society*, London: Sage Publications.

Spier, R. (1995) "Ethical aspects of the university-industry interface," *Science and Engineering Ethics* 1: 151–62.

Steiner, D. (1996) "Conflicting interests: the need to control conflicts of interest in biomedical research," *Science and Engineering Ethics* 2: 457–68.

Stevens, W. (1996) "Greenhouse effect bunk, says respected scientist," *Denver Post*, 23 June, 1996: A22.

Stix, G. (1995) "Fighting future wars," *Scientific American* 273, 6: 92–101.

Stone, M. and Marshall, E. (1994) "Imanishi-Kari case: ORI finds fraud," *Science* 266: 1468–69.

Swisher, K. (ed.) (1995a) *What is Sexual Harassment?*, San Diego: Greenhaven Press.

—— (1995b), "Businesses should clearly define sexual harassment," in K. Swisher (1995a).

Thomsen, M. (ed.) (1993) *Proceedings of the Ethical Issues in Physics Workshop*, Ypsilanti, MI: Eastern Michigan University.

Tomoskovic-Devey, T. (ed.) (1993) *Gender and Racial Inequality at Work*, Ithaca, NY: ILR Press.

Traweek, S. (1988) *Beamtimes and Lifetimes*, Cambridge, MA: Harvard University Press.

—— (1993) "The culture of physics," paper presented to the Gender and Science Colloquium, University of Wyoming, 19 March.

United Nations Scientific and Cultural Organization (UNESCO) (1983) *Racism, Science, and Pseudo-Science*, Paris: UNESCO.

US Congress, House Committee on Science and Technology, Subcommittee on Investigations and Oversight (1990) *Maintaining the Integrity of Scientific Research, Hearings, One Hundred and First Congress, First Session*, Washington, DC: US Government Printing Office.

Varner, G. (1994) "The prospects for consensus and convergence in the animal rights debate," *Hastings Center Report* 24, 1: 24–28.

Veatch, R. (1987) *The Patient as Partner*, Bloomington, IN: Indiana University Press.

—— (1995) "Abandoning Informed Consent," *Hastings Center Report* 25, 2: 5–12.

—— (ed.) (1997) *Medical Ethics*, 2nd edn, Boston: Jones and Bartlett.

Volti, R. (1995) *Society and Technological Change*, 3rd edn, New York: St. Martin's Press.

von Hippel, F. (1991) *Citizen Scientist*, New York: American Institute of Physics.

Wadman, M. (1996) "Drug company suppressed publication of research," *Nature* 381: 4.

Wallerstein, M. (1984) "US participation in international science and technology cooperation: a framework for analysis," in *Scientific and Technological Cooperation Among Industrialized Countries*, Washington, DC: National Academy Press.

Wasserman, D. (1995) "Science and social harm: genetic research into crime and violence," *Philosophy and Public Policy* 15, 1: 14–19.

Webb, S. (1995) "Sexual harassment should be defined broadly," in K. Swisher (1995a).

Weaver, D., Reis, M., Albanese, C., Costantini, F., Baltimore, D., and Imanishi-Kari, T. (1986) "Altered repertoire of endogenous immmunoglobin gene expression in transgenic mice containing a rearranged MY heavy chain gene," *Cell* 45: 247–59.

Weil, V. and Snapper, J. (eds) (1989) *Owning Scientific and Technical Information*, New Brunswick, NJ: Rutgers University Press.

Weinberg, A. (1967) *Reflections on Big Science*, Cambridge, MA: MIT Press.

Weiner, T. (1994a) "US plans overhaul on secrecy, seeking to open millions of files," *New York Times*, 18 March: A1, B6.

—— (1994b) "Inquiry finds 'Star Wars' plan tried to exaggerate test results," *New York Times*, 22 July: A1, 26.

Weiss, R. (1996) "Proposed shifts in misconduct reviews unsettle many scientists," *Washington Post*, 30 June: A6.

Weisskpof, V. (1994) "Endangered support of basic science," *Scientific American* 270, 3: 128.

Westrum, R. (1991) *Technologies and Society*, Belmont, CA: Wadsworth.

Whitbeck, C. (1995a) "Teaching ethics to scientists and engineers: moral agents and moral problems," *Science and Engineering Ethics* 1: 299–308.

—— (1995b) "Truth and trustworthiness in research," *Science and Engineering Ethics* 1: 403–16.

Williams, G. (1995) "America's food cup," *Denver Post*, 31 August, E1–2.

Wilmut, I., Schnieke, A., McWhir, J., Kind, A., and Campbell, K. (1997) "Viable offspring derived from fetal and adult mammalian cells [letter]," *Nature* 385: 769, 771.

Wilkins, L. and Paterson, P. (1991) *Risky Business*, New York: Greenwood Press.

Woodward, J. and Goodstein, D. (1996) "Conduct, misconduct, and the structure of science," *American Scientist* (September/October): 479–90.

Wueste, D. (ed.) (1994) *Professional Ethics and Social Responsibility*, Lanham, MD: Rowam and Littlefield.

Ziman, J. (1984) *An Introduction to Science Studies*, Cambridge: Cambridge University Press.

Zolla-Parker, S. (1994) "The professor, the university, and industry," *Scientific American* 270, 3: 120.

Zuckerman, S. (1966) *Scientists and War*, New York: Harper and Row.

Index

patents 109–10, 112–13; of genes 113–14
paternalism 120–1
peer review 4, 46–9, 96–101, 182
personal relationships in science 190; *see also* mentoring
philosophy 13; moral 14; political 16; and relativism 29
placebo effect 138
plagiarism 62, 185; and credit 104; and honesty 62; self- 203; unintentional 104
Plato 50
pluralism 21, 24
politics and ethics 16–17; and science 147–72
post-modernism 201–2
preferential treatment 66–7, 128–30; *see also* affirmative action, discrimination
principles of conduct in science 53–73; and professional codes 72–3; skepticism about 71–2
priority 91, 182 *see also* co-discovery, credit, patents
privacy 22, 134
professions: characteristics of 35–7; and codes of conduct 35, 72–3; and ethics 15, 35, 72–3; science and 31–8, 177
pseudoscience *see* junk science
public misunderstanding of science 117–18, 154–5, 187–8; science and 147–72; support for science 63–5, 147–8
publication: electronic 47, 103; history of 43–9; and the least publishable unit 67, 102; quality 101–3; quantity 102–3; and the rush to publish 92; *see also* authorship, credit, peer review
publish or perish 3, 44–5, 102
pure research 39, 169–70

racism 66, 85, 127–30, 143–4, 172, 196
rationalism 32
record keeping 6–8, 76, 136, 180
reflective equilibrium 18
relativism: definition of 27–8; ethical 28; legal 28; moral 28–33, 194–5; scientific 56, 201–2
religion and ethics 17, 19, 29, 32; and science 172
research: AIDS 170, 177, 192, 203; animal 67, 140–6; applied 39, 168–9; on children 135; environment 3, 41–5, 178; fetal

tissue 170; groups 42–3; human subjects 67, 133–40; industrial 89, 112–13; interdisciplinary 44, 70; military 161–7; as a public good 170; pure 39, 169–70; restrictions on 8–10, 170–2, 200; *see also* science, scientific
responsibility 60–1, 63–5; *see also* accountability, social responsibility
resource use 130–2, 184
Royal Society 45
RU-486 151

Sagan, C. 118–19
science: academic 38; big 43; as a career 39–40; goals of 38–41; junk 63, 147–8, 205; and the media 11–12, 114–21; methods of 40; Nazi 133, 164, 183–4, 189; objectivity and 40, 42; and the public 118–21; and public policy 148–51, 171–2, 197; as a profession 31–8; and relativism 201–2; and religion 172; Soviet 61, 91, 168; *see also* research, scientific, scientists
scientific: communication 45–9; creativity 37; journals 4, 45–9; judgment 55–6, 76–7, 88–9; knowledge 39; merit 131–2; methods 49–52; objectivity 40, 42; societies 45–6; *see also* research, science, scientists
scientists: amateurs 37, 177; as citizen-advocates 148–51, 197; goals of 39–40; as professionals 31–8; as role models 122–4, 128–30, 174
secrecy *see* industrial research, military research, openness
self-deception 11–12, 57–8, 82–4
self-interest and cooperation 59, 91
sexism 66, 85, 123–4, 127–9, 172, 196, 203–4
Singer, P. 143
situational ethics 22–3, 26
social constructivism 201–2
social contract theory 20
social responsibility 63–5, 147–51, 188, 197–200
Sokal, A. 56
speciesism 143–4
statistics: and honesty 76, 180; and scientific method 51
steam engine 155